THE CARDINAL KING

Prince Henry Stuart, Cardinal Duke of York

The Cardinal King

BRIAN FOTHERGILL

This edition first published in 2010
by Faber and Faber Ltd
Bloomsbury House, 74–77 Great Russell Street
London WC1B 3DA

Printed by Books on Demand GmbH, Norderstedt

All rights reserved
© Brian Fothergill, 1958

The right of Brian Fothergill to be identified as author of this work
has been asserted in accordance with Section 77 of the
Copyright, Designs and Patents Act 1988

This book is sold subject to the condition that it shall not, by way of
trade or otherwise, be lent, resold, hired out or otherwise circulated
without the publisher's prior consent in any form of binding or cover other than
that in which it is published and without a similar condition including this
condition being imposed on the subsequent purchaser

A CIP record for this book is available from the British Library

ISBN 978–0–571–25955–7

To
URSULA SOMERVELL

Acknowledgments

I must thank the Right Revd. Monsignor W. R. Clapperton, Rector of the Pontifical Scots College at Rome, for his kindness in placing the library of the College at my disposal and for showing me various Stuart relics preserved there. I am also grateful to the Revd. Dom Silvester Houédard, O.S.B., of St. Michael's Abbey, Farnborough, for help and advice on certain ecclesiastical matters, and to Mr. G. Anthony Dawson, and Mr. Albert Gallichan for their assistance in preparing my manuscript for publication.

I must also express my indebtedness to the Right Revd. Monsignor A. N. Gilbey for kindly allowing me to reproduce the picture of the Cardinal Duke of York by J. Giles, and to the Director of the National Portrait Gallery, London, and the Board of Trustees for the National Galleries of Scotland for permitting me to make use of reproductions of pictures in their Galleries as illustrations to this book.

Contents

1.	THE YOUNGEST PRETENDER	page 13
2.	THE HELMET AND THE HAT	34
3.	A PRINCE OF THE CHURCH	62
4.	THE FIGHT FOR RECOGNITION	89
5.	SPLENDID TRANQUILLITY	110
6.	THE MARRIAGE OF PRINCE CHARLES	118
7.	POET AND PRINCESS	139
8.	THE ROYAL NIECE	168
9.	KING HENRY THE NINTH	188
10.	REVOLUTION AND RUIN	208
11.	THE PENSION	226
12.	THE END OF A DYNASTY	243
	BIBLIOGRAPHY	267
	INDEX	269

Illustrations

1. PRINCE HENRY STUART, CARDINAL DUKE OF YORK
   From the picture by Pompeo Batoni in the National
   Portrait Gallery, London   *frontispiece*

2. PRINCE HENRY STUART AS A CHILD
   From the picture attributed to Antonio David in the
   National Portrait Gallery, London   *facing page* 26

3. PRINCE CHARLES EDWARD STUART IN MIDDLE AGE
   From the picture by Pompeo Batoni in the National
   Portrait Gallery, London   104

4. CHARLOTTE STUART, DUCHESS OF ALBANY
   From the picture in the Scottish National Portrait Gallery, Edinburgh   170

5. THE CARDINAL OF YORK AS KING
   Copy by J. Giles, R.S.A., of the original formerly at the
   Scots College, Rome. (*Photograph by Ramsey & Muspratt, Ltd., Cambridge.*)   198

1

The Youngest Pretender

I

It is perhaps surprising to think that not quite twelve years separate the death of the last male descendant of the House of Stuart from the birth of Queen Victoria; yet so forgotten is the career of 'Henry IX' that few people recall how close in time is the death of this last upholder of the doctrine of Divine Right to the birth of the great exponent and interpreter of the idea of Constitutional Monarchy. Yet this grandson of James II, who was heir in line to the Tudors and Plantagenets, did not renounce his claim to the British throne though he chose to live the life of an Italian ecclesiastic and never, like his brother Prince Charles Edward, asserted his claims on the field of battle, or even set foot on British soil. The neglect of foreign courts; the reticence of the Papacy to acknowledge him; the loss of all worldly possessions in the upheaval of the French Revolution; poverty and flight in extreme old age; none of these things served in any way to undermine his belief in the justice of the Cause for which he and his family had lived in exile for so many years; and when his brother died, though he continued to be known by his ducal title, he let it be known that he considered it to be only a title of incognito under cover of which he reigned, if only in private, as King of Great Britain, France and Ireland, *'non desideriis hominum sed voluntate Dei'*—not by the desire of man but by the will of God.

This Prince, best known to posterity by his title of Cardinal of York, was born on the 6th of March, 1725, in the Palazzo Muti-Papazurri at Rome. This palace in the Piazza dei Santi Apostoli had been given to James Francis Edward Stuart, titular James III, by Pope Clement XI and here, after his marriage in 1719 to the

The Cardinal King

Princess Clementina Sobieska, his two sons were born. The elder, Charles Edward, whose birth in 1720 had restored hope to the cause still smarting from the humiliations of the Fifteen, was already nearly five years old when his younger brother entered this world a month before his expected time.

2

The father of the young Princes, although not yet forty, had spent almost the whole of his life in exile and had already tasted adversity to such a degree that he had earned from his opponents the name of Old Mister Misfortune. He was born at St. James's Palace on the 10th of June, 1688, the sixth child but only surviving son of King James II by his second wife Mary Beatrice of Modena; and despite the fact that the event was witnessed by sixty-seven people the story of the warming-pan baby was soon spread to discredit his claim to be the true child of his mother, and was to be believed, at least for a while, by his own half-sister the Princess Anne, who had nothing to gain by the arrival of a Catholic heir to the throne. In six months' time his father was in flight. The throne was declared vacant and offered to the deposed King's own daughter and son-in-law the Prince of Orange, while the King himself with his wife and infant son found refuge at the court of Louis XIV.

It was at Saint Germain-en-Laye, the château given to the exiled English Royal Family by the French king, that the young Prince of Wales was proclaimed King of England, Scotland and Ireland on the death of James II in 1701. Though contrary to treaty agreements there is no doubt that this proclamation was a source of considerable satisfaction to his Most Christian Majesty as it was of mortification to William III who, as Saint-Simon tells us, 'went red in the face and pulled his hat down over his eyes' when he heard the news. James was now to serve with the French armies as the Chevalier de St. George, and as such was to campaign against his half-sister's great general the Duke of Marlborough. His military career was to end in the failure of the attempt to wrest his throne from the Elector of Hanover in 1715.

The Youngest Pretender

From the disappointments of Scotland he returned a man of deep and increasing melancholy.

That devotion to the principles of the Roman Catholic faith which had lost James II his crown was to prevent his son from ever regaining it. After the Fifteen his devotion increased as his hopes diminished. But the charge of bigotry brought against him by Whigs in England was untrue; in this respect he differed from his father. The attitude of the Chevalier to those not of his own faith is clearly expressed in a letter written to his mother, the widowed Mary of Modena, in February 1718, shortly before his marriage.

'I am a Catholic, but I am a king, and subjects, of what ever religion they may be, have an equal right to be protected. I am a king; but as the Pope himself told me, I am not an apostle. I am not bound to convert my people otherwise than by my example, nor to show apparent partiality to Catholics, which would only serve to injure them later.'

These are not the words of a bigoted man. If James II had with similar good sense followed the advice of the Pope the history of England and of the House of Stuart might have been very different.

After the Chevalier's return from Scotland the question of his marriage became important. Both the courts of France and of Spain were eager to see the Stuart dynasty perpetuated. A rival heir was too useful a weapon against England to be neglected, and so the search began for a wife of suitable rank and title. Since the death of Louis XIV the Regent of France had entered into an understanding with the Government of George I; none the less the thought of possible future embarrassment to the Court of St. James in such a marriage was not distasteful to him. Romans were later to refer to James and the monarch in London as 'the king here' and 'the king there', and the possibility of being able to change one for the other was always an agreeable idea to those who watched the growth of British power under the House of Hanover with little or no enthusiasm. A wife must therefore be found for the King over the Water. One of Tzar Peter the Great's daughters was considered, but the fact that the Russian Grand

The Cardinal King

Duchess was probably illegitimate did not help to recommend her, and as she was only thirteen the difference in age between the parties was excessive. Other aspirants for the royal hand seemed to vie with each other in their peculiarities: the daughter of the Elector of Saxony, unlike the Grand Duchess, was considered too old; the Princess of Furstenburg had a red nose, while the Princess of Baden (upon the colour of whose nose history is silent) was unsuitable for another reason: she was a dwarf. Daughters of the French Regent, the Landgrave of Hesse, and King Charles XII of Sweden were also considered but did not show any great eagerness to be united to the King unless he was first reunited to his Kingdom.

The final choice rested upon the daughter of Prince James Sobieski, son of King John III of Poland, the valiant defender of Christendom against the Turks. This prince had married Princess Hedwige Elizabeth Amelia of Bavaria-Neuburg by whom he had two daughters, Maria-Charlotte, who became Duchess of Bouillon, and Maria Clementina Sophia, who was to marry James Stuart and become the mother of Prince Charles and Prince Henry Benedict.

3

This marriage, which accorded so well with the schemes of the King of Spain and the Regent of France, was less pleasing to the bridegroom's distant cousin George I and his ally the Emperor Charles VI, who, prompted by his English ally in whose debt he stood to a considerable extent, positively refused his consent to the marriage, and to ensure that his orders were not disregarded had the Princess and her mother confined in the fortress of Innsbruck. The story of the Princess's dramatic escape, planned and executed by Charles Wogan, and of her flight through the Emperor's hostile dominions to safety in the States of the Church, is sufficiently well known and need not be repeated here, except as a testimony to the ardent and romantic nature of the young girl who was soon to be united to a Prince whose gloomy nature was already manifesting itself.

The flight of the Princess had coincided with a general outbreak

The Youngest Pretender

of European hostilities. Austria and Spain were at war and at the end of 1718 England, joined somewhat reluctantly by France, came in on the Austrian side. Cardinal Alberoni, the Spanish minister, at once planned an attempt on Scotland and James, managing to escape from Italy with the help of Captain Cammock (who had taken the Prince across the sea to an unsuccessful venture upon a previous and more famous occasion) contrived to escape the vigilance of the British fleet and present himself at the Court of Madrid where he was received with every mark of royal respect and cousinly affection by his Catholic Majesty, but with little else to his purpose. Thus when Clementina eventually reached Bologna after her dangerous journey she was met not by a bridegroom but by the elderly Papal Legate, and after a marriage by proxy to her absent Prince, continued her journey to Rome, where Cardinal Acquaviva had arranged for her to be received in the Ursuline Convent until her husband should return. There she quickly won the hearts of the nuns who were soon referring to their royal guest as their Mother Superior. To the cloistered sisters this visit must have brought a breath of excitement from the great world outside: it was not to be Clementina's last visit to the Sisters of St. Ursula.

Meanwhile James was achieving little or nothing in Spain, where it was becoming increasingly obvious that Philip V and Alberoni had abandoned any hope of a further attempt on Scotland, and the presence of the Chevalier de St. George was becoming something of an embarrassment both to himself and to his hosts. He decided to leave Spain and sent a messenger on before him to warn his bride and to ask her to wait for him at Viterbo. They were married on September 1st, 1719, in the Cathedral of Montefiascone. Clementina had just celebrated her eighteenth birthday; James was thirty-one. Their first child, Charles Edward Louis Philip Casimir Silvester Maria, Prince of Wales to all still loyal to the old dynasty, was born at Rome at the end of the following year.

The Cardinal King

4

The difference in age, combined with an incompatibility of temperament that was soon to display itself, did not make the marriage a happy one. The emotional tension which had been increased by the dramatic means of Clementina's escape from the Emperor's intended confinement at Innsbruck, combined with her determination to be a queen, did not survive the disillusionment which life in the gloomy Muti Palace was to bring. This court of shadows, of empty royalty supported by a diminishing hope and surrounded by courtiers often only eager for the empty honours which were now all their king could bestow, was far removed from the splendour of her imaginings when she had set out on the journey to her royal husband to fulfil the ambition of her childhood when she had liked to be called Queen of England. How different the reality was! James must have seemed older to her than his actual years. He must have cut a sad figure in comparison with the handsome and dashing Irishman who had been the companion of her flight. The marriage began with difficulties. The son of James II no less than the grand-daughter of John Sobieski was nothing if not stubborn and obstinate. Moreover, always a prodigious letter-writer, he had the habit which his young wife must have found most irritating (as her elder son certainly did at a later date) of addressing lengthy screeds to her which carried more of the tone of a father than of a husband. It was not that James's nature was lacking in affection but that his affection was of the detached sort, while his propensity to improve the occasion whenever the opportunity presented itself must have been irritating beyond measure to an impulsive young wife.

Clementina's character, on the other hand, was vehement in the extreme. Her likes and dislikes were sudden, violent and unreasonable. Her religious life, always strong, was in the early days of their marriage emotional rather than profound and this resulted in a strong prejudice against the Protestants in her husband's household, especially in so far as they might have influence over her sons' education. To these Protestant gentlemen of his court

The Youngest Pretender

James himself, as was his principle, always adopted an attitude of scrupulous fairness, providing them with a chaplain and a place for worship. Pope Clement XII was later to take Clementina to task for her uncharitable attitude to the Protestants in her husband's entourage, pointing out that James was bound to provide for their religious needs. It was also perhaps a source of private disappointment to her that James never consulted her in the vast correspondence and the ever changing plans, schemes, plots and intrigues that made up his political life. Already fully immersed in these activities at the time of his marriage, and never really able to delegate authority until his virtual abdication at the time of the Forty-Five, it probably never occurred to him that his wife might be a help to him in this respect. The slightly hysterical side to her nature which showed itself after the birth of her second son perhaps made him abandon such ideas if indeed he had ever entertained them.

In appearance Clementina must have had great charm, with a delicate, gentle expression later to be characterized as saintly. Her hair was 'a bright brown'. Her features, of a slightly Polish cast, were distinguished by fine eyes and a general air of intelligence and regal dignity. In Rome she was much admired not only for her grace but also for her piety, a quality which Romans had not always observed, and indeed had scarcely come to expect, in ladies of distinguished birth. She was also not lacking in education and could speak Polish, German, Italian and English with equal fluency.

Portraits of James belie the libel of the warming-pan story by showing a strong resemblance to his father and his Stuart ancestors. This was, indeed, confirmed by Sir Godfrey Kneller who saw, with the trained eye of a portraitist, a strong resemblance between father and son. He is described as tall, thin, and somewhat awkward of movement by unfriendly Hanoverian observers, who did not scruple to add that he had 'extremely the looks and air of an idiot particularly when he laughs or prays.' Thus Thomas Gray describes him in 1740, adding of his mirth and devotions 'the first he does not often, the latter continually.' The notion of a king at prayer must have seemed strange indeed to someone familiar

The Cardinal King

with the court of the first two Georges. That James Stuart had something of the vacant expression which is all too often a characteristic of ancient lineage is not impossible (his second son was not unlike him in this respect), yet the qualities of understanding shown in his lengthy correspondence display a mind that was not lacking in intellectual endowments. Furthermore he lived a life which, in comparison with that usual in princes of his day and age, was one of irreproachable rectitude. In this respect he was in marked contrast to his German cousins whose preference for ladies of mountainous charm brought a Rubenesque air of blowsy obesity to the life of the British Court. But that the Chevalier did not possess a face of radiant intelligence is born out by the unprejudiced report of the President de Brosses who, comparing him with his half-brother the Marshal Duke of Berwick, remarks that 'the Marshal's face was sad and severe while that of the Pretender is sad and silly.' He makes some amends by adding: 'The Pretender's dignity of manner is extraordinary; I never beheld any Prince preside over a great assembly so well or so gracefully.'

Thus both physically and temperamentally the Stuart King and Queen were ill suited to each other. Their two natures, the vehemently enthusiastic and the more phlegmatic and pedestrian, were to be strangely intermixed in the characters of their two sons.

5

The marriage was verging into a state of crisis when Prince Henry was born, a month prematurely, in 1725. The event was hailed with enthusiasm by Jacobites everywhere while Cardinals and Roman princes hastened to pay their respects and compliments at the Muti Palace. The Pope, Benedict XIII, who was at prayer in his private oratory when the news was brought to him, arrived at once to baptize the infant who was shown to him by James with the proud words: 'I present the Duke of York to Your Holiness that you may make him a Christian.' This the Holy Father did without delay, himself sponsoring the child, whom he baptized in the names of Henry Benedict Thomas Edward Maria Clement Francis Xavier. The only person in Rome who seemed to be put

The Youngest Pretender

out by the event was the Baron von Stosch, better known as Walton the Spy and described by Sir Compton Mackenzie as 'an expatriated Prussian sodomite', who had only recently excelled himself by informing the British Government that Clementina was incapable of bearing any more children. Not only had another son been born to the House of Stuart but the same child was to remain a person of some consequence in European affairs for the next eighty-two years.

6

Domestic storms soon gathered round the royal infant's cradle. On November 19th in the same year Clementina, overcome by unreasonable jealousy, left her husband for the Ursuline Convent of St. Cecilia. The cause of the trouble centred in the violent dislike she had suddenly taken to John Hay, whom James had appointed as his Secretary of State with the title of Earl of Inverness. Not only did she turn against the new Earl but more especially against his Countess who she imagined to be James's mistress. This lady, the sister of James Murray, had before been on such good terms with Clementina that when on a private visit to England she had been imprisoned in Newgate, the Jacobite Queen had asked the Duchess of Bourbon to secure her release through the good offices of the French Ambassador, so that Mrs. Hay (as Lady Inverness then was) might be present at Clementina's next confinement.

The Queen's desertion of her husband and the groundless charge made against him was put to good use by the enemies of the Stuart cause and all Europe rang with the scandal of it. It was not until 1727 when Inverness, at his own request, retired to Avignon with his wife that Clementina would consent to return to her husband. And so, for the first two years of his life, the young Prince Henry Benedict was a stranger to his mother. Fortunately the Prince was too young to be much disturbed by these events. That Europe was amusing itself at the expense of the matrimonial difficulties of an exiled king and queen was of less importance to Henry Stuart than the fact that in the year of his mother's return Winifred Lady Nithsdale was appointed his governess. This was

The Cardinal King

the heroic lady who had boldly rescued her husband from the Tower of London where he was awaiting sentence of execution for his part in the Fifteen.

The year 1727 was important to the House of Stuart for a yet more pressing event than the return of a wife or the appointment of a governess. In June George I left London for Hanover, travelling some of the way with his German mistress, the hideous and grotesque Ehrengard von Schulenberg, Duchess of Kendal (who was as thin and scraggy as his other mistress, more in the Hanoverian tradition, was gross and fat). Not far from Osnabruck he was struck down by a fatal seizure. As the coach rumbled across his German principality the last coherent thoughts of the dying Elector were occupied, it was said, not with the throne he had usurped but with the wife he had wronged. For the tale was soon being spread of a mysterious letter thrust into his coach; a letter of appeal and reproach written before her death by Dorothea of Zell whom he had for thirty years held prisoner in the castle of Ahlden on the suspicion of an intrigue with Count Königsmark. The shock of this appeal from his wife, already dead a year, was said to have called the King to his final account. The attendants found him with his face contorted and his speech gone. In this state he died soon afterwards. The legend of the letter, whether true of whether merely the result of the rumours that arise from the awe that surrounds the death of kings, brings a note of poetic justice to the end of this unloved monarch who could so punish a wife whose guilt, if indeed established, was inconspicuous in comparison with his own. At her death he had even tried to prevent her burial in consecrated ground. Now his own death had overtaken him unawares. Yet death was a sudden visitor to the House of Hanover. The Electress Sophia had been found dead, sitting in an arbour where she had gone to shelter from a thunderstorm, only a few weeks before the death of the Queen she was so eager to succeed on the throne of England. George II was to die equally suddenly at Kensington Palace in 1760.

With the passing of King George the Chevalier had gone at once to Lorraine and his movements were closely watched by the Government in London. He was thus not in Rome to be united

The Youngest Pretender

to his wife when she left the Convent to return to her husband and children. But for all the good it did he might as well have stayed in the Eternal City, for George II succeeded without opposition to his father's throne and the hopes of the Jacobites were again destroyed.

It must have been about this time that he received the letter from his eldest son which contains the quaint phrase that throws a sad light on the state of his mother's nerves:

DEAR PAPA,
    I thank you mightily for your kind letter. I shall strive to obey you in all things. I will be very dutifull to Mamma, and not jump too near her. I shall be much obliged to the Cardinal for his animals. I long to see you soon and in good health.
    I am, dear Papa,
        Your most dutifull and affectionate son,
            CHARLES P.

The rest of Clementina's short life was to be given over almost entirely to works of charity and to an increasing and deepening devotion to her religion. She was undoubtedly neurotic, and twice before her death was to announce that she was again pregnant though it was only her fancy that made her think so. She was quite unfitted to care for her children whose happiest days were spent in their father's company at Albano where they retired for the summer months. His children gave him a great deal of comfort, and he already seems to have shown a special love for the younger. Writing to Lord Inverness in 1729 he says: 'I am really in love with the little duke, for he is the finest child can be seen.'

Clementina died on the 18th of January, 1735, being thirty-three years of age. In her last years she had been under the spiritual direction of Father Leonard of Port Maurice, a Franciscan Friar later canonized. Her devotion had the same fervour about it that she had previously shown in her likes and dislikes. She would kneel without support on the hard stone floor of a church during the long ceremonial of the Mass, often hearing more than one Mass in a day. It was a familiar sight to see her coach in Rome, with the royal arms of England emblazoned on its panels, rushing from church to church in order that its mistress might assist at as many Benedictions of the Blessed Sacrament as the speed of the coach and the hours of the service would allow. It was nothing for her to hear three or four Masses and attend as many Benedictions in the same day. Urged by Clement XII to a more practical expression of devotion she wrote a letter of reconciliation to Lady Inverness. To the poor she was a generous benefactress, but it must be confessed that so far as her sons were concerned her influence consisted chiefly in frustrating her husband's plans for their education; for the fear of the Protestant members of the court never left her mind.

7

The Pope allowed her the same funeral rights as those accorded to Queen Christina of Sweden in 1689. These royal funeral pomps may well have impressed the young minds of her children with a greater impact than any event in her actual life, for now the shadowy royalty to which they were accustomed became a vivid reality in this moment of death and burial. Hundreds of wax tapers surrounded the magnificent catafalque as it rested in the choir of the Basilica of the Holy Apostles close to the Muti Palace where for three days, attended by the Irish Dominicans, it was watched by a royal escort of the Papal Guard with drawn swords. Then, crowned and holding the sceptre and golden orb, the lifeless figure was clothed in the purple velvet and ermine of royalty and taken in solemn procession to St. Peter's attended by thirty-two Cardinals in their mourning robes of violet silk. Here, in the vast Basilica of the Vatican, draped in black velvet displaying the arms of England, Scotland, Ireland and Poland, the last rites were performed. Then the Queen, her regal purple changed for the simple black and white habit of a Dominican Tertiary, was sealed in her coffin and finally buried in the crypt. The heart alone was enclosed in a marble urn and placed in the Church of the Holy Apostles. For the rest of his long life James Stuart would spend hours in prayer by this shrine.

The Youngest Pretender

8

All accounts of the Stuart children during their boyhood and early youth tell of their lively and engaging manners and of their pleasant good looks. The portrait of the Duke of York as a boy by Antonio David now in the National Portrait Gallery in London shows him in gala dress with the blue sash of the Order of the Garter. The face has a marked likeness to his mother's. He is described as short and strongly built, dark almost to swarthiness like his father and his great-uncle Charles II. Both as a child and as a man his features were more Polish than Stuart though Pompeo Batoni's portrait of the Duke in later life, wearing the robes of a Cardinal, has a distinct resemblance about the eyes and nose to Charles I as we see him in the masterpieces of Van Dyck. Despite his sturdy build Henry was always delicate, but like many people of fragile constitution he was to outlive his more robust brother by many years.

As a boy Henry was undoubtedly the better looking of the two, with a more vivacious air than the Prince of Wales. De Brosses notes that 'the younger is the more popular of the two in Rome on account of his handsome face and charming manners.' At the same time he was to show something of his mother's hot temper. When the elder brother had gone to the siege of Gaeta with the Infante Charles of Spain (afterwards King of the Two Sicilies) and the Duke of Liria, the nine-year-old Duke of York flung his sword across the room in anger at having to remain at home. The King picked up the little sword at the same time removing the Star of the Garter from the Prince's coat, saying that the one could not be worn without the other. This admonition the Duke must have taken to heart for we rarely hear of outbursts of temper in his later years, though there were occasions when he would act in a hasty and irresponsible way.

It had been suggested that the younger Stuart prince should be brought up at the Spanish Court but this plan was strongly opposed by Clementina. It is perhaps odd that she should have taken up this attitude as in the atmosphere of Madrid or the Escorial the likelihood of any contamination by Protestant ideas, such as she

The Cardinal King

dreaded at her husband's court, would hardly have arisen. Perhaps she feared the influence of the strong-minded Elizabeth Farnese, consort of the indolent Philip V, whose reputation as 'the termagant' may have awakened a latent feeling of maternal protection for the young prince. More probably it was simply unreasonable obstinacy. For whatever cause the plan was soon abandoned; Clementina, as we have seen, was not accustomed to react in a reasonable way to anything that concerned her children. The same fate befell the offer of candidature for the crown of Poland, made to James for his younger son on the death of Augustus of Saxony in 1733. Henry was considered too young for the nomination, for all that, as his father wrote, 'the blood of the Sobieski's runs in his veins and by what may be judged of a child of such tender years, he will not be unworthy of it.'

The children were taught to speak English and always spoke together in that language in the family much as their distant cousins at St. James's spoke in German. They spoke it with a pure accent though the letters of Henry as an old man suggest that by then his command of the language was more that of a foreigner, than a native. James brought them up to love open-air activities and they were never happier than when hunting in the hills around Albano. It is possible that the more academic side of their education was somewhat neglected, for contemporary observers suggest that they were not up to the standard of other princes of their age in matters of book learning. Charles never had the reputation for being studious and his spelling to the end of his days was characteristically original. (In one of his letters he writes 'God nose' for 'God knows'.) Henry, though later a great patron of learning and the liberal arts was never more than an average scholar. His first unaided letter to his father was written when he was ten years old and compares favourably with his brother's compositions at the same age:

My Dear Papa,
    The impatience I am in to see you makes me write this letter which I hope will be acceptable, being I writ without any assistance, by your most dutiful son,
Henry

PRINCE HENRY STUART AS A CHILD

The Youngest Pretender

The Earl Marischal visited the Muti Palace in 1731 where James received him with great pleasure and honour as befitting the hereditary Great Marshal of Scotland and one who had been with him in the Fifteen and had shared his disappointment in Alberoni's disastrous expedition to Glenshiel. The Earl was greatly delighted with the Chevalier's younger son and much amused at the Prince's determination to have a journal kept of his activities. He writes to his brother Marshal James Keith, the great soldier, 'The Duke of York believes I send you a journal of his actions; he stands in great awe of it, lest his faults should be published in Europe and Asia, and is very fond to do any good thing to be put in the journal' It is interesting to compare this childish fancy with the *Diario del Cardinale Duca di York*, that long and generally tedious record of his day to day life which he caused to be kept by his secretary when he was Bishop of Frascati.

The young Princes made themselves very accessible to English travellers in Rome, and as no treason as yet attached itself to the cultivation of their acquaintance, as it did to their father's, the subjects of King George II were generally curious to meet these representatives of the direct royal line. From the accounts of travellers we learn not only of the Princes' delight in hunting and dancing but also of their prowess in the art of music. Both were to love music all their lives. Charles would play upon the 'cello while Henry was noted for the sweetness of his voice. Writing from Rome in 1739 Samuel Crisp tells us: 'I think I may say with truth they are two as fine youths as ever I saw; particularly the youngest, who has more beauty and dignity in him than ever one can form to oneself in idea. He danced miraculously, as they say he does all exercises, singing, so I am told, most sweetly, and accompanies himself and is, in short, the admiration of everybody.' Lest this enthusiasm should savour of Jacobitism the writer cannot resist (or perhaps thought it prudent to include) a dig at the Chevalier in his next sentence. 'These accomplishments,' he discreetly adds, 'must come to him by the mother, for I take the father to be a poor, mean, cowardly bigot, and nothing more.' But perhaps this last remark was intended as a present to the

The Cardinal King

Hanoverian spies in case they should chance to intercept a letter complimentary to the rival heirs.

In the same letter there is a description of the Duke of York at a reception in honour of the Prince of Poland held during the Roman carnival. 'I never saw anything so genteel as this young one's paying his court to the Electoral Prince; his looks, his gesture, all was the finest and most expressive that can be imagined.'

From these observations we can judge that as youths the princes were well mannered and at ease in society; open and friendly; and especially ready to charm visitors from the distant kingdom from which they were excluded but over which they believed themselves to be born to rule. We can also see that at this age it was often the younger who stole the scene from the elder.

9

History, which has always been more interested in the elder of the two brothers, has little to tell us about the younger between his fourteenth and his seventeenth year. This was the time that Prince Charles was making his grand tour of Italy and beginning to cut a figure in the great world, winning golden opinions wherever he went. He travelled incognito as Count of Albany, the title by which he was to be known during the last tragic years of his life, visiting Bologna, Parma, Reggio, Milan, Genoa, Venice and other Italian cities, being received everywhere as a great prince, despite the incognito. Henry, presumably, remained at Rome with his father.

Prince James Sobieski died in 1737 leaving his grandsons his historic jewels, including the famous rubies from the crown jewels of Poland, as well as a considerable sum of money. But like so many legacies the bequest brought with it a long process of litigation with the princes' aunt the Duchess of Bouillon, though fortunately without any interruption in the friendship which existed between the two branches of the family. The future Cardinal was to be famous for the brilliant diamonds in his pectoral cross which he wore as a bishop; and later, in poverty and exile, a fugitive

The Youngest Pretender

from the advancing armies of revolution, these jewels (or what remained of them) were to be his last source of subsistence until help came from an even more unexpected quarter.

There is a description of the Duke preserved among the Stuart Papers at Windsor which was written in 1742 when he was seventeen years old. During the years since we last saw him as a gay and lighthearted prince delighting all who met him a great change has taken place. It is Charles now whom all find irresistible; the younger brother has become a neurotic, unsettled and exaggeratedly pious young man, restless and listless in manner, showing to an alarming degree some of the less admirable characteristics of his mother. James Murray, Earl of Dunbar, the Prince's Protestant tutor, sends a long and rather incoherent report about the Duke of York to his father which must be quoted at some length for the light it throws upon his personality as he verges on manhood.

'I offer to your Majesty [writes Dunbar] the following account of the manner in which the Duke [is] used to spend his time. He is called by special order a quarter of an hour before six in the morning, rises at six and sometimes says some prayers in his bed during this quarter of an hour or a little more. He commonly spends about three quarters of an hour in washing his face and hands and putting on his shoes and stockings, for he does not dress till afterwards. After this he employs one hour at prayers of which one half in his little closet and the other in walking in his bed-chamber. Always says them aloud, so that when he is in his bed-chamber with the doors shut, they hear him in the next room. Next to this he takes his breakfast, which lasts about half a quarter of an hour or ten minutes.

'Father Ildefonso comes about half an hour after seven and always waits a good half hour during his prayers and the time of his breakfast. He stays with him generally an hour, sometimes an hour and a quarter and sometimes, but seldom, an hour and a half . . . after which he danced and fenced, but sometimes when the dancing master was in the way, he danced two little minuets with him before he began with Father Ildefonso which lasted but a few minutes, because he has lost the inclination he had to that exercise. When he rid a horseback he went out immediately after his lesson with Father Ildefonso. Then he dressed and went to Mass of which he heard two and sometimes three on holidays and Sunday last four—to wit two with yr Majesty one with the Prince and one by himself. When he hears Mass with the Prince he stays at prayers in the Chapel about a quarter of an hour thereafter when the hour of dinner permits it. Since Lent he has heard sermon always twice, sometimes thrice and once four times in a week, but of this last they can not be absolutely positive.

'When dinner is over, he waits a certain time with the watch in his hand and then goes into the chapel where he stays at his prayers as in the morning about three quarters of an hour and sometimes a little more. Then he goes abroad and generally goes to church (but sometimes he does not) where he remains about half an hour. I have remarked it by my watch and have observed sometimes seven or eight minutes less and sometimes three or four.

'He comes home about four hours, goes to his chapel again where he remains always an hour and some times an hour and a half. It is to be remarked that in reciting or reacting his prayers he puts his mind in agitation, pronounces his words aloud, and crowds them with great precipitation one upon another and I often remark him when he goes abroad after dinner with a blackness about his eyes, his head quite fatigued and his hands hot and the same thing when he comes from his prayers at night . . .

'It is observable that the Duke is the whole day in constant inquietude for fear of not having time for all he ought to do and very often has his watch in his hand on that account. His temper and inclination is so far changed that to propose to carry him of an evening as next Sunday to an assembly, in place of doing him a pleasure it gives him pain and he seems to have no pleasure in anything.

'It deserves serious attention that he undergoes much greater application of mind than his delicate health can bear, yet there is little of it directed towards forming his judgement or adorning his mind with knowledge of things suitable to his station. His small study with Father Ravillos may be reckoned of this sort, and

The Youngest Pretender

though Father Ildefonso teaches him a language yet as he reads a little history in that language by which he may form sentiment, I also comprehend it. But this is a small matter and though he has always a perfect goodwill to apply while he is with him he is often unable to do it otherwise than with interuptions of ten minutes at a time. During the rest of the day he never reads a word on any subject nor could he probably do it, so that were not the course he is in noxious to his health, as it certainly is, he would arrive at the age of twenty-two without having cultivated his understanding or acquired a reasonable degree of such knowledge as is the chief duty of station at present both towards God and man.

'In this manner, the first capacity in the world with a wonderful memory would be lost, and this I take to be a very great evil and what wants a prudent and affectual remedy. I will add to this that when he is not employed as above he is always singing, which I am far from thinking indifferent in regard of his breast. . . .

'I take it for granted that the Duke's only pleasure is in the exercise of his devotions in which he is employed, that it is become a passion and that the contradicting him in it will have a very violent effect upon him, and therefore this matter I think is very delicate and required to be considered very maturely.'

What is one to make of a youth of seventeen who spends upwards of three and a half hours in prayer in addition to two or three visits to Mass in the course of a normal day? How can we account for the changed picture this letter presents from that happy young prince who had so entranced all who saw him as a boy? A love of dancing is a natural enough expression of youthful exuberance but a love of sermons is surely a curious taste among the old, let alone the young, and one (or two at the very most) a week is generally considered sufficient meat for the average spritual digestion. One can sense something of the irritation of the unfortunate Dunbar as he stands outside a church, watch in hand, while his devout young charge kneels inside in seemingly endless prayer. In the circumstances it appears unfair that the Duke should not be allowed to enjoy the pleasure of singing for fear of his delicate chest.

It is common knowledge that the period of adolescence often

results in marked changes of personality, and in the case of Henry Stuart it is possible that this was accentuated by a conflict in his mind; a conflict which did not resolve itself until the failure of the Forty-Five made his path clear to him. The preoccupations which Dunbar describes show that the Prince was already conscious of a religious vocation even though his bent in this direction was to some extent due simply to a condition not unusual, though rarely so marked, at his particular time of life. To follow such a bent would present no difficulties to any other young man but to Henry the call to a religious vocation was irreconcilable with the life that was expected of him as a Stuart prince. He must have known that he was likely soon to be called upon to help his father and brother in another bid for the crown; his whole life up to this time, all the influences which had surrounded his upbringing, had been dominated by the idea of Divine Right, of the three Kingdoms to be regained for those who God willed should rule them. This notion was in the very air he breathed; every action of his life, as in his brother's life then and always, was encinctured by the thought. Across this now came a conflicting call. Something of his mother's fanatical spirit was at work in him, and it was to cut across the single line which all Stuart policy had pursued since his grandfather's flight from St. James's in December 1688.

If his sense of vocation was perhaps not yet fully realized the memory of his mother's intense religiosity and the life of real devotion to which it ultimately led her, as well as the hints of sanctity that had accumulated round her name after death, must have given strength to it. At the same time he must have felt himself enjoined to deny its fulfilment and hold himself bound to the other cause (no less sacred) of securing the ancient heritage of his family. It is not surprising that his mind was in the grip of conflicting ideas which, in one always young for his years, resulted in the neurotic behaviour the King was to read about in Lord Dunbar's revealing letter.

10

The changing political scene in Europe began to show signs favourable to another venture in the great Cause. It found Prince

The Youngest Pretender

Charles more than ready for the fray. When the hope of a large military expedition failed he at once set off almost alone and came so near to gaining his end that even the opportunist ministers of George II were in a frenzy of uncertainty less they had backed the wrong side. Henry lacked the daring of his brother. That he was ready to help him in all that was reasonable was never, as we shall see, in any doubt; but the spirit that would rush to hazard all on the mere expectation of success (with nothing to back it up but faith in the countrymen he had never seen) was not in Henry's nature any more than it was in his father's. He was altogether too introspective for such feats. 'You may perhaps gain the Kingdom of Heaven by your prayers,' the Duc de Richelieu was later to remark to him, 'but never the Kingdom of Great Britain.'

2

The Helmet and the Hat

1

The year 1740 saw Prince Charles on the threshold of manhood, already taking an increasingly important part in the political intrigues of his father and zealous to adventure for the cause. Henry was equally devoted to the interests of his family though as a younger son he had already accustomed himself to a less active role. His purpose was to support the plans made by others, to follow rather than to lead. The events of this year were to offer James and his elder son the opening they and their supporters had so long awaited and which was to lead at last to the ultimate disaster of Culloden. Yet even a year or two after this, when their plans were far advanced, a rising in support of the Stuarts was so little expected by the complacent government of George II that when Lord Chesterfield, then Lord Lieutenant of Ireland, was roused from sleep by an excited bishop with the news that the Jacobites were about to rise he replied, glancing wearily at the time-piece, 'I fancy they are, my Lord, for it is nine o'clock.'

2

Two deaths this year were to have far-reaching effects on the destinies of more than one ruling house. In Prussia, still comparatively new to the dignity of a kingdom but already beginning to show those predatory tendencies that were to bring European civilization so near to extinction in the course of the next two hundred years, Frederick William, a monarch who liked to discipline his subjects in person by laying about him freely with his cane, died, and was succeeded by his son, Frederick II, sometimes

The Helmet and the Hat

called the Great. The new King might have been expected to show some gratitude to the House of Austria, for had it not been for the intervention of the Emperor the young Frederick would almost certainly have been punished with death for what his father had considered as military insubordination when, at the age of eighteen, the Prince had attempted to escape from his insane father's belabouring cane to the comparative safety and shelter of the British court. But gratitude was not apparently a Hohenzollern virtue, as events were to show. Nor indeed were any other virtues particularly conspicuous in Frederick, who combined a flair for bad verse with an arid genius for waging what nowadays would be described as 'total war'.

A few months later died Charles VI of Hapsburg, Holy Roman Emperor, Apostolic King of Hungary, and last in the male line of the House of Austria. By means of the Pragmatic Sanction, agreed to by the Powers, he had secured the succession of his vast dominions to his daughter the Archduchess Maria Theresa who had married her cousin Francis of Lorraine. The Pragmatic Sanction was accepted by England, France, Spain, Russia, Poland, Prussia, Sweden, Denmark and the other German states. Its almost immediate breach by Bavaria, Prussia and Spain, aided and abetted by France, although granting an opportunity to Stuart hopes in the resulting general confusion, was a callous crime of a type with which Europe was at that time less familiar than we are to-day. Ambition was placed before honour and opportunism before the sacred rights of Treaties freely agreed to. Frederick II, the man who thus held the accepted rules of international law in open contempt, could remark complacently of his invasion of Silesia: 'Ambition, interest, the desire of making people talk about me, carried the day; and I decided for war.'

The very nature of the position of the House of Stuart as an exiled dynasty forced on them an opportunist attitude to the war that resulted over the question of the Austrian succession. The government of George II fulfilled their obligations under treaty and came to the support of the Queen of Hungary, and the fact that George II as a German prince had personal irons in the fire in connection with his Hanoverian Electorate does not detract in

The Cardinal King

any way from the correctness of his attitude in the hostilities that followed. But in aligning himself with Louis XV James was not concerned with the claims of Maria Theresa as Queen of Hungary; he was concerned only with the claims of James Stuart as King of England, Scotland and Ireland.

In 1742 the Elector of Bavaria was elected to the Imperial Throne as Charles VII to the mortification of Maria Theresa who expected that dignity to come to her husband (as it eventually did) and to the delight of James whose wife had been a cousin of the Bavarian prince and who enjoyed something of the real pomps of royalty when the Imperial Ambassador at Naples waited on him in full state to announce the accession of the new Kaiser to the King of England. As the threat of war spread through Europe a little of his melancholy must have lifted as he saw dawning the hope that he might once again set eyes on the land of his birth. Another personage of importance was also ready to see the Stuarts restored to their kingdoms; though it was said of the Cardinal Prospero Lambertini, elected in 1740 to the Chair of St. Peter as Benedict XIV, that his zeal for their cause was not solely based on its intrinsic merit but also on his strong desire to get rid of them from Rome.

Other happenings seemed destined to raise the hopes of the conspirators at the Muti Palace. In 1742 Sir Robert Walpole, that inveterate enemy of the Stuarts (except when it served his interests to correspond with them) and undoubted lover of peace, resigned, and passed into the Gilded Chamber as Earl of Orford; while in France Cardinal de Fleury, a minister equally devoted to peace, died the next year and was succeeded in office by Cardinal de Tencin, a prelate who owed his Red Hat to James's influence at Rome and who was sincerely attached to the House of Stuart. In the same year the battle of Dettingen, where George II personally inflicted a severe and humiliating defeat on the French forces under the Duc de Noailles, so particularly annoyed Louis XV (who had always been loth to recognize the Hanoverian succession in England) that his somewhat slothful attention to affairs of state now turned in the direction of an invasion of King George's territory across the channel assisted by a Jacobite rising from within,

The Helmet and the Hat

and Cardinal Tencin deemed that the time had come for Prince Charles to show himself in Paris.

3

In these days of their boyhood and youth in Rome the two Princes were without doubt very devoted to each other. 'Few brothers love as we do,' Charles wrote to Henry from Scotland, and we can gather from contemporary accounts that the younger tended to hero-worship the elder. So when in 1744 the plans were laid for Charles to escape to France Henry was told nothing of the scheme lest his anxiety for his brother's safety, which he would find difficult to conceal, should show itself in his face and discover the plot to the ever watchful eyes of the Hanoverian agents. For the Princes had enemies as well as friends among the cosmopolitan inhabitants of Rome. Just before this time, when fate seemed to promise so well for them, a mysterious attempt was made to sow discord between the brothers and their father who, in marked contrast to the bitter feelings between the king then reigning in England and his son and heir Frederick, Prince of Wales, had always been so united in affection. Partly it was due to those influences, always secretly at work and once so dreaded by their mother, to sunder the young princes from their allegiance to the Catholic Church. Two members of the Stuart Court, Francis Strickland and John Towneley, were said to be leading them into irreligious ways. It was thought that if they could not make them Protestants outright, then tender consciences in England and Scotland might at least take comfort in the thought that they were not over zealous in their obedience to Papal superstitions. With Charles, who, as Walton the Spy noted, 'wanted to amuse himself in his own way', they had some success. Even at this stage in his career, before the disappointments of later life had embittered him, it must be admitted that he was fond of a glass too much; and he was never at any time a man of strong religious convictions.

Certainly about 1742 James was seriously alarmed at his son's behaviour and was troubled by the bad influence of some of his friends. Henry, being considered of a delicate constitution, did not join in the dissipations of his brother and his boon companions, and in any case his more serious disposition witheld him from easily joining in the sort of entertainment that amused them. The Prince's enemies were not slow in spreading rumours against the Duke, depicting him as a sanctimonious kill-joy, and because he was not prepared to be diverted by their sottish behaviour gave him out to be wholly lost to the 'bondage and foolishness of popery.'

Fortunately the unity of the royal family was not seriously upset by these attempts; James's fears were allayed and the brothers' friendship suffered no more than a momentary disruption. By the beginning of 1744, when Charles took leave of his father, all was peace again. As the Prince left Italy in search, as he put it, of three crowns, his ageing father thought only of the safety of his 'dearest Carluccio'. 'Heaven forbid' he answered, 'that all the crowns in the world should rob me of my son.' Thus the Prince left on the beginning of that journey which was to end at Culloden. His father never set eyes on him again.

4

The plans for Charles's departure had been carefully laid and kept a close secret. The Pope himself did not know that so distinguished a guest was about to leave his territory and was not a little annoyed to discover it after the event. Henry, as we have said, was not in the secret, and only the ambassadors of Spain and Malta, Cardinal Acquaviva and the Duke of Gaetani knew of the true destination of the Prince when it was given out that Charles and his brother had gone to the Duke's country estate at Cisterna for a boar-hunt. When Henry woke on the morning of January 10th, 1744, he was told that his brother, eager for the chase, had gone on before him. He was only told the true story when it was thought that Charles would be safe from all pursuit.

If the Duke of York was angry at being excluded from the plan there is no record of it. His father wrote to explain why he had

The Helmet and the Hat

not been told, adding that it would be wise for him to remain in the country so that the deception could be kept up as long as possible. His reply, written from Fogliano on January 15th, shows an almost too dutiful acquiescence.

'I am much obliged to your Majesty for the honour of your two letters, your goodness has really been very great in giving me reasons for not revealing to me earlier this Affair. You may be very well assured, Sir, that I can never be anxious to know anything but what you think fit I should know, and that also but when you please; certainly the thoughts of such a separation could not but at first have some impression on me, but that lasted very little, for those very reflections which your Majesty put under my Eyes in your letter, as also many other joyful prospects, immediately came into my mind, and not only put me at ease, but filled me with vast content and satisfaction, so that the Road which of itself is very long, passed away without my almost perceiving it. I have, however, had a good deal of anxiety whilst I was at Cisterna, for I really did not think it a good air in the present conjuncture, but now that we are, thank God, at Fogliano, as I think out of all harm's way, and that I perceive by your Majesty's letter that all things continue quiet at Rome, I am very happy, but I am at the same time very impatient to hear news of our Dear Traveller which news I do not doubt will be but good, for the hand of God seems to be remarkably upon him on this occasion. The pretence of staying here longer is very natural and easy, so that I shall stay with a great deal of pleasure as long as your Majesty shall think fit, were it to be of any use in this occasion I would really be locked up very willingly in the old Tower till Easter. I am very much ashamed of myself for not having writ sooner to your Majesty as I have no good reason to give for my excuse I shall say nothing but only ask your pardon for my negligence.

'Begging your blessing I am your most dutiful son,

'HENRY'

Next month, returned to Rome, he was able to write to Charles who had now reached France in safety. This letter shows the

The Cardinal King

affection which the brothers still had for each other and the eagerness of Henry to help his elder brother in any way he could should circumstances permit it.

'I really had not the heart to write to you before I heard of your safe arrival at Antibes, but as soon as I got that comfortable news, I have seized on the first occasion, for to return you many thanks for the great goodness you have showed me on this occasion. I can assure you, Dear Brother, that I am here without you like a fish out of water, the only thing which makes me bear our separation with patience and even with Pleasure is the reflection of its being at present so necessary for your honour, Reputation, and (I hope) Advantage, and besides all that, I hope in God it shall not be for long. I have already thanked the King and I also thank you particularly for not having told me the secret of your journey beforehand, for certainly the great love I have for you could not but have show'd itself. . . . I wish you cou'd see all the content and satisfaction my heart feels every time I hear anything that can rebound to your honour and glory, and that I am sure proceeds from the Respectrous love and tenderness I have for you, which I can assure you, Dear Brother, were the King but to permit me wou'd make me fly through fire and water to be with you . . .'

In Paris Charles's position was nothing if not enigmatical as Louis XV, while still ready to make use of the Stuarts as a convenient weapon against George II, insisted upon Charles observing a strict incognito and would not consent even to receive him. Work was set in progress, none the less, for an assault upon the English coast and a force was assembled at Brest and Dunkirk under Marshal Count Maurice de Saxe, a natural son of Augustus, Elector of Saxony and King of Poland, to whose Polish throne Henry had once almost been nominated. Also a nephew of Count Königsmark, the lover of Dorothea of Zell, he had no reason himself to love the House of Hanover, and was destined later to inflict no less than three military defeats upon the 'butcher' Duke of Cumberland. Charles, with the commission of Regent from his father, settled himself in a small house near Paris until he could join Marshal de Saxe on the coast. Sir Thomas Sheridan, who

The Helmet and the Hat

joined the Prince in February, describes later how he appeared in a letter to James dated June 8th, the same year.

'The Prince is lodged in a pretty little house near Montmartre where the prospect and air are very good. He has all his conveniency and room enough for so small a company as his. I found him in very good health and he seemed to me both taller and broader than when I saw him last. He is certainly increased in bulk, but for his height, when I seemed surprised at it, he let me into the secret. He showed me the heals of his shoes which he wears now of the usual size, whereas before he wore them remarkably lower than other people.

'In fine, he has altogether a much more manly air than he had when he began his travels. His sentiments towards your Majesty are such as could be wished.'

We must not here pursue the well known story of the fate that overcame the tempest-stricken invasion fleet when disaster struck at it and scattered to the winds the great force gathered for the invasion of England; or follow Charles when, impatient of delay, he set off with his few companions in the ships *Elizabeth* and *Du Teillay* (the 'Doutelle' as she is sometimes called) for the distant Hebrides. We must return to Rome where King James and the Duke of York were anxiously waiting for news of the adventure, the latter all impatience to follow should occasion permit, the elder man, with his long experience of disappointment, hopeful, yet resigned for whatever blows fate might still have in store for him as he sat in the gloom of the Muti Palace listening for tidings of his son.

5

The European situation while Charles passed his time at Paris 'much hurried between balls and business' before embarking for Scotland, was in a highly complex state, to say the least. 'Now at last,' writes Alice Shield in her life of Cardinal York, 'a French fleet lay off Brest and Dunkirk under Admiral Rocquefeuil to transport troops under Count Maurice de Saxe for the invasion of England, to dethrone France's official ally, the Hanoverian occupant of the British throne: all under the Supreme Command

The Cardinal King

of Charles, Prince of Wales, Regent for His Majesty James III and VIII, whom Louis XV must not so much as speak to.' But by the beginning of 1745, before Charles set out for Scotland with the Seven Men of Moidart instead of fifteen thousand soldiers commanded by a Marshal of France, the Emperor Charles VII had died (to be succeeded by Maria Theresa's husband as Francis I) and Britain and France were openly at war with each other, so that the Prince could shed the cloak of anonymity he had had to wear.

Eventually the old King at Rome was to hear the news he both hoped and feared to receive written by his son at the moment of sailing; a letter which he had kept open until the last minute 'so that I may add a note to it iff being sea sick does not hinder.' It is dated from 'Ye mouth of ye Loire', 2nd of July, 1745.

'We have nothing to do now [the letter ends] but to hope in ye Almyties favouring uss. And recompencing our troubles which as you may see by the nature of ye thing were not small. I hope in God my next will bring comfortable news. In ye mean time I remain, laying myself at Your Majesty's feet most humbly asking blessing your most dutiful son,

'CHARLES P.'

Charles's landing brought George II hurrying back from his beloved Hanover to London where he was greeted by a new patriotic song beginning with the words 'God save great George our King' which was later, in a slightly modified form, to become the National Anthem of the British Empire; but the same event only succeeded slightly in lifting the melancholy that surrounded the old Chevalier. He had mistrusted the rashness of his elder son's action after the destruction of the invasion fleet, and though he found some comfort in the enthusiasm which greeted the bold attempt in Paris and Rome (where for a time people could talk of nothing else) he never seems to have escaped from the forebodings of failure which had by now become a part of his very nature. Not long after the news of Charles's landing in Scotland reached him (bringing back, as it must have done, sad memories of the Fifteen) he was received in Audience by the Pope. 'The poor King of

The Helmet and the Hat

England' wrote Benedict XIV afterwards, 'is verily an object of compassion, unable to neglect his son's affairs, yet not knowing where to turn for help.'

Henry was eager to join his brother as soon as possible. On August the 29th he left Rome under conditions of great secrecy, it having been given out that he was suffering from the small-pox to keep curious visitors at bay. Meanwhile James had written to his cousin Louis XV explaining that age and ill health kept him in Rome but recommending his younger son to the French King. 'He cannot endure the idea of having to remain in Rome while his brother is in Scotland,' the King wrote, 'and although the dangers and difficulties of escaping from Italy have grown greater than ever, he will take the very earliest opportunity of making his way to Avignon, so as to await the orders of Your Majesty in that city.'

Despite the secrecy that surrounded his departure the British Government soon got wind of it. At the court of the Grand Duke of Tuscany (or the 'Great Duke' as he is styled in the official correspondence of the time) his Brittanic Majesty was now represented by Sir Horace Mann whose unfailing vigilance was, for fifty years, to keep his government well informed on the affairs, both political and domestic, of the exiled Stuarts; while his correspondence with Horace Walpole was to preserve for posterity some of the less diplomatic aspects of their lives that might be likely to cause a shrill giggle to echo in the mock-gothic cloisters of Strawberry Hill. 'The second son,' wrote Mann, 'departed from Rome on the 29th at night, with as much mystery as his Demetrius did last year. . . . At three hours in the night he set out with the Valet de Chambre of Bailli Tencin who attended his brother, whom some believe he has gone to join. An opinion prevails that the Pretender himself will set out soon.'

The result of this warning, and other information supplied to the British Minister at Florence by Cardinal Alessandro Albani, a bitter enemy of the Stuarts who represented the interests of the Austrian party at the Court of Rome, was that the British squadron off the coast of Genoa was ordered to intercept any small vessels they might find heading in the direction of France. It is rather

The Cardinal King

ironical that in a letter sent to his father on September 3rd Henry should comment on the charms of the prospect of Genoa and its coast and the badness of the roads which were none the less worth passing once 'for curiosity's sake'. He does not say whether he saw any sails on the horizon. No doubt Mann's curiosity would have been gratified to learn of the Duke's appreciation of the Genoese scenery. This letter, so different from the curt mis-spelt scrawls of Prince Charles, is interesting not only for its account of his adventures as in illustrating the different characters of the two brothers. Charles writes like one impatient of delay; his are the letters of a man of action. Henry, on the other hand, tended to be garrulous on paper, a tendency which increased with age.

Genova. Sept. 3. 1745.

SIR,

I arrived here about one and a half in the afternoon. I chose that time on purpose that I might find few people in the streets and from the place where I lay last night it was impossible for me to get here as early in the morning as would have been requisite for the same purpose. So I have taken my party to keep close and stay here all to-night and tomorrow; at the opening of the Gates I shall set out for Savona, where I reckon I shall be two or three days before the news of my departure from Rome reaches this place. I must not omit to tell Your Majesty that as we passed by Pogibonii (*sic*) the post-master had liked to have obliged us to pass by Florence, as all courriers must do and had it not been for the Cleverness of my courrier I believe we never should have escaped that useless and troublesome detour for, as it was, I perceived he somewhat suspected our *bona fide*. After that we arrived at Pisa at a very untimely hour for it was just about four and twenty, all the world abroad and flocking about to ask news of the 'Pretendente'. We were very anxious to get away as you may well believe and, for all the sights of that town pleased me extremely, yet I was not sorry to find myself well out of it. I have been enchanted with the sights of Genoa and the Coast about it, but I cannot say the same about the roads which really are much worse than ever I could have imagined and yet I think they deserve to be passed

The Helmet and the Hat

once for curiosity's sake. The Post master in a village betwixt Sarzana and this, where I lay a night, as soon as he had seen me told the courrier that the young Gentleman was very like the Prince of Wales whom he had seen there as he passed on his way to France. I was much surprised at this for I never thought we had been like one another. I am now pretty well rested and as I have nothing more—Humbly asking yr Majesty's blessing,

I remain,

HENRY

From the Genoese coast, despite the watching Squadron, Henry made his way by ship to Antibes, the same port where his brother had landed a year and a half before him, and from there proceeded to Avignon, a town much frequented by Jacobites which at this date was still Papal territory. Here he was made welcome by the old Duke of Ormonde, whose life was nearly over. At Avignon the Duke fell ill of a fever and was delayed for two months. This at least gave him time to consider his next move, whether to continue to Paris where preparations were being made in a rather leisurely way for another attempted invasion of England, or to go to Madrid, where the commission of an Admiral in the Spanish service would be given him with the command of a fleet destined for an attack on the Irish coast. Influenced perhaps by his brother's example Henry decided in favour of France, and when his health had sufficiently recovered set out on his journey again.

6

The Duke of York arrived at the French capital at an auspicious moment, for the good news of Prince Charles's advances in Scotland inclined Louis and his ministers to regard the Stuart Cause with a certain amount of favour. This was of particular importance for the enthusiasm of the House of Bourbon for the legitimate sovereigns of Great Britain had been largely academic since the death of Louis XIV. But if Louis XV, like the Almighty, could be expected to help those who helped themselves, then the successful campaign in Scotland (now almost entirely in the hands of the

The Cardinal King

Jacobite army) might be hoped to put him in a generous mood when the question of material help was raised. Moreover the British army in the Netherlands was receiving heavy blows at the hands of Marshal de Saxe while in England itself people were getting tired of what they considered as a primarily 'Hanoverian' war.

Though it was not considered expedient for the Duke to appear openly at the French Court an audience of the King was arranged through the influence of the Duc de Fitz-James, a cousin of Henry's, and the Marquis d'Argenson, the Minister of War. The Duke of York was presented incognito as Count of Albany, Albany being the title held traditionally by the second son of the King of Scots. The audience did not go as smoothly as the shy and inexperienced young Duke might have hoped, but his Stuart charm and natural good breeding carried him through the ordeal with considerable credit. The court was at Fontainebleau. Louis XV, in his dilatory way, quite forgot about the whole interview until well on in the day, when suddenly recalling the presence of his young cousin in the Château, commanded the Duc de Gesvres to present 'the Prince' at once, without specifying in any more particular way what prince he meant. The bewildered Gesvres hurried away and managed to discover by discreet if somewhat frenzied enquiry that a young foreigner had been waiting in a small ante-chamber for some considerable time and though his name was not known it was thought he might perhaps be the prince of England. We can only wonder what Henry went through during his long anxious wait in a small chamber of the Château, while Louis, happily forgetful of his presence, let the long hours slip by. Only twenty years old, and unused to the world outside his father's small and dismal court at Rome, he might well have been overpowered by the ritual and grandeur that surrounded the French monarchy and been reduced to a state of nervous collapse before he so much as reached the presence of the King. How long he was left to his own thoughts we do not know but surely it was quite long enough. No doubt with many apologies the Duc de Gesvres conducted him into the royal presence.

Louis XV was easily embarrassed in the company of strangers and his uneasiness must have been increased by the knowledge

The Helmet and the Hat

that he had acted discourteously to his guest by keeping him waiting for so long. The embarrassment was not eased by the anomalous character in which the English prince was made to appear. As a cousin and a member of a royal family he was entitled to the royal embrace but as he was supposed to be incognito the problem of etiquette added considerably to the King's discomfort. Henry, however, unwittingly saved the situation by walking so confidently up to the monarch that Louis found himself kissing the incognito Duke whether he liked it or not. The Duc de Luynes, who was present on the occasion, was favourably impressed by the noble air and charming manners of the young prince, and the great good sense he showed in his conversation with the King. He expressed the gratitude of his family towards the House of France which had always stood staunchly by them since his grandfather's flight in 1688; and went on to describe his brother's great success in Scotland and to press that more aid might be forthcoming now that the Prince had crossed over into England. Loyalty to his brother made him, perhaps unwisely, remind the King how Prince Charles had attempted unsuccessfully to gain an audience before joining Marshal de Saxe and his invasion army on the coast. On this delicate issue his Most Christian Majesty did not vouchsafe any reply but with regard to the main points in Henry's conversation with him he declared his own conviction in the justice of the Stuart cause and promised that they might rely on his continued favour.

After this the conversation flagged and an awkward silence ensued. It was filled by a few commonplace courtesies. Was not the Duke, asked Louis, a godson of the Pope? Henry, remembering that the Holy Father and the Eldest Son of the Church were not always on the most filial of terms, replied cautiously that though he had been given the name of Benedict among many others he liked to be known by the name of the eight kings of England who were his forbears. He might have considered that the eighth Henry was no particular credit to the Catholic House of Stuart nor the fifth Henry one to introduce tactfully into a conversation carried on in the presence of the descendant of Charles VI of France; Louis, however, passed on to other topics and subjected his guest to a polite but tedious enquiry into the details of his education and upbringing. This perhaps reminded him of his own son, for he asked that the Dauphin should be sent for.

Monseigneur entered the room in some consternation, for not only had his father forgotten the Duke of York's presence at Fontainebleau until late in the day, but he had also completely omitted to tell his son that the Duke was coming at all. No doubt a few hurried whispers from the embarrassed courtiers helped the Dauphin to sum up the situation as best he could, and hearing how his father had greeted the royal stranger himself embraced him with a kiss. This only served to add to the general discomfort.

The Duke contrived to meet the situation without losing his composure, and congratulated Monseigneur on his campaign in Flanders, at the same time thanking the King for permitting him to meet his son. Louis bowed his acknowledgement and the conversation again reached a stand-still. Henry, only lately recovered from a fever and his self-possession now somewhat undermined by the strain of the interview and the long wait that had preceded it, began at this point to shiver, which gave the Duc de Gesvres his opportunity to remark to the King that the young prince had so recently been ill and was perhaps in need of rest. The King, one may imagine with a sigh of relief, brought the audience to an end and Henry retired from the royal presence with a low bow but with no more kisses. Outside the royal apartment Henry had to wait until the Duc de Gesvres was free to conduct him away as no one had bothered to show him the way out. So the interview with Louis the Well-beloved came to an end.

If Henry was a little depressed by his not very encouraging talk with the King of France from which nothing tangible seemed likely to develop, he must have been pleased and grateful when he was sent for by the Queen. This was Marie Leczinska, herself the daughter of a one-time King of Poland who took a kindly interest in the children of that other Polish princess Clementina Sobieska. The Princess de Conti, whose husband was related to the Stuart princes through their grandmother Mary of Modena, introduced the Duke into the presence of the Queen and the Dauphiness, and as the incognito did not apply in private there was no bar to the exchange of royal greetings. This audience, being private, was short and devoid of political significance but passed off without any of the awkward moments that had attended his meeting with the King.

7

Despite the rather unsatisfactory nature of the audience with Louis XV and the vague nature of the promises made, an expedition was prepared on the channel coast under the Duc de Richelieu with the Duke of York in nominal command. This was to consist of eleven thousand men together with artillery and the necessary ships to transport them over to England. These preparations must have given heart to the young Duke whose one ambition at this time was to give all the help he could to his brother, but he seems to have thought that Louis might have been more generous in his assistance, for when the Prince de Montauban asked to serve with him as an aide-de-camp Henry agreed, but refused to ask the King's consent, saying that he would ask no more favours after the treatment he had received. This rather petulant behaviour received from Louis XV the response one might have expected: if the Duke of York did not see fit to ask for Monsieur de Montauban's service he could do without it. On Christmas day, 1745, Henry left Paris for Dunkirk without his aide-de-camp.

It was perhaps unfortunate that the Duc de Richelieu, of all commanders in France, should have been placed over this army in association with the Duke of York. This distinguished nobleman, who enjoyed very appropriately the office of First Gentleman of the Bedchamber and whose reputation for victories of a decidedly non-military nature has caused him to be described as the champion rake of eighteenth-century France, was hardly likely to have much in common with the pious young prince whose passion for religious observances had given rise to some amusement at the French court where even making the sign of the cross was considered evidence of excessive devotion. Richelieu, who whiled away the months of delay at Dunkirk by carrying on an amorous correspondence with the reigning mistress at Versailles, was moved to exasperation by a prince who, in the words of the Marquis d'Argenson, 'never passes before a crucifix or an altar without genuflecting like a sacristan.' Henry soon became the 'Italian bigot' in the eyes of the Duc de Richelieu, whose sneering references to the former's relative chances of gaining the Kingdoms of Heaven or Great Britain have already been referred to.

It might be remarked that Henry was something of a prig at this time, but on the other hand this was his first experience of life outside the shelter of his father's court at Rome with its rather oppressive atmosphere of piety, and the contrast of this simple life with the air of elegant promiscuity that pervaded the environment of the Most Christian King and his First Gentleman of the Bedchamber must have overwhelmed the young inexperienced Duke of York. As Cardinal Alberoni informed Sir Horace Mann: 'He was as much scandalised by his French experiences as the French Court was bored with his own absurd prejudices.' It is not surprising therefore that there was little harmony in the councils of war; that accusations of every sort were made; that the English retinue of the Prince, weary of delay, thought Richelieu had no real intention of invading; while to the French Henry appeared, in the words of d'Argenson, 'untrustworthy, thoroughly Italian, deceitful, superstitious, miserly, and fond of his comforts.' This was quite a startling array of epithets to be collected by a young man scarcely twenty years old whose character was as yet hardly formed.

Henry had not been at Dunkirk long before he received a letter from his father dated from Rome on January 4th, 1746. Though the retreat from Derby had started on December 6th it would seem that news of this had not yet reached the King.

'I hope in God, my dearest Harry, that this will find you in England. . . . It is a great comfort to me to see things in such a forwardness for the English expedition. The persons lately come from England and Scotland will, to be sure, yet more hasten the execution, but till that is done and that I know you once safely arrived in England, you may imagine my anxiety for your Brother and you. In the mean time it is a great comfort to me to receive such good accounts of you as I do. . . . I am glad you are pleased

The Helmet and the Hat

with me, and I believe there is little danger of our ever being otherwise than satisfied with one another.'

The Stuart King's hope of finding his second son in England was to remain unfulfilled. The French force was closely watched by Admiral Vernon and a chance to slip out under cover of fog just before the New Year had been abandoned as too risky. (Later the Duke of York was to be blamed for this decision.) When the son of Lord Derwentwater was captured from a ship in the channel it was thought at first that he was Prince Henry, and he was subjected to a violent demonstration by the London mob only just recovered from the panic occasioned by the presence of Prince Charles's army at Derby. There were other equally false claims to his capture: 'We think we have got the second son under the name of Macdonald,' Horace Walpole wrote, but in fact the Prince never left French soil. Throughout the winter he remained on the coast, but the hope of any action grew less and less so that eventually the Duc de Richelieu returned to Paris with many bitter complaints about the Duke of York's piety which he considered almost as much a calamity as the failure of the expedition. France had obviously given up hope in the Stuart cause after the news of the retreat from Derby had reached Paris, and even the victory at Falkirk failed to move them. James wrote again from Rome urging Henry to keep the good will of France at all costs, though it is clear that he, too, was beginning to lose hope.

'But in all events [he concludes] what is I think of the greatest importance is to use all possible means to preserve the King of France and his Ministers in the good disposition they are towards us, and to conceal with care our being sensible that the Prince miscarrying in his present enterprise is manifestly owing to their being so long in assisting him. It is to be hoped the King of France will make it a point of honour to be kind to your Brother and you whatever may happen.'

Henry remained on the coast until the fatal news of Culloden was brought to him, and it was not until then that he turned his back on the distant view of the English coast, those white cliffs which were all he would ever see of the ancient Kingdom of his ancestors.

The Cardinal King

8

It was a great disappointment to the Duke of York that he had been unable to offer any more positive help to his brother, and he must also have been aware that he had enemies at the Court of France who were ready to attribute the failure of the Dunkirk expedition to the indecisions of the Duke of York rather than to the inertia of the French command. It was perhaps for this reason that Henry sought permission from Louis XV to serve with the army in Flanders where the Marshal de Saxe was conducting his brilliant campaign. Leave was eventually given to the Duke and in May he was able to write to his father to tell him of his appointment to the staff of the Comte de Clermont who was then with the French army before Antwerp.

Ghant. Mai ye 20*th*, 1746.

SIR,

Your Majesty must pardon the hurry and shortness of this letter, but really I have not one moment's time having just got leave to go to the Army under Ct Clermont's orders that is going to Besiege the Citadel of Antwerp. I part in a few hours. The affliction and anxiety I am in for my dearest Brother makes me enjoy the pleasure of this leave much less than I wou'd have done had things gone better in the North than I fear they do. My constant attention shall be for the Prince's personal safety; that I think is the chief point at present. Most humbly begging Your Majesty's blessing I remain with the utmost respect

Your most dutiful son,

HENRY

In the siege of Antwerp he saw his only active service and he must have carried himself bravely enough for even d'Argenson, whose previous uncomplimentary description of the Duke has been quoted, was to write of his conduct here that 'he behaved with a valour which was at once natural and hereditary.'

But though the Duke must have been glad of an opportunity to show his worth on the field of battle, his main purpose, as the

The Helmet and the Hat

letter quoted above shows, was to contrive means for his brother's safe return from Scotland. From this time we find the Duke becoming more sure of himself and his character strengthening. Perhaps the experience of battle or the thought of being able to help Charles in his hour of need had contributed to this, or more probably the fact that he alone of the Stuarts was to see the full significance of the defeat at Culloden as a final blow to their Cause; but whatever the reason he was no longer lacking in decision either in bringing assistance to his brother or in determining his own future course. Plans were at once discussed for fetching Prince Charles back to France and in this Henry took a leading part, urging the French Government to dispatch ships to the Scottish coast and showing much impatience at the delays. 'It is a cruel thing,' he wrote to his father at the end of July, 'these frigates are so long a-going, and I am sure it is not for want of pressing.' From the Château de Navarre, near Evreux, where Henry was staying with his cousin the Duc de Bouillon after returning from the Antwerp campaign, Colonel Warren was able to report to King James in August of the progress of their plans. 'The present orders were intimated to me,' he records of the latest scheme, 'just as I was about to depart for Navarre, there to make my court to His Royal Highness the Duke, and to receive from him due instructions relative to the present circumstances: it's wonderful how capable he is of giving good ones though so young.'

It was not until October, when Henry was living at Clichy near Paris where Louis had given him a house, that news reached him of his brother's safe arrival at Roscoff on the Breton coast. Henry lost no time in rushing to meet the brother whom he had not seen for nearly three years. Back at Clichy he sent off an account of their meeting to Rome where James was all anxiety for information.

'The very morning after I writ you my last, I had the happiness of meeting with my dearest brother. He did not know me at first sight, but I am sure I knew him very well, for he is not in the least altered since I saw him, except grown somewhat broader and fatter, which is incomprehensible after all the fatigues he has endured. Your Majesty may conceive better than I can express in writing the tenderness of our first meeting. Those that were present said they never saw the like in their lives; and, indeed, I defy the whole world to show another brother so kind and so loving as he is to me. . . . The Prince sees and scarce will see anybody but myself for a few days, that he may have a little time to rest before he is plagued by all the world, as to be sure he will, when once he sees company. I go every day to dine with him. Yesterday I brought him privately to see my house; and I perceive he has as much *goût* for the chase as ever he had.'

This cheerful letter, so full of affection and pride in the achievements of the elder brother, must have gladdened the heart of the melancholy old King for all that the return of Prince Charles meant the failure once again of all their hopes. None the less he must have been thankful that his two sons were so happily united. This happiness was not to last.

9

It is not unusual for brothers, united in childhood, to find themselves at variance with each other in later years. We have already noted how the Duke of York's character had strengthened and taken on a new sense of direction since he had heard the news of Culloden and had had time to assess its significance. The end to which this new sense of purpose was to lead him was soon to be made known and the relationship between the brothers was never to be the same as a result of it. Charles returned from Scotland expecting to find in Henry the same admiring younger brother always ready to play the lesser rôle and to accept without question the elder's leadership. Furthermore Charles's character bore the scars of his bitter experiences in Scotland. To the end of his days he would never efface from his memory the recollection of the barbaric cruelties inflicted on his defeated troops by the soldiers of the brutal Duke of Cumberland. Sir Charles Petrie has given us some idea of the atrocities that followed Culloden, when 'the wounded were dragged from their hiding-places, drawn up in line, and despatched by platoon firing; the few who survived had their brains beaten out by the stocks of the victors' muskets.' Or

The Helmet and the Hat

again: 'A barn in which several wounded Highlanders had taken refuge was set on fire, and as the unhappy inmates, half suffocated by the smoke, tried to get out, they were driven back at the point of the bayonet by the soldiers stationed round the shed, and roasted in the flames.' These, and other horrors, haunted Charles's memory to such an extent that, even as an old man, he could never recall them without emotion. His mind, coloured by such terrible experiences together with those involved in his final escape to France, could not appreciate the more detached attitude which his brother was able to adopt to the whole affair; yet for all this it was the Duke who appealed to the Marquis d'Argenson to intercede with the British Government when news of the dreadful penalties meted out to the prisoners of the Forty-Five became known in Paris. The latter saw in the battle of Culloden the end of all his family's political hope, and he felt himself free to follow his own destiny. Charles, for the remainder of his life, was to be haunted by a phantom hope that he would once again lead his Highlanders to victory and a crown.

To begin with the brothers were friendly enough, but jealousies and petty irritations soon began to separate them, though for all this there was an underlying affection which could be relied upon to heal most breaches sooner or later. Charles was hailed in Paris as a hero and even the chilly reception of the Court, which would only receive the two princes as Lord Renfrew and Earl of Albany respectively, did nothing to check the enthusiasm of the people who turned out in great numbers to cheer the Prince as he drove to Fontainebleau with his orders glittering on a coat of rose-coloured velvet and silver lace. Louis XV received him with personal cordiality but with obvious reluctance to make any promises or offers of help in the political sphere. France had already expended vast sums on the Scottish enterprise and one can hardly blame Louis for not putting the cause of his Stuart cousins before that of his own Kingdom. But Charles was angry, both at the refusal to recognize him as Prince Regent of Great Britain, and at the offer of nothing more than empty promises instead of material assistance. His irritation was such that he took offence at his brother's sharing his honours at the French Court and would not

The Cardinal King

speak to the King of his affairs until he could have an audience at which Henry was not present.

The Duke of York had done little to merit this treatment, but there were plenty of people in Paris ready to suggest to Charles that his brother's efforts to assist him in the Dunkirk enterprise had been nothing if not half-hearted; while the Marquis d'Argenson, who admired Charles as much as he despised Henry, was not above accusing the latter of actual cowardice in refusing to embark from Dunkirk under cover of fog. Furthermore Henry's growing preoccupation with his own future plans made Charles suspect him of scheming on his own account, and the confidence of the two brothers in each other grew less.

In Rome James began to hear of the quarrels and wrote urging a reconciliation. To this Charles replied that his brother 'does not open his heart to me, and yet I perceive he is grieved, which must proceed from malicious people putting things in his head, and preventing him against me.' James, in answer, pointed out the regrettable effect such a breach would have on the cause and even suggested that he might ask Henry to return to Rome, without actually ordering him back there, as the way matters now stood he might be of more service there than in Paris. There were, no doubt, faults on both sides, and the King ends: '*Enfin*, my Dear Child, my whole thoughts are turned to provide as much as is possible for the real good and advantage of both of you.'

Thinking, as his letter had hinted, that the brothers might be happier apart, James decided to send Henry on a mission to Spain. But this only served to annoy Charles the more, being at the time on his way to Avignon having left his brother in charge of affairs at Paris. He wrote in some anger to his father complaining that he should make such a move without first consulting him, and pointing out that the trip was unnecessary anyway as he was going to Spain himself. It is more than likely that the idea of going there had never occurred to him until he heard that Henry was to go, and in any event he might have spared himself the trouble as the visit to Madrid only resulted in further humiliations. He returned to Paris in March 1747 to fling himself into a bout of dissipation as an escape from the mounting frustrations which were becoming more and more a feature of his political existence.

Henry could only view his brother's conduct with horror, and the thought of the plight to which his disappointments had reduced him (though Charles's fits of intemperance were nothing yet compared with what they were to become) very probably influenced him yet more in taking the step he had for so long comtemplated, and on April 29th he left Paris for Rome with as much secrecy as he had originally left Rome for Paris.

Henry's manner of discovering his flight to Charles was tactless and cruel in a way quite out of character with his nature, and can only be accounted for by the fact that the urgency of his motive must have made him inconsiderate of its effect on one who, despite all their differences, had until that moment a considerable affection for him. On the evening of the 29th Charles arrived by special invitation to dine at the Duke's house at Clichy, but on arrival was deeply disturbed to find that his host was not there despite the fact that the meal was ready and that every preparation had been made for his reception. Very much alarmed by the thought that his brother might have been kidnapped or even assassinated, he was not to be informed until next morning of the true cause of the absence, and even then he was only told that his brother had left for Rome. It was not until several weeks had passed and after the fatal step had been taken that a letter from King James announced to him the true reason for the Duke of York's flight to Rome; that he had embraced the ecclesiastical state upon nomination by Pope Benedict XIV to the Sacred College of Cardinals.

10

If Charles was kept in ignorance of his brother's intentions so, it must be added, was all the world. Sir Horace Mann was at a loss to account for the young Prince's sudden arrival at Rome and guessed that arrangements were being discussed for a French pension. 'The young Prince seems very quiet at present,' he wrote, 'but he has certainly something in his head which will soon flash out.' No one was more horrified and disgusted when the news did

The Cardinal King

at length 'flash out' than the new Cardinal's elder brother whose fury was such that he was even ready to believe that Cardinal de Tencin, the French Minister, had been bribed by the British Government to favour the plan. To the long and closely reasoned letter of explanation sent to him by his father the outraged Prince could only reply: 'Had I got a Dager throw my heart it would not have been mor sensible to me than ye Contents.'

James in his letter explains in patient detail the reasons which in his consideration justified the action of Henry in accepting the Red Hat. It is clear that he anticipated the hostility with which the news would be received by his elder son, and made every endeavour to explain things fully. At the same time he had so arranged matters that Charles need not associate himself in any way with an action of which he could claim complete ignorance. The letter also shows the earnest desire of the father to preserve the unity of the family, already so shaken:

Albano. June 13.1747.

I know not whether you will be surprised, my dearest Carluccio, when I tell you that your brother will be made a Cardinal the first days of next month. Naturally speaking, you should have been consulted about a resolution of that kind before it had been executed; but, as the Duke and I were unalterably determined on the matter, and as we forsaw you might probably not approve of it, we thought it might be showing you more regard, and that it would be even more agreeable to you, that the thing should be done before your answer could come here, and to have it in your power to say it was done without your knowledge and approbation. It is very true I did not expect to see the Duke here so soon, and that his tenderness and affection for me prompted him to undertake that journey; but after I had seen him, I soon found that his chief motive for it was to discourse with me fully and freely on the vocation he had long had to embrace an ecclesiastical state, and which he had so long concealed from me, and kept to himself, with a view, no doubt, of having it in his power of being of some use to you in the late conjectures. But the case is now altered: and as I am fully convinced of the sincerity and solidity of his

The Helmet and the Hat

vocation, I should consider it a resisting the Will of God, and acting directly against my conscience, if I should pretend to constrain him in a matter which so nearly concerns him. The maxims I have bred you up in, and have always followed, of not constraining others in matters of religion, did not a little help to determine me on the present occasion, since it would be a monstrous proposition that a King should be a father to his people and a tyrant to his children.

After this, I will not conceal from you, my dearest Carluccio, that motives of conscience and equity have not alone determined me in this particular; and that when I seriously consider all that has passed in relation to the Duke for some years bye-gone, had he not had the vocation he has, I should have used my best endeavours, and all arguments, to have induced him to have embraced that state. If Providence has made you the elder brother, he is as much my son as you, and my parental care and affection are equally to be extended to you and him, so that I should have thought I had greatly failed in both towards him, had I not endeavoured by all means to secure to him, as much as in me lay, that tranquility and happiness which I was sensible it was not possible for him to enjoy in any other state. You will understand all that I mean without my enlarging further on this last so disagreeable article; and you cannot, I am sure, complain that I deprive you of any service the Duke might have been to you, since you must be sensible that, all things considered, he would have been useless to you remaining in the world.

But let us look forward, and not backward. The resolution is taken, and will be executed before your answer to this can come here. If you think proper to say you were ignorant of it, and do not approve it, I shall not take it amiss of you; but, for God's sake, let not a step which naturally should secure peace and union amongst us for the rest of our days, become a subject for scandal and *éclat*, which would fall heavier upon you than upon us in our present situation, and which a filial and brotherly conduct in you will easily prevent. . . .

I am all yours,
JAMES R.

The Cardinal King

The brief and angry reply to this letter, already noted, left no one in doubt as to Prince Charles's reaction to it. To Henry he wrote not a word, nor would he have his name mentioned in his presence nor his health drunk at his table, and ignored completely the letter that closely followed upon his father's.

Albano, June 20th, 1747.

DEAR BROTHER,

Tho I have still the mortification to be without hearing from you I think it my duty to continue to write to you and to assure you of my most respectful and tender love and affection, until you let me know more plainly that by the silence of a few weeks that my letters will not be acceptable, but I trust in God that will never happen, and that you will never do me and, give me leave to say, yourself, the wrong of breaking with a Brother who you will be sensible at last is not unworthy of your kindness. I remain, dear Brother, with the utmost respect,

your most loving Brother,

HENRY

Though the Duke of York might wish to remain a most loving brother, as far as Charles was concerned the breach was final, and it was indeed almost eighteen years before the brothers were finally reconciled to each other.

The damage done to the Stuart Cause by Henry's nomination as a Cardinal was certainly greater than either the King or the Duke would seem to have expected, and if the rumours circulated in Paris of a bribe from the British Government to encourage the scheme were inaccurate, it is none the less true that few things were more likely to please the House of Hanover than this intimate association of the native dynasty with the feared and distrusted Church of Rome. Only Charles understood the extent to which the Roman Catholic Church was still detested by the majority in England (and more especially in Scotland) and he knew from personal experience how great a blow this step would be to the vast bulk of Anglican opinion in England which was still at heart largely loyal to the Stuarts. The point is clearly expressed by Mann, who could remark to Horace Walpole with as

The Helmet and the Hat

much satisfaction as truth that 'Cardinal Stuart by putting on the Cowle has done more to extinguish his party than would have been effected by putting to death many thousand of deluded followers.'

The truth of Mann's observation is corroborated by the protest addressed to King James by Father Myles McDonnell, Rector of the Scots College at Paris, on what he refers to as 'his R.H. the Duke of York's late change of condition'. He makes no pretence in condemning the Duke's action as being a 'mortal deadly stroke at the cause'; strong words indeed for a subject to address to his sovereign. He points out how occasion will be made in England to renew the old bugbears of Popery and bigotry, and suggests that 'discreet persons' should be sent at once across the channel in an endeavour to justify the step and 'ward off if possible the dreadful storm the cause is threaten'd with'.

Against all these remonstrations, so fully justified from the practical point of view, we can only set the plain fact of Henry Stuart's genuine vocation to the religious life. Some people have suggested that a love of ease and the attractions of the lazy existence which could then still be enjoyed by a Roman ecclesiastic had commended this mode of life to the Prince; but his subsequent energetic execution of his duties as Bishop of Frascati and as Camerlengo are in themselves proof to the contrary. The truth of the matter is that Henry saw more clearly than either his father or his brother (and especially more so than Charles) that the Stuart Cause in so far as it represented any real chance to regain actual possession of the British Crown was now for ever lost; that he must therefore accept the realities of the situation and, while not renouncing one jot of his hereditary rights, face the future in the knowledge that it would never be the destiny of his family to return to the Kingdom from which his grandfather had made such a hurried exit. This being so, there was nothing to prevent him from fulfilling the vocation nearest to his heart which was also one in which his life could be passed in useful service. If we compare his career with the subsequent tragic rôle of his brother there surely can be little doubt as to which made the wiser assessment of the future or followed the better course.

3

A Prince of the Church

1

Henry Benedict Stuart in assuming the Roman Purple was creating no precedent in the long annals of British royalty. From Norman days to the Reformation the reigning dynasty had from time to time given Cardinals to the Church. Odo, Earl of Kent, half-brother to William of Normandy, was Cardinal-Bishop of Bayeux; Henry of Blois, brother to the unfortunate King Stephen, was Bishop of Winchester and Legate. Of the House of Plantagenet was Henry Cardinal Beaufort, son of John of Gaunt, and later came Reginald Cardinal Pole, last Catholic Archbishop of Canterbury and also the man who came nearest to being the second English Pope. It is perhaps ironical that the only other royal Henry, prior to the Cardinal Duke of York, destined for the Red Hat was the Tudor prince who later became King Henry VIII, who was originally intended for an ecclesiastical career had his elder brother not died. It is tempting to speculate on the possible course of events had Prince Arthur lived and Henry worn the robes of Wolsey or perhaps even the tiara of Leo X.

2

Before the traditional ceremonies of admission to the Sacred College could be completed it was necessary for the Duke to receive the Tonsure, the bestowal of which set a person aside as an ecclesiastic though it did not confer any sacred character in the sense of Holy Orders. It should here be pointed out that the Cardinalate, being a rank or dignity of the Roman Church, was not of necessity synonymous with the priesthood, and many Cardinals (such as Ministers of foreign states or Papal Secretaries)

A Prince of the Church

whose activities were largely of a secular nature never entered the priesthood at all but remained in Minor Orders from which they could, on occasion, be released. This practice remained until the time of Pius IX; one of the last Cardinals to be only in Minor Orders being his famous Secretary of State Giacomo Antonelli. It is probable that James Stuart himself expected his son to remain in Minor Orders when he originally agreed to his nomination, looking upon the office as something that would provide the Duke with ample revenues and a position of dignity, but also as something that could be laid aside should destiny call him to be head of the family through the death of his brother without heirs. Indeed even priestly vows had been dispensed with when the question of succession to a crown arose, as in the case of Casimir the Monk, King of Poland. But whatever James may have thought it had little influence on his son who had undoubtedly decided from the beginning to embrace the ecclesiastical life in the fullest sense.

On June 30th, 1747, Henry Stuart received the Tonsure at the hands of the Sovereign Pontiff himself in the presence of King James and his Court and the Cardinal-Protectors of England, Scotland and Ireland. Benedict XIV, one of the most distinguished, tolerant and enlightened Popes of the Eighteenth Century, was no doubt pleased to show this mark of favour to the House of Stuart, the justice of whose cause he had always upheld. He had a devotion to James Stuart which sprang not only from a respect for his qualities of character but also from an admiration for his loyalty to the Catholic Faith but for which he might have worn the crown of three kingdoms. It is possible that the Pope did not feel the same affection for the proud young Duke who now knelt before him; he was to know him only as a rather opioninated churchman of difficult temper often, in these early days of his ecclesiastical career, all too ready to take offence. It was this Pope who, after a long and rather tedious Audience granted to the young Cardinal, is said to have remarked that if all the Stuarts were as boring as Cardinal York he did not wonder that the English had driven them out.

On July 3rd Henry proceeded in state to the Vatican, wearing

The Cardinal King

for the first time the splendid scarlet robes of his new office, where at the altar of the Sistine Chapel he received the Red Hat, having already received the red skull-cap and biretta. The Pope, in his allocution, after recalling the piety of the postulant's mother and the services rendered to the Church by his father and grandfather, declared that the glory of the Sacred College could only be increased by admitting the son of such parents. The assembled Princes of the Church, not a few of whom resented the royal pretensions of their new colleague, may have listened to these words with less enthusiasm than the members of the Jacobite Court who were present at the ceremony, and many of the latter must have doubted the wisdom of the entire proceedings. In excusing the excessive youth of the Duke—he was only twenty-two—the Pontiff reminded their Eminences that the saintly Charles Borromeo was no older when raised to the same dignity; that Peter of Luxemburg had been only sixteen and Robert de Nobilibus no more than twelve. It was perhaps fortunate that the Holy Father did not make his list more inclusive, for Caesar Borgia had also become a Cardinal at the age of sixteen, as did the cunning Giulio de' Medici who, as Clement VII, had brought upon Rome its greatest disaster since the days of the barbarians. Possibly only Cardinal Alessandro Albani considered such parallels. As a staunch supporter of the House of Hanover he sent an account of the proceedings to Horace Mann in which he declared that the speech was extremely ridiculed in Rome—an opinion that is not born out by any other testimony. At the end of the allocution the Pope put the traditional question to the Sacred College—*Quid vobis videtur?*—and as no objections were raised the Duke was duly appointed a Cardinal Deacon of the Holy Roman Church with the title of Santa Maria in Campitelli. This church, near the theatre of Marcellus, is one of those parish churches of Rome which are held according to ancient tradition by the various members of the College of Cardinals as their titular churches. In honour of this occasion King James endowed prayers to be said in this church at noon every Saturday for the conversion of England.

A week after this the new Cardinal attended the Pope at the Apostolic Palace of the Quirinal where the curious rite of opening

A Prince of the Church

and shutting the mouth was performed in token of the discretion required of the Cardinal in his capacity of an adviser to the Sovereign Pontiff; and here he also received the sapphire ring which, from the words of Isaiah, 'I will lay thy stones with fair colours and thy foundations with sapphires' had become the symbol of the Cardinalate.

These great ceremonies completed, other less important matters pressed for attention. The thorny problems of precedence always cause considerable heart-burn in ecclesiastical circles, and there was no exception in the case of the Cardinal Duke. From Mann, who was informed by Albani, we learn that at a special Congregation it was decided that the Duke should have no special precedence but that his style of address should be 'Royal Highness and Eminence', and nothing was calculated to annoy the royal Cardinal more than when the former of these distinctions was purposely or inadvertently omitted. Further trouble arose over the coat of arms: should the Hat be over or beneath the prince's crown? Here a victory was won for the spiritual symbol and on the Cardinal Duke's escutcheon we find the tasselled Hat placed above the princely coronet. The curious may still see the royal arms of England thus displayed in the Church of Santa Maria in Trastevere over the arch at the East end of the right-hand aisle of the nave; it can also be seen at various places in the little town of Frascati where the Cardinal Duke was later to be bishop. Lest King James should think that his son's royal rank had been overlooked or belittled the Pope gave orders that when the other Cardinals came to make their ceremonial call of congratulation on their new colleague they should wear their full scarlet robes of state and not the customary black cassock distinguished only by the red buttons and sash.

While the Cardinal was receiving these visitors Sir Horace Mann was busily writing to his friend Horace Walpole of all the latest excitements at Rome. 'They say,' wrote the Envoy of the new Cardinal, 'he is to be Legate of Avignon for life, and that he is to have the Archbishoprick of Monte Reale, which Acquaviva had, and which they say is worth near 100,000 Ducats a year—is not he vastly in the right to become Cardinal?'

The Cardinal King

3

At the age of twenty-two the Cardinal Duke of York emerged as a personality in his own right, though in order to establish his independence he was soon engaged in squabbles with his father often undignified and sometimes ridiculous which must have called to mind among the older members of the Court the earlier disagreements between James and his wife.

Both father and son suffered from ill-health. James's almost congenital melancholia was accompanied by a less distinguished malady; he was a chronic dyspeptic. The periodical outbursts of exasperation at what he considered to be his son's inconsiderate behaviour were not made easier to bear by the attacks of violent indigestion they occasioned. Henry, too, was in weak health. His chest was never strong and he was liable to fainting fits; at times he was seen coughing and spitting blood. The threatened consumption can never, however, have been a serious menace in a man who lived a life of considerable activity to beyond his eightieth year. His complaints were more probably nervous and he may well have taken refuge in ill-health as a protection against his father's intransigence, for it was unreasonable of James to expect his son to live under the same roof as himself now that the Cardinal had a position of his own to maintain, and tastes and interests of a very different sort from his father's. Henry liked to frequent the literary and artistic circles of Rome, having inherited something of the connoisseurship of his great-grandfather Charles I. While never a first-class scholar he became a patron of learning and his collection of books (now in the Vatican Library) was famous. The present of a rare edition was a sure way to gain the Cardinal Duke's favour, as Count Alfieri later discovered. James, on the other hand, read little and had no interest in the arts. Though once discovered reading Voltaire (had not Benedict XIV, after all, accepted the dedication of 'Mahomet'?) his main pleasure seems to have been derived from the works of the Fathers, a taste that may be good for the cultivation of piety but is not calculated to make one the life and soul of a literary symposium; and when

A Prince of the Church

artistic friends of the Duke appeared at the Muti Palace it is not surprising that the dyspeptic old King complained that his son was keeping low company. But such a charge is not a tactful one to bring against a Prince of the Church though he be only in his twenties and one's own son into the bargain, and there were days when the Cardinal and the King met daily at table without so much as speaking to each other. Sometimes the tension was such that James, torn between rage and gastric discomfort, went to bed without his supper.

Since childhood Henry had been devoted to music and now he was able to indulge his taste in a practical way. He organized musical concerts and commissioned special Masses and Oratorios for his titular church where he appointed Buranello (Baldassare Galuppi) as his choirmaster. It was also his custom to give receptions every Thursday evening and these became so popular that latecomers were often unable to gain admission owing to the throng.

Despite these successful social gatherings the Duke seems to have gained a reputation for haughtiness and for adopting unnecessarily stately airs during these early years of his Cardinalate. His was an unduly sensitive nature, and on top of this he had to bear the slights he was occasionally subjected to by persons who went out of their way to ignore his royal rank, to which, like all dispossessed royalty, he attached an exaggerated importance. The desire to avoid such occasions made him more unapproachable than he need have been, though to genuine friends (like Cardinal Giovanni Francesco Albani, a cousin of Alessandro already referred to, but as friendly to Henry as the other was opposed), he was open enough; and the fact that artists and musicians sat down at table with him shows that in some respects at least he was more 'democratic' than many people at that time whose social position was considerably less exalted than his own. King James was, after all, only expressing the sentiment of his time in considering such like as 'low company'. But with strangers who were attracted to him solely by curiosity the Cardinal Duke was cold, for the old King and his son were looked upon as one of the sights of Rome by the many British travellers who flocked to the Eternal City in increas-

The Cardinal King

ing numbers; and while these avid sight-seers were only too pleased to find themselves in the presence of their sovereign by right of lineal descent, or to watch his son participating in some great function of the Church, they were careful to accord them none of the natural respect which their royal blood warranted. Thus, two years after Henry Stuart became a Cardinal, we find the Earl of Chesterfield offering this advice to his natural son who was about to visit Rome: 'When you speak of the Old Pretender, you will call him only the Chevalier de St. George; but mention him as seldom as possible. Should he chance to speak to you at any assembly (as, I am told, he sometimes does in English), be sure that you seem not to know him; and answer him civilly, but always either in French, or in Italian; and give him, in the former, the appellation of Monsieur, and in the latter, of Signore. Should you meet with the Cardinal of York, you will be under no difficulty; for he has, as Cardinal, an undoubted right to Eminenza.' To this we might add that as the grandson of a reigning English monarch he had an undoubted right to Royal Highness, and the neglect of this obvious courtesy by British visitors was a mortifying experience to the proud young prince who had not yet learnt by experience to accept these rebuffs with the patience and dignity which never deserted his father on any occasion.

When the Cardinal was an old man he was visited by George III's son Augustus Frederick, Duke of Sussex. It is to the credit of this prince that he was scrupulous in addressing his aged relative by his proper title, and when the Cardinal returned the call the prince conducted him to the only chair in the room and himself remained standing. It is said that George III had suggested this gesture and it is characteristic of the good heart of that monarch if the story is true. It is, of course, equally true that at the time when the young Cardinal was smarting under the calculated slights of George II's subjects the House of Hanover could ill afford to make gallant gestures to the banished Stuarts.

Among his fellow members of the Roman Curia the Cardinal caused further annoyance by wearing ermine on his cappa, or scarlet cape, as a sign of royalty. Cardinal Ruffo made a special journey in all the heat of the Italian summer to expostulate with the Pope on the subject at Castelgandolfo; but Benedict XIV, it would seem, had more important things to think about. But this was not all; his household was next announced and this, if we may believe Mann, was additional reason for jealous murmurings. 'He is to have a Monsignore Leigh for a Maestro di Camera,' Mann informed Walpole, 'a very noble Irishman born at Cadiz of a little merchant there; two Sicilian Marquises for his Major-Domo and Cupbearer; and an Abbé Falingieri for Segretario dell' Embasciata. You know that the Cardinals have people about them with these titles, but as all the above are supposed to be vastly noble, the other Cardinals grumble at it.' The grumbling was not confined to the Cardinals: soon James himself was running to the Pope with complaints about his son's entourage.

4

The Cardinal Duke was ordained Priest on September 1st, 1748. It is probable, as we have suggested already, that his father had not expected him to take this step, but Henry was determined and James did not withhold his consent. Certainly no opposition was offered by the Pope who nearly wept, we are told, on hearing of what he described as the 'heroic resolution of this holy youth'. When the news reached Charles, on the other hand, he was furious and renewed his resolution never to set eyes on his brother again. Henry said his first Mass the day after his ordination in the King's private chapel, and his first sung Mass, or *Missa Cantata*, in the Sistine Chapel on the Feast of the Holy Innocents in the presence of James and twenty-two Cardinals. Twelve days after his ordination he was elevated to the office of Cardinal Priest but retained his former titular church. Commenting on these changes in the Cardinal's condition Mann was able to report: 'The Cardinal is all devotion. He fasts and prays as much as his mother used to do, and, they say, has ruined his constitution already.'

The Basilica of the Holy Apostles, that church with so many associations with the House of Stuart in their days of exile and in which the heart of Queen Clementina lies entombed, was now transferred to the Cardinal Duke, while the Kings of France and

The Cardinal King

Spain bestowed benefices upon him so that Henry's financial position began to improve until he was able to occupy for a time a place unique in the annals of history; a rich Stuart. He was at one time, indeed, to be computed the richest member of the Sacred College. The generosity of Louis XV may well have been prompted by a desire to make up for his ungrateful treatment of the Cardinal's brother. For in the same year that Henry became a priest Charles, under the severe terms of the Treaty of Aix-la-Chapelle, was arrested after attending the opera in Paris and hurried out of the French King's territory with a minimum of ceremony. Charles might have saved his cousin this unpleasant duty had he agreed to leave voluntarily as Louis more than once asked him to; but the Prince refused to believe that the French Court would treat him with such ingratitude, and stubbornly remained in Paris. Gratitude, however, is not a quality widely known in the game of politics, and as the Prince refused to budge of his own accord Louis was forced to sign the warrant. 'How hard it is for a King to be a friend,' he said as he signed it, and then fell silent. The Prince was removed to Avignon, from which place he started on his restless wanderings, sometimes disappearing for long periods when neither the Government in London nor the exiled Court at Rome had any idea of his whereabouts. He was to continue in this unsettled state until his father's death.

King James and the Cardinal seem to have been little moved by the news of Charles's expulsion. It is true that they made a pilgrimage to Loretto on behalf of the Prince; but as this was made in connection with a vow for his safe return from Scotland it is rather strange that they should only have fulfilled it at the time of the Prince's rejection from France. The breach between Prince Charles and his family grew wider with each passing year and often, as we have seen, neither the King nor the Duke had the remotest idea where he was, and had to be content with the report of rumour and the occasional undated and unaddressed notes that reached them from the Prince. There is something of tragedy in the thought of the old Chevalier asking for enquiries to be made of Cardinal Alessandro Albani, whom he knew to be the implacable enemy of his House, to see if he had any information on the

A Prince of the Church

whereabouts of his elder son. But Charles's disappearance was, for the moment, complete. Neither friend nor enemy knew where he was.

5

In the year following his ordination to the priesthood the Cardinal Duke dismissed Monsignor Leigh, his English Maestro di Camera or Chamberlain, and replaced him by a Genoese priest named Lercari. The latter was nephew to one of Henry's fellow Cardinals; a man, presumably, whose birth was above the sneers of Sir Horace Mann. This act, innocent in itself, greatly annoyed King James, who blamed the Cardinal's confessor, Father Ildefonso, for setting his son against the English. He further accused his son of unnecessary extravagance. Father and son still kept a common table at the Muti Palace and James now determined that Henry should increase his contribution towards the expenses of hospitality. At the same time he gave orders that Father Ildefonso was to be refused admittance. Henry, in a rage, retired to Nocera, where he announced that he was taking the waters for his health and threatened not to return unless he could have a separate establishment from his father. The waters of Nocera, however, seem to have calmed him, for he forgot his threat and eventually rejoined his father at Albano, though they did not speak to each other until Henry had recovered from the mortifying experience of having his confessor changed, and replaced by a candidate more suitable to the King's taste. For in these skirmishes the King generally had the Pope on his side and he did not let the grass grow under his feet while Henry was sulking at Nocera. If the unfortunate Ildefonso, who now found himself dismissed, was the same priest we read of in Lord Dunbar's letter of 1742 describing the adolescence of the Duke, he may well have had cause to complain of his treatment after such long service in the royal household, and Henry's loyalty does him credit. Furthermore, James himself was not in a strong position to remonstrate with his son on the ground of partiality to foreigners, for shortly after this he took as his secretary Monsignor Lascaris, a Polish priest who had previously been agent to Prince Radziwill.

The Cardinal King

The reconciliation was only temporary for James, with typical Stuart obstinacy, was still determined on the dismissal of Lercari, while Henry (who could add a good measure of Sobieski obstinacy to his already considerable store of the Stuart variety) was equally determined to keep him. It was perhaps to give the Cardinal a little more independence that in 1751 the Pope appointed him Archpriest of the Vatican Basilica, an office which included an official residence in the Piazza della Sagrestia, and a considerable amount of patronage connected with the many ecclesiastical appointments at St. Peter's. But the Cardinal still lived at the Muti Palace and the quarrel, so humiliating to the Duke's dignity and disastrous to the King's digestion, continued on both sides.

Under pressure from the Pope Henry was compelled to dismiss his Chamberlain, who was banished from Papal territory, while Father Ildefonso was permitted to return to Rome but not to the Stuart Palace. The Cardinal's suppressed annoyance at these rebuffs told on his health, and when James insisted that all correspondence with Lercari and Ildefonso should cease Henry, like his mother before him, shut himself up in a monastery and refused to see anybody on the excuse that he was making a retreat, and shortly afterwards returned again to Nocera hoping that the therapeutic character of the water might cure more than mere ill-health.

From Nocera the Cardinal went to Bologna, where he was received in great state by the Legate, Cardinal Doria, and here he made a show of entertaining himself in the pleasant society of that town if only to annoy his father, who was still fuming at Rome, and constantly plaguing the Pope with complaints about his son's conduct. Lest anyone should think that he was not enjoying himself at Bologna the Cardinal sent to Rome for his most splendid vestments so that he could take part in the ceremonies in connection with the Feast of the Nativity of the Blessed Virgin Mary, but for this received a rebuke from the Pope, who informed him that he could not pontificate in a Papal diocese. If Henry could not have his vestments he still did not mean to come home without Lercari, so he sent for his winter clothes instead, as well as his

A Prince of the Church

silver, and hinted to the Pope that if he could not be independent in Rome he was quite content to remain where he was.

The much tried Pontiff now decided that the quarrel had gone on quite long enough. Having reminded Henry that Cardinals must live in Rome unless they are Legates or bishops, he ordered him back at once, telling him that he owed entire obedience to his father. 'I beg you to reflect,' he went on in a more fatherly tone, 'upon the triumph that heretics would feel in seeing a great prince of the Cardinal Senate ready to quarrel with the Head of his Church, although keeping himself sound in the faith of his ancestors and thereby renouncing a splendid Crown; and also to consider what lamentable effects would be produced in the minds of the followers of his royal House by such regrettable dissensions.'

The Cardinal was moved by this direct appeal from Benedict XIV; his obstinacy gave way to a more submissive temper, and he wrote to his father in a chastened mood. The King, having gained his point, replied in affectionate terms:

'It is very true, my dear son, that your leaving me has been a subject of grief and affliction to me, chiefly on your account, for these four months past, so that you may easily imagine with what satisfaction I perused your letter. . . . I am sensible your absense was the effect of ill advice; but I have the comfort to see that your return is your own work alone. Return, therefore, my dear child, without delay and with all confidence, into the arms of a tender father and true friend, who will forget what is past, and who will be as he always has been, wholly taken up with whatever may contribute to your real good and satisfaction. I beseech God to bless you and give you a good journey, and tenderly embrace you, my dear child.'

It might be pointed out that Henry had done no more than wish to have an independent establishment and control over his own household, which was hardly unreasonable for a person of his age and position. James seems still to have treated him as a child, which Henry must have found increasingly exasperating. But however just his cause, there can be little excuse in his conduct in rushing off to Bologna; it was, indeed, a childish gesture. The Cardinal returned in a subdued mood. But he got his separate table to which he could invite whoever he pleased. As for Monsignor Lercari, he remained in Genoa. What objections James had to him, beyond the fact that he was not an Englishman (a fact for which he could hardly be held responsible) has never been very clear. But perhaps he did the best of all out of these obscure and rather pointless family dissensions, for the Pope made him Bishop of Brunato for no other reason than to keep him away from the Cardinal Duke, and later he became Archbishop of his native Genoa.

While all these disturbances were causing excitement in Italy, Prince Charles was taking to himself a mistress in the person of Clementina Walkinshaw, a lady he had first met in Scotland at the time of the Forty-Five and who was named after his own mother. She seems to have sprung from a family of divided loyalty, for her sister was a Lady in Waiting to the Hanoverian Princess of Wales. This, and the Prince's rumoured apostacy, was a cause of great grief to James, but the Cardinal at this time seems to have been more concerned that he should not share his father's table than to care who shared his brother's bed. The consequences of this liaison were to cause him a good deal of trouble in years to come. Meanwhile all Europe enjoyed itself at the expense of these family rows, and in England Horace Walpole noted the latest epigram on the subject:

> *In royal veins how blood resembling runs!*
> *Like any George, James quarrels with his sons.*
> *Faith! I believe could he his crown resume,*
> *He'd hanker for his Herrenhausen, Rome!*

6

While King and Cardinal quarrelled at Rome, Charles was busy destroying his reputation as the 'bonnie Prince Charlie' which his gallant exploits in Scotland had gained for him. His somewhat tempestuous affair with the Princess de Talmond (herself of Polish birth, being a cousin of Queen Marie Leczinska) had ended in violent scenes in which they are said to have come to blows, and the Prince had asked Clementina Walkinshaw to keep her promise made during the Forty-Five to go to him where ever Providence might lead. In this instance Providence was expected to lead her

A Prince of the Church

from the religious seclusion of a Convent for Noble Ladies in the Netherlands where she was living as a Canoness into the arms of a lover still bruised—both mentally and physically—from the treatment of the temperamental Princess.

Charles and Miss Walkinshaw set up house in Ghent where they chose, with singularly little romantic imagination, to be known as the Count and Countess de Johnson. Here, in October 1753, a daughter was born to them and baptized under the name of Charlotte Johnson. Domestic peace, however, seemed to be as unobtainable for the unfortunate Charles as the Crown of Great Britain. Rumours of their drunken quarrels were soon current in Europe, where British envoys delighted to notify the Secretary of State of the latest bit of gossip about the 'Young Pretender' and his mistress to enliven an otherwise colourless dispatch. Three weeks after the birth of Charlotte violent scenes caused the parents to part company; (Clementina Walkinshaw, like the Princess she had succeeded, became a target for the Prince's blows, and as likely as not returned them, though in this respect she probably lacked some of the verve of Madame de Talmond), but they were soon reunited again, this time at Basle. The reunion was not destined to be either peaceful or long-lived. The couple were not above quarrelling in public and Lord Marischal records how they were recognized in a 'low tavern' where they poured drunken abuse at each other to the amazement of the onlookers.

Certainly their circumstances were not conducive to any sort of settled existence at this time. Charles was constantly on the move, often in disguise (sometimes, we are told, wearing a false nose) and there is no doubt that he was drinking considerably. This intemperance, which his many misfortunes may explain and in some measure excuse, was made no easier to bear by his quite extraordinary fits of jealousy, which took a form which would have been more suitable to comic opera. So little did he trust his mistress's virtue that he would surround her bed with chairs set on tables, while on the chairs themselves he would place little bells whose tinklings would warn him of the approach of any unauthorized stranger. Clementina was further subjected to the

The Cardinal King

dislike and distrust of her jealous lover's political associates who suspected her of correspondence with her sister who, as we have seen, was in attendance on the Hanoverian Princess of Wales: and as though this were not enough, she was further attacked for being a Catholic, for at this time Charles was posing as a Protestant having gone through some form of submission to the Church of England during a secret visit to London in 1750. It must be admitted that religious conviction, whether Catholic or Protestant in complexion, was not a strong characteristic of the Prince's personality, and his 'conversion', which was of a purely political nature, did not last long. Whether his return to the faith was any more sincere it is difficult to say.

It is not surprising that Clementina Walkinshaw eventually found the *ménage* of the Prince more than she could stand, and in 1760 she left him, retiring with her daughter to a convent at Paris where she was known as Countess Alberstrof, a dignity bestowed on her by the Emperor and certainly of a more reassuring sound for a lady living in conventual retirement than Countess de Johnson. The Prince gave nothing for her support; it remained for the Cardinal of York to provide her with a pension. Charles never saw her again, and it was many years before he remembered the existence of his daughter.

While these interesting events were in progress the Cardinal Duke was continuing to advance in the Church while the old Chevalier declined slowly towards his grave. News of Prince Charles only occasionally reached Rome and then it was usually either bad or unwelcome. James was deeply shocked by his elder son's conduct and sought, when ever he was able to write to him, to urge him to mend his ways and to marry. Charles himself cared less and less about his father or his brother and conducted his affairs as though the old King were already dead and he himself the head of the family. James was too old and too ill to object. In the same year that Clementina Walkinshaw left Charles, Horace Mann reported to London that James's end was expected at any time. 'He is so emaciated and weak' wrote Mann, 'that it is not natural to suppose that he can hold out long. He seems of late totally indifferent to all affairs both of a public or of a domestic

A Prince of the Church

nature, and leaves the management of both to his son the Cardinal and Mr. Grimes (whom they call Lord Alford) who receives and answers all his letters.' Apart from helping his father in these details the Cardinal became more and more engrossed in his own affairs as his career in the Church increased in importance.

7

The Cardinal Duke did not enjoy his various appointments in the Church as mere sinecures. He had marked his incumbency as Archpriest of the Vatican Basilica by presenting St. Peter's with a fine gold chalice studded with precious stones; but if the clerics over whom he exercized authority expected his rule to be merely decorative they were sadly misinformed. One of his first acts was to rebuke a Canon for appearing in choir with his hair powdered, and he angered the Canons generally by making them stand when giving him information where former Cardinals had permitted them to sit. This insistence on respect for his royal presence was not likely to endear him to the members of the Chapter, but his dislike for priests in powder was confirmed in the next reign when the Pope proscribed the use of powder and ruffles for all ecclesiastical persons.

From about this time the health of James began to fail seriously and he retired more and more into the solitude of his own rooms in the Muti Palace. He was dispensed by the Pope from the rules of fasting—the same privileges that had been granted to the Emporor Charles V after his abdication—on account of his frail condition, while the gloom of his final years was deepened by the occasional information that reached him about Prince Charles, whose intemperate ways were a source of increasing distress to his father. With his eldest son all but lost to him, and often angered and irritated by the conduct of the younger, the old King became a pathetic figure as his last years were dragged out in the gloomy surroundings of his Roman palace. Sometimes his health would improve a little and he would appear at one of the Cardinal's musical receptions, but he found little in common with the company that thronged his son's apartments—the same 'low company', many of them, whom he had previously deplored—and he remained an aloof figure with his long, sad face, and dark clothes relieved only by the pale blue sash of the Order of the Garter (for it was George I who had changed the ribbon to the darker blue to distinguish his knights from those created by the Stuart King): but for the most part he remained in his rooms with only Lascaris and his secretary John Graeme, whom he had created Earl of Alford, for company. It was this latter, to whom Mann refers as 'Mr. Grimes', who now, with the Cardinal, managed most of James's affairs. But despite his weakness and melancholy the old Chevalier lingered on and was sufficiently interested in this world to beg the important office of Vice-Chancellor of the Holy Roman Church for his son when it fell vacant. The Pope refused the request and James, indignant at the refusal, removed his ailing body to Albano without taking ceremonial leave of the Holy Father or availing himself of his customary escort of Papal troops.

Benedict XIV took no offence at the old invalid's show of temper and to demonstrate his good will to the House of Stuart appointed Henry Camerlengo in April 1758. This is an office of great dignity and considerable importance during the vacancy of the Holy See, for it is the duty of the Cardinal Camerlengo at such times to arrange for the Conclave which elects a new Pope; and during the *Sede Vacante*, as head of the Treasury, he may mint his own coins. Such coins, bearing the arms of the Cardinal Duke of York, still survive. In giving this office to the Cardinal of York Pope Benedict was performing one of his last public acts. A month later he died, at the age of eighty-three, the wisest and most respected Pope of his century. Even Protestant countries found much to admire in this occupant of the Throne of the Apostle whose learning and tolerance were equalled by his wit. Horace Walpole had a statue of him on the pedestal of which, in a floridly expressed inscription, he described the Pope as 'a Priest without insolence or interestedness, a prince without favourites, a Pope without nepotism, in short a man whom neither wit nor power could spoil.' When these rather patronizing phrases were repeated to Benedict he replied with a smile that he was more like the statues in the Piazza of St. Peter's, admirable at a distance, but monstrous when seen at close quarters. With the death of this Pope James lost a staunch and faithful friend, and Henry a patron who had sponsored his first years as an ecclesiastic with splendid generosity.

As soon as the news of the Pope's death was known to Henry he made his way to the Apostolic Palace where, as Cardinal Camerlengo, he entered the death chamber and after remaining some time in prayer removed the white veil from the face of the Pontiff and after calling his name three times, according to the ancient custom, announced to the assembled members of the Court: 'The Pope is dead indeed.' Then, removing the Fisherman's ring from the lifeless finger, he broke it with a golden hammer. Finally he took possession of the Vatican in the name of the Sacred College and sent a detachment of Swiss Guards to secure the gates of the city and the Castle of St. Angelo.

The Conclave met on June 4th and did not elect a successor to Benedict XIV until July 6th. It was the first Papal election to be attended by the Cardinal Duke. Almost at once he was faced with a mortifying experience when welcoming the Cardinal of Turin, for while paying his respects to the Camerlengo this prelate referred to him only by the title of *Eminenza* and pointedly omitted the coveted *Altezza Reale*. The Cardinal Duke managed to stifle his resentment but when his Eminence of Turin came at the appointed time to the Cardinal Duke's cell to return the call in full ceremony he found the door shut in his face and himself refused admission.

The question of the future of the Society of Jesus, which the Bourbon Courts wished to suppress, was the great issue at the two last Conclaves of the Eighteenth Century, and Henry greatly angered his father when it became known that he had spoken in favour of the Austrian candidate rather than the one favoured by the Bourbons. James's resentment was justified in so far as his family owed so much to the House of France, but when his rebuke reached the Cardinal the latter replied, with some complacency, that he would sooner lose his head than act against his conscience. James was seriously ill at Albano at the time and an effort was made to allow the Cardinal Duke to leave the Conclave in order to visit his father whose death was said to be expected at any moment. Henry refused to avail himself of any such permission, for not only was it without precedent to leave a Conclave before the final vote had been cast, but he also guessed, perhaps rightly, that pressure would be brought to bear on him in respect of his own vote. So the Cardinal remained in the Vatican and James remained alive. Both King and Cardinal might have spared themselves anxiety for the candidate favoured by the latter was unsuccessful in the scrutiny and his rival, Cardinal Rezzonico, was elected under the name of Clement XIII. In fact he did little to further the suppression of the Jesuits but showed great favour to the Cardinal of York who had voted against him, for in November 1758 he consecrated him Archbishop of Corinth *in partibus infidelium*.

8

The consecration took place on November 19th in the Basilica of the Holy Apostles, the new Pontiff himself performing the ceremony. A description of the occasion was entered into the journal which was started about this time to record the day to day acts of the Duke under the sonorous title of 'A Diary of the Sacred Functions and of the Illustrious Acts of His Royal Highness and Eminence the Lord Cardinal Duke of York'. From the Palace of the Quirinal the Pope drove to the Basilica with the Cardinal Duke seated beside him in the place of honour together with the Dean of the Sacred College. A troop of cavalry and cuirassiers escorted the carriage which was guarded by a detachment of Swiss Guards in their picturesque uniforms of yellow, blue, and red. After the coach followed a train of prelates and Roman nobles on horseback. The church had been decorated with hangings of crimson velvet and cloth-of-gold, and a splendid pontifical throne was erected in the Sanctuary with a chair of state for King James placed near it. This chair, however, was to remain empty. The Chevalier was now reconciled with his son again after their latest quarrel but ill-health prevented him from being present to assist at the consecration, to his great sadness and concern. The presence of twenty-five Cardinals helped to make up for the absence of the

A Prince of the Church

King and added, with the splendour of their scarlet, to the pomp and solemnity of the scene. With them were a vast number of bishops, princes, ladies and nobles, and a great concourse of the Roman populace. In the midst of this colourful and distinguished throng Henry knelt to receive episcopal consecration, and at the conclusion of the long ceremonial, advanced to the papal throne to give public thanks for the new dignity conferred upon him. Clement XIII, in a gesture of generosity, gave orders that the vestments of cloth-of-silver heavily embroidered with gold thread that he had himself worn should be presented to the new bishop.

Following this sacred ceremony the Pope and his Court returned to the Quirinal where a great banquet was given at which Henry again had the place of honour. As the guests dined they were entertained with the singing of sacred motets by the Papal Choir to the accompaniment of an organ and a stringed orchestra. Thus, lulled by the music he loved so much, ended this great day in the life of Henry Stuart, Duke of York and Cardinal-Archbishop of Corinth. To the rest of Europe, engaged in the bitter struggle of the Seven Years' War, the fact than an exiled Stuart prince had just become a bishop was a matter of very little importance.

9

While the Cardinal of York was gaining ecclesiastical honours; while King James was falling into his last long illness; while Prince Charles was drowning his sorrows in drink or engaging in sordid quarrels with his mistress, the House of Hanover was never more securely seated on the British throne. King George II, that brave but rather ridiculous monarch, died at a moment when the world resounded to the glory of British arms. The great Year of Victories had culminated in the capture of Quebec in September 1759, while France's plans to revenge herself received a decisive check in the action of Quiberon Bay in October. When George II died a year later as a result of a sudden stroke while seated on his *chaise-percée* he passed to his heavenly reward in a blaze of glory despite the somewhat grotesque nature of his demise. His armies were everywhere successful, his navy was victorious, and

The Cardinal King

his country about to enter on a period of great prosperity. At the accession of George I the Chevalier de St. George had come near to gaining his throne and had issued a Proclamation naming fifty-seven people with a prior claim to it by right of birth than the Elector of Hanover; at George II's accession his actions had caused some concern to the government of the Hanoverian King. But by the time that the great-grandson of George I mounted the throne a new age had dawned which had already almost forgotten that the son of James II was still alive. James III, *de jure* King of Great Britain, France and Ireland, issued a protest against the succession of George III but so little notice was taken of it that even Sir Horace Mann was unable to obtain a copy of it.

One of the chief claims of James against the first two Georges was that he was a native-born prince while they were German in speech and thought as well as by birth. George II was not a person to inspire either loyalty or affection. Fussy, irascible, something of a martinet, though able to converse in guttural English he would always prefer either French or German, and usually spoke in the former to his English ministers. His love for Hanover was known to predominate over his love for England as his love for other women did over his love for his wife. When that intelligent and strong-minded woman urged him, on her death-bed, to marry again out of fear for the influence less regular relationship might have over him, the monarch amazed his courtiers by replying through his sobs, '*Non, non; j'aurai des maîtresses!*' Only on the field of battle could he hold his own without fear of unfortunate comparisons, for his personal bravery was never in question. Not only did he lead his troops at Dettingen but at Oudenarde he and the Chevalier de St. George had fought in the opposing armies with equal valour. The grandson who succeeded this absurd old monarch was a young man of upright character, and if he possessed much of the obstinacy and poverty of intellect latent in his family heritage, he was at least morally irreproachable; and when in old age his clouded perception was eventually driven beyond the boundaries of sanity he remained a figure of genuine tragedy beyond range of the ridicule that never entirely escaped the personalities of his predecessor or his heir.

A Prince of the Church

It is not surprising that the enthusiasm which greeted the accession of such a prince should have found an outlet in verse, some of which was more noticeable for the sincerity of its sentiments than the sublimity of its expression. One of the more curious of these pieces came from the pen of the Laureate Laurence Eusden:

> *Hail, mighty Monarch; whom desert alone*
> *Would, without birthright, raise up to the throne;*
> *Thy virtues shine particularly nice,*
> *Ungloomed with a confinity to vice.*

That the inspired poet should stress the monarch's right of descent shows the extent to which James and his two sons had been forgotten as King George III began his reign of sixty years; for while he could boast with justifiable pride that he had been born and educated in Britain the aged King over the Water was already on his death bed while his Italian-born sons could no longer inveigh against the German birth of their rival. The House of Stuart had become more alien than the House of Hanover, and in no one was this alien spirit better expressed than in the Stuart Duke who had become a Prince of the Roman Church which still remained to the average English or Scots mind, foreign, suspect, and utterly incompatible with loyalty to the Protestant Succession, that chief prop and bulwark of the reigning dynasty. With the accession of George III Jacobitism ceased to be a Cause and became merely a whim.

10

In 1761 the See of Frascati, some fifteen miles outside Rome, became vacant through the translation of Cardinal Camillus Paolucci to the See of Porto and Santa Ruffina, and the vacant diocese was presented by Clement XIII to the Cardinal Duke. In accepting this appointment Henry resigned his titular Archbishopric of Corinth together with the *commendam* of the Church of the Holy Apostles. Frascati is one of the six suburban Sees of Rome —the others being Ostia, Porto, Sabina, Palestrina and Albano— which are held by the six Cardinal Bishops who in virtue of

The Cardinal King

their office are the senior members of the College of Cardinals which, when complete in its seventy members, consists of six Cardinal Bishops, fifty Cardinal Priests, and fourteen Cardinal Deacons. The Cardinal Priests may in fact be in episcopal orders and hold important Sees, but it is only the incumbents of these six dioceses who enjoy the title of Cardinal Bishop, the senior of whom, the Bishop of Ostia, is Dean of the Sacred College.

About a thousand feet above sea level, Frascati is one of those small towns in the Alban Hills south of Rome known as the *Castelli Romani*, among which are Albano itself (which had long been the summer residence of the Stuart Court); Castelgandolfo, where the Pope's château dominates the little village high above Lake Albano; Rocca di Papa and Grottaferrata, famous for its wine, where a thousand-year-old Abbey of the Greek Rite testifies to the days when the Eastern and Western Churches were united round the Throne of St. Peter.

It is not surprising that Frascati became the Cardinal Duke's favourite place of residence. Crowding the hill-side with its narrow streets and gaily painted houses the little town clusters picturesquely round the Duomo or Cathedral and the Piazza, below which stretches the vast campagna with its sweeping views culminating in the distant prospect of Rome itself dominated by Michaelangelo's massive dome. From time immemorial Frascati was the haunt of the Roman nobility escaping from the summer heat of the city. Here was the villa of Lucullus, while the Princes of the Renaissance, following ancient tradition, chose the environs of this town to build their splendid villas. The bishop himself occupied the medieval castle of La Rocca, so named from its commanding position and fortress-like appearance. Known as the See of Tusculum from the name of the ancient city close to whose ruins modern Frascati stands, the first bishop was one Vitalianus about the year 680, and in subsequent centuries at least three of its bishops had risen to the Papal throne under the names of John XXI, Paul III (who issued in 1538 the Bull of Excommunication against Henry VIII), and Clement XII who reigned during the boyhood and youth of the Cardinal Duke. Henry was to remain Bishop of Frascati for close on fifty years and came to be deeply

A Prince of the Church

loved and venerated by its inhabitants, who took great pride in their royal bishop whose lavish hospitality and great munificence brought much prosperity to the town. The poor soon began to benefit from his generosity. Writing at a time when memories still survived of 'the amiable and beneficent Cardinal Henry' another Englishman, Cardinal Wiseman, remarked that 'whatever else may have been wanting for his title, to a royal heart he was no pretender. His charities were without bounds: poverty and distress were unknown in his see.'

Henry entered into his new diocese the day before his enthronement, which took place on the 13th of July, 1761. All day eager and expectant crowds had thronged the Piazza and gazed out across the plain for a sign of the approaching cavalcade. At last, towards evening, his coach was seen at the foot of the steep ascent leading up to the town, with a troop of cuirassiers galloping ahead as a guard of honour. As the carriage rattled over the cobbled streets the people caught a first glimpse of their new bishop as he passed with hand raised in benediction. The Cardinal-Bishop was thirty-six years old and looked younger still; the oval face was saved from weakness by the finely shaped nose and might indeed have passed for handsome save for his Royal Highness and Eminence's habit of keeping his lips slightly parted when in repose which gave a rather vacant expression to an otherwise distinguished appearance. On his breast a cross of immense diamonds caught the rays of the setting sun in a dazzling blaze of fire. As he alighted before his episcopal palace the leading citizens were presented to him and the Canons of the Cathedral knelt to kiss the sapphire ring.

Next day the Cardinal Duke drove to the Cathedral through decorated streets in a coach and six with other coaches containing his household and suite following. In the Piazza Carpegna he received a deputation of magistrates and municipal dignitaries. At the door of the Cathedral the coach again stopped and the Cardinal stepped out. Here in his rich episcopal vestments he knelt on a gold-embroidered cushion and kissed a crucifix held out to him by a priest. The façade of the Cathedral, the work of Girolamo Fontana, made a perfect setting for this baroque scene. The interior

The Cardinal King

of the building had been draped in crimson damask and hung with cut-glass chandeliers as is the custom still in Italian churches on great occasions. Down the aisle of this church, blazing with lighted candles and filled with the singing of the choir, the Cardinal was escorted to the sanctuary where he was solemnly seated on his episcopal throne. One Stuart at least had gained a throne, if not that of a kingdom. In the evening a great banquet was held at the Palace of La Rocca, the whole town was illuminated, and blankets, clothes and money were distributed among the poor.

Henry Stuart brought the same earnestness and thoroughness to his duties as a diocesan bishop as he had to the office of Archpriest of St. Peter's. Though, in the manner of his age, he lived magnificently as a Prince of the Church and a Royal Duke, maintaining, his biographer Don Alessandro Atti tells us, 'grooms, lacqueys and serving-men without number, all of pleasing appearance and of commanding stature, as a great Prince should,' at the same time he kept a stern eye on the condition of the clergy and a few years after his appointment called a Synod at which various reforms were proposed and disciplinary measures enforced. Here, we read, the royal bishop was not afraid to show 'a certain emphasis or vehemence of paternal sternness, also a desire for ancient discipline in recalling his clergy to their proper sphere.' If some of the laxer clergy (and at this period we may be certain that they were not a few) winced under the lash of the Cardinal Duke's reforming spirit, they could at least console themselves in the fact that while the Synod lasted the entire clergy were entertained at their bishop's expense at the Villa Aldobrandini which he had taken especially for the purpose. In these elegant surroundings thoughts of 'ancient discipline' took on a less disturbing complexion, and could happily be put off until tomorrow. The Cardinal, however, had no intention of letting the decrees of his Synod become a dead letter, and had them published in a handsome quarto volume.

The poor and destitute were not overlooked by the new bishop, as Cardinal Wiseman has shown. Indeed he took a keen interest in their welfare which must have been considered unusual at a time when the higher clergy were not particularly renowned for apos-

A Prince of the Church

tolic zeal. In his diocese was a district known as Morala where casual winter labourers and other poor or unemployed wanderers collected. Not being local inhabitants, but forming a small group of people gathered there in the hope of employment or casual labour, they were ignored by the rest of the community and their squalid little settlement—known as Le Capanne from the tumble-down cabins in which they lived—did not even have a priest to minister to their spiritual needs.

When the Cardinal Duke heard of the existence of this black spot in his diocese he determined to visit it himself. The out-cast settlement which so far had not seen so much as a priest now beheld the bishop himself in their midst bringing them the Blessed Sacrament which he carried under a canopy of cloth-of-gold. Henry did not content himself with a single spectacular visit to this place; he ordered the ruined church to be repaired and a presbytery to be built, and arranged for the children to be given proper instruction. His interest in their welfare continued, so that in time he became a legendary figure among a people who were previously dismissed as being no better than cut-throats. The Cardinal, they firmly believed, would sooner sell his great diamond cross than see them again suffer starvation and neglect.

In 1763 the office of Vice-Chancellor again fell vacant and this time the Cardinal Duke was appointed to fill the place which his father had previously asked for him in vain. With this post went the magnificent palace of the Cancelleria, built by Bramante for a nephew of Sixtus IV, so that Henry now had a splendid residence in Rome as well as his fortified palace at Frascati. Though he chose to live chiefly at the latter place business often called him to Rome, and he delighted to travel at great speed between the town in the Alban Hills and the great city below. The Cardinal's coach and six would tear across the *campagna* in a cloud of dust as fast as the horses could gallop, while running footmen in the royal livery dashed alongside. An empty coach and four brought up the rear; a precaution the Cardinal insisted upon in case of accident. In this way he would also clatter through the city and nothing caused him greater satisfaction than to draw up with a flourish before the door of some great palazzo. Indeed he caused much offence to the

The Cardinal King

august Princess Rezzonico when arriving at a reception given by the Cardinal de Bernis to celebrate the birth of an heir to the House of France. As both coaches were about to arrive at the same moment one of the Cardinal's footmen flung his torch at the feet of the Princess's horses so that his master's equipage could gallop up first to the door. The furious Princess was so angry that she could only be persuaded with difficulty to enter the house. Next day the Cardinal had to write a letter of apology for his footman's over-zealous behaviour.

As Vice-Chancellor the Cardinal Duke's name had to appear in matters relating to foreign Courts and the question of his claim to the Dukedom of York caused some embarrassment. It was, however, retained in his official style, with his bishopric coming first and the Chancellorship at the end of the list. It is in this order that his titles appear on the coin struck at the time of his father's death, where he is described as HENRICUS M.D. EP.TUSC. CARD.DUX EBOR. S.R.E.V.CANC. (Bishop of Tusculum, Cardinal Duke of York, Vice-Chancellor of the Holy Roman Church.)

The embarrassment caused by the Cardinal Duke's titles among foreign Courts was nothing to the embarrassment of the Cardinal himself when Edward Duke of York, brother to King George III, arrived in Rome in 1764. Rather than find himself involved in an awkward situation Henry discreetly left for the country until the visit was over, while the Hanoverian Duke was fêted everywhere to the considerable exasperation of the Stuart Court. It cannot, however, be claimed to the advantage of any party that this prince brought much credit to the ancient northern city whose name he bore, for three years later he drank himself to death at Monaco. As for the old, ailing King James, he was beyond taking pride in his son's new honours or offence at the visit to Rome of an usurping prince; for his long life was now fast drawing to its close.

4

The Fight for Recognition

I

The last illness of James Stuart dragged on for many years during which time reports and rumours of his imminent departure from life formed a regular feature of the correspondence of the British Envoy at the Court of Tuscany. Thus, as early as 1758, Sir Horace Mann reported that James's health was much impaired by 'some organick disorder in his stomack' and that it was the general opinion that he would not live long. With typical Stuart obstinacy the old King survived this dismal prophecy by nearly eight years. Two years later his end was again expected when Mann informed Walpole that 'the Cardinal, his son, who is never so happy as when he is acting the Priest, had the consolation of administering the Viaticum to him, with all the ceremony and solemnity that such a function is capable of.' Through the efficacy of this Sacrament, or perhaps just to spite Sir Horace Mann, the King again rallied, and another interval of two years passed before Mann ventured to return to the rather unprofitable theme of the Pretender's death. In October 1762 he wrote: 'The Pretender seems to be at the last period of his life. He has lately had two apoplecktic fits, by which his mouth is much drawn aside, and his speech is hardly intelligible. His devout son contents himself with praying for him. The other will probably get drunk to drown his sorrow.' Once again the old man failed to conform with the morbid prognostications of the Envoy, and for more than three years he lingered on.

The next bulletin from Florence concerned itself with the health of the Cardinal, who was troubled with a 'fluxion in his eyes' for which his doctors advised him to leave Rome where he was in constant attendance on his father and remove himself to the purer air of Frascati. As soon as his health and his physicians allowed him to return the Cardinal Duke, realizing that his father must soon die, set about securing a reconciliation with his brother whose presence in Rome he considered essential at this crisis in the affairs of their family.

As early as 1760, when his health first began to give cause for serious alarm, James had himself written to his elder son begging him to come back. 'If I have not writ to you for some time, my dear Son,' went the King's letter, 'you would wrong me if you attributed it to want of sincere concern and tenderness for you. They increase with my age and make me more desirous than ever to see and embrace you once more before I die.' 'I am continually thinking of you,' the letter concludes, 'and have nothing so much at heart as your welfare and happiness.' This plea brought no response from the wandering prince, and the Cardinal, now that the case was so much more urgent, appealed not only to the Prince's heart but also to his pocket, in the hope of bringing him to his father's deathbed. With characteristic generosity he surrendered to Charles the pension of 12,000 crowns which he enjoyed from the Apostolic Chamber, and further promised to renounce in his brother's favour any money he might inherit under his father's will. He also, perhaps rather tactlessly, mentioned the Princess de Talmond who, he wrote, 'complains she never can hear of you, and thinks she deserves a share in your remembrance.' The Cardinal, who in worldly matters was a simple man, probably did not realize that a share in the Princess's remembrance was more than likely the one thing the Prince most wished to avoid. To these inducements, filial, financial and feminine, the Cardinal was able to add the invitation of the Pope himself; but Charles made it a condition that the Pontiff must recognize him as King in succession to his father before he would enter Rome, a condition that Clement XIII was not prepared to accept.

Thus deprived of the presence of his 'dearest Carluccio' James Francis Edward Stuart ended his *de jure* reign of sixty-four years, three months, and fifteen days on the night of the 1st of January, 1766, being in his seventy-eighth year. The Cardinal had attended

The Fight for Recognition

him constantly in his last hours, though at the actual moment of death he was not present, having gone to rest after many hours of watching by the dying man's bed. His friend Cardinal Giovanni Francesco Albani, who had witnessed the death, went immediately to the Palace of the Cancelleria with the news, but hearing that the Cardinal Duke had retired to rest it was considered prudent to delay breaking the melancholy news until the morning. After so long an illness it was no great shock to Henry when the sad news was told. 'With the deepest grief His Royal Highness received the account of His Majesty's decease,' states the *Diario* for January 2nd, 'but he bore the blow with marvellous calmness, and at once began to make arrangements for the holding of funeral services for his dead father's soul in the Palace chapel and in the Church of the Holy Apostles, as also in the churches of San Lorenzo in Damaso, San Clemente, Sant' Isidoro and in the chapels of the National Colleges.'

There is something immeasurably sad in the passing of this lonely old exile whose entire life had been devoted to the fruitless pursuit of a crown which was his by right of birth. Fortune had constantly gone against him; even the elements themselves had seemed to oppose him, for again and again violent storms and contrary winds had delayed or frustrated his plans with as much evil consequence to his cause as the worst wiles of his enemies. The tragedy of his life was not of his own doing; had he succeeded to the crown in the normal way instead of being the heir to his father's mistakes he might have been remembered as one of the wisest of kings and the most worthy of his House; for his conception of the duties of a monarch was free from the bigotry which had condemned James II from the start, while he was the soul of honesty and conscientiousness. It was his principle, as he once explained in a letter to Prince Charles, not to transgress the rules of justice and prudence; and while the former resolution is commendable at all times the latter is not perhaps the most suitable virtue for one whom history has cast in the rôle of a Pretender. It was this prudence, which his father had so conspicuously lacked and which might have served the son so well as a limited or constitutional monarch, that accounted for much, if not all, of

The Cardinal King

the failure of his political ambitions. But above all else it was his devotion to the Old Religion that cost him the sacrifice of all his earthly hopes. He was not prepared to deny his faith for a crown, and from this point of view his life assumes a moral grandeur which in an opportunist age was a source of amazement or of ridicule to his contemporaries, but to the eyes of posterity brings to the ethereal crown of James III a lustre few can share. To the Catholic religion he always remained faithful and it was that Church alone which recognized him as a reigning sovereign when death finally overcame him. The world had long forgotten him but from the Church he received the last rites as befitted a sovereign prince wearing, in death, the crown which in life he had never worn.

2

Thus crowned and clad in royal robes the body of James Stuart lay in state in the chapel of the Muti Palace for five days. Meanwhile a bed of state had been erected in the neighbouring church of the Holy Apostles with hangings of purple velvet and gold lace. Above was a canopy upon which angels supported the British crown under which ran the legend JACOBUS TERTIUS MAGNAE BRITANNIAE REX ANNO MDCCLXVI. A macabre touch to this imposing catafalque was introduced by bronze skeleton figures of Death clutching candelabra and boughs of yew which were placed at intervals round the sanctuary. The body was conducted solemnly to the church from the palace by a procession including twenty Cardinals, and here were performed the obsequies as for a king who had actually reigned. It was the Papacy's last gesture to a king whose cause they hoped to see buried with his body. On January 7th, still clothed in royal robes and with the stars of the Garter and the Thistle shining on its breast, the body was removed to burial in the grotto of St. Peter's, being escorted through the streets of Rome by a guard of honour of Papal troops and a procession of over five hundred students from the English, Scots and Irish colleges carrying torches.

The Cardinal Duke of York was the chief mourner at these last rites: Prince Charles preferred to delay his arrival in Rome until he

The Fight for Recognition

could be received there in a style that befitted his new dignity as King Charles III of Great Britain, France and Ireland; and it was to the gaining of such recognition that the Cardinal now set himself with a determination that showed no resentment for the neglect and scorn he had suffered from his brother for so many years.

3

Immediately after his father's death the Cardinal Duke sent official notification of the fact to the Marquis d'Aubeterre, Ambassador of France, and also to the Spanish Ambassador and to Cardinal Orsini, who represented the interests of the Kingdom of Naples at the Court of Rome. From these Ministers of the Bourbon Courts the Cardinal no doubt expected a lead that might influence the wavering Clement XIII in favour of recognizing his brother. All three ambassadors received the Cardinal's representations favourably and suggested a direct approach to the Pope. Cardinal Giovanni Francesco Albani had already sounded the Holy Father at the urgent request of the Cardinal Duke but the Pope had refused to commit himself. Henry now drew up a Memorandum on 'The indispensable necessity for the Holy See to recognize the House of Stuart as the only true and legitimate Sovereigns of the Kingdom of England,' and this he presented to the Pope 'in the most pathetic and becoming manner' as James's old secretary Andrew Lumisden wrote to inform his new master.

Clement XIII protested his personal sympathy with the plight of the Cardinal and his brother (whom he would gladly receive as Prince of Wales) and professed, as indeed was hardly necessary, his belief in the principles of legitimacy, but he remained unmoved in his determination not to give official recognition to the House of Stuart unless other European Courts did so first. He did, however, agree to call a Congregation of Cardinals to discuss the matter and allowed Henry to circulate copies of his Memorandum to anyone he might think proper.

Meanwhile Monsieur d'Aubeterre exerted himself in every way to favour the policy of recognition despite the fact that he had received no authority to do so from his own Court. He demanded

The Cardinal King

an audience with the Cardinal Secretary of State in which he expressed his surprise at the Pope's delays and difficulties in acknowledging the new king and contrived to intimate, without any exact confirmation, that such an acknowledgement would be highly acceptable to his Court. But in saying this he was acting without instructions and the failure of the French government to back him up was soon to place him in a highly equivocal and embarrassing position. For another busy schemer was at work: one who had already been responsible for upsetting some of the most cherished designs of the exiled dynasty. This was Cardinal Alessandro Albani, the elder of the two Albani cousins who took such opposing sides in all issues concerning their fellow prelate the Cardinal of York. From the moment James III had breathed his last the elder Albani had been in regular correspondence with Sir Horace Mann, keeping him in touch with the moves and counter-moves in these delicate negotiations: for, as Mann knew only too well and as he made plain in his despatch to London, 'everything is carried on at Rome by cabals and intrigues'.

Mann's scheme to thwart the Cardinal Duke as his brother's advocate was simple and ingenious, and to this end he made sure that his letters to Cardinal Alessandro Albani would receive a wide publicity among the prelates assembled for the Congregation. The effects of this he described, with pardonable complacency, in a letter he wrote later to Walpole.

'In my letters to old Cardinal Albani, which were read in the consistory held on the subject, I asserted that the French ambassador could not have received orders from his court, whose engagements with that of England had made it inconsistent with its honour to insist upon it; that the ambassador had laid a snare for the Pope, which he might avoid by only waiting for an answer from Paris, which I was very sure would bring disavowal of the ambassador's conduct. That encouraged the Pope to tell him that if his master would be the first, he would be the second to acknowledge him under the title he contended for. The answer from France was such as I foretold; and General Conway, who was then Secretary of State, conveyed to me the king's approbation for what I had done.'

The Fight for Recognition

This simple reasoning was sufficient to convince the Pope and the Congregation of Cardinals who, as Mann pointed out, 'are for the most part excessively ignorant of Courts and of the world'. The French Ambassador never forgave the British Envoy, whom he described as '*Ce diable Monsieur Mann*', for his successful intervention, while it is not surprising that this same '*diable*' described the elder Albani as being 'staunch as a heretic in our favour'.

Mann's victory was certainly complete. Though Henry had, as a last resort, himself written to the Kings of France, Spain and Naples, it was of no avail. The Marquis d'Aubeterre received a severe rebuke from His Most Christian Majesty and was told to have nothing further to do with the affair, while the Pope took Cardinal Orsini to task for meddling in matters without first waiting for the directions of the Sovereign he served.

For once the interests of the House of Hanover had triumphed at Rome. But in fairness to the Pope it should be remembered that at this particular time his relations with the Courts of France, Spain, and Naples were far from happy, while he had every reason to wish to remain on good terms with George III who, as a result of the Seven Years' War, now had a vastly increased number of Catholic subjects, especially in Canada, and the Holy See had no wish to see the spiritual welfare of these Catholics placed in jeopardy. With regard to the Bourbon Courts, their quarrel with the Papacy over the demand for the suppression of the Society of Jesus was now in a critical stage. In this dispute they were joined by the Kingdom of Portugal from which the Jesuits had already been expelled by the Marquis de Pombal, while Spain was soon to follow suit, deporting the Fathers of the Society wholesale to the States of the Church where, though their spiritual plight was sympathized with, their physical presence was not particularly welcome.

In this dilemma, poised between his delicate relations with the Catholic powers and his desire not to offend the Government of Great Britain, Clement XIII could ill afford to adopt a policy which would give either party an excuse for hostile action against him. These problems weighed heavily on the shoulders of the Supreme Pontiff, and though he must have wished to assist the

The Cardinal King

Cardinal Duke of York who stood high in his favour, the dangers of his situation prevented him. Already broken-hearted at the situation with regard to the Jesuits the Pope was soon to find the burden of life too much for him and to die leaving his many problems, among which the question of the status of Charles Edward was the least, as a legacy to his successor. Sir Horace Mann, on the other hand, could afford to be magnanimous at the expense of the Prince whose designs he had so neatly frustrated:

'I have as much compassion for the young man as anybody [he wrote to Walpole] nor would I disturb him in anything, but his vanity is the sole point that relates to us. He is rich, and if he is capable of being in any degree happy, the being deprived at Rome of a title which was denied to his father in every other part of the globe, ought not to make him otherwise.'

As a moralizer Mann was less happy than as a diplomat; though to confuse the claims of legitimacy with vanity was probably the only interpretation open to a servant of the Hanoverian dynasty. Charles Edward was either right or he was a fool, and Sir Horace Mann did not entertain any doubt on the subject.

4

While the Cardinal Duke was thus employed at Rome his brother, cloaking his unacknowledged royalty under the pseudonym of Baron Douglas, was posting in the direction of the same city which he had previously refused to enter without the title of King. The roads were in a deplorable state and the *de jure* reign of Charles III, so inauspiciously begun, came almost to an untimely end when the coach and its august occupant was upset over a precipice. No serious harm was done, however, though the traveller's legs were painfully swollen as much from the confinement of the carriage as from the accident.

On January 23rd news was brought to the Cardinal of his brother's approach and he set out at once to meet him. They had last seen each other in Paris in 1747 when the elder prince had just returned from his gallant exploits in Scotland, and was still the romantic hero of the hour. Did Henry remember, as he was galloped at speed across the dusty plain, that journey they had taken together to Fontainebleau when his brave and handsome brother had sat next to him with glittering orders on his breast as they rode to meet the King of France? If so, indeed, what must have been his thoughts when, arrived at the small inn on the Flaminian road some miles from the Porto del Popolo, he was confronted with this travel-weary man of forty-nine who already looked considerably older and who could walk only with the assistance of his valet owing to the condition of his legs? How marked a contrast there was between these two brothers! Charles, gloomy and irascible, embittered by unfulfilled ambition, his constitution already undermined by heavy drinking and his once handsome features bloated and gone to seed, now found himself in the presence of a dignified and gracious Prince of the Church, a handsome figure in his flowing Roman purple with his jewelled ring and cross; a poised and urbane prelate who must have borne little resemblance to the awkward and self-conscious youth he had once been.

The *Diario del Cardinale Duca* records their meeting simply enough: 'His Royal Highness dismounted from his coach and walked up the steps of the inn, where the two brothers embraced each other affectionately, obtaining an infinite joy in meeting again after an absence of eighteen years and a half.' In this embrace the long years of misunderstanding and separation seemed to be at an end and something of the affection of their early years found expression once more. Charles was sincerely grateful for the Cardinal's disinterested exertions on his behalf, for all their present lack of success, and in Henry a naturally affectionate nature was augmented by the respect he owed to the man whom he must now venerate as his sovereign and the head of his House.

After eating a meal at the inn Charles and Henry seated themselves in the latter's coach and set out for Rome two hours before sunset. Curiosity had compelled a small crowd to gather outside the Palace in the Piazza dei Santi Apostoli, and perhaps even a few were ready to shout 'God save the King' as Charles Edward alighted and was helped into the Palace where he had been born nearly fifty years before and where his father's dead body had so

The Cardinal King

recently lain in state. A few of the Roman nobility and those whom death had spared of the dwindling Jacobite Court were waiting in the antechamber to pay their respects to the new King. Charles remained a few moments with them and then retired to his room where he rested for two days in bed to recover from the strain and exhaustion of the journey.

5

While the Prince remained confined in the Muti Palace regaining his strength the Cardinal Duke made a further attempt to win over Clement XIII, but the Pope was now quite determined in his refusals, drawing attention (much to the embarrassment of the Cardinal) to Charles's renunciation of the Catholic Faith in 1750. Henry's assurances that his royal brother was now once more a good Catholic did not do much to encourage a belief in the solidity of the latter's religious convictions; while Charles himself was to complain that in Rome he was abhorred as a Protestant while in England he was dismissed as a rank Papist. It is perhaps no wonder that he kept to his bed.

As it became clear that the Pope was not to be moved the Cardinal resolved upon a bold and foolish demonstration of independence, his one and only gesture of defiance against the known wishes of the Head of the Church since the days when as a young prelate he had so sorely tried the patience of Benedict XIV. As soon as the Prince was well enough to leave his palace he and the Cardinal were to be seen driving about Rome in the latter's coach with Prince Charles sitting on his brother's right hand. By the etiquette of the Papal Court it was the custom for Cardinals to give this place only to crowned heads, so that the sight of the two royal brothers driving out with the Prince of the Church giving the place of honour to the unacknowledged King amounted to a public challenge to the decree of the Pope. It need hardly be said that Clement was furious when he learnt of this demonstration, and he decided to put a stop to any more scenes that might compromise his dignity in his own city.

And so the Congregation of Cardinals was assembled once more (this time more in anger than in sorrow), and the Dean of the

The Fight for Recognition

Sacred College was ordered to send a messenger to all the Cardinals not present and to the heads of the Orders informing them explicitly that the Holy See did not recognize Prince Charles Edward Stuart as King of England, Scotland, and Ireland, and that it was expected that all His Holiness's subjects should conduct themselves in accordance with this decision. The Pope also made certain, on the advice of Cardinal Alessandro Albani, that the Nuncio in Florence should be directed to inform his Britannic Majesty's Envoy there of these arrangements so that the intelligence might be passed on to London; a task highly agreeable to Sir Horace Mann who could now announce with a certain degree of smugness that 'it was as much treason to call Monsieur le Baron Douglas king in Rome as at London'.

The Cardinal Duke's impulsive gesture had done little to help his brother, yet for no one else would he have risked the displeasure of the Pope by such an act, and it surely answers those who maintain that in adopting an ecclesiastical career he had abandoned his family's cause for ever. His wish to cede precedence to the brother whom he now must regard as his King made it desirable for them to travel in future in separate coaches rather than risk a further clash with the Pontiff upon whose charity the Prince depended for his palace in Rome as well as the greater part of his income, and to whom the Cardinal owed canonical obedience. The royal titles which had once been accorded throughout the States of the Church must now be confined to the rooms of the Muti Palace and the Cardinal's villa at Frascati, while only from his servants and the few members of his Court could Charles hope to hear himself addressed by the coveted style of 'Your Majesty'.

But his humiliations were not at an end. When the Pope heard that Charles Edward had been prayed for as King Charles III at the English and Scots Colleges and by the Irish Dominicans and Franciscans he banished the heads of these institutions and orders from the city. Finally, to remove any shadow of doubt that might still linger as to his intentions, he ordered the arms of Great Britain and the Roman Senate that adorned the entrance to the Muti Palace to be taken down while the Prince was away from Rome on a visit to his brother at Frascati.

The Cardinal King

The Cardinal bore these rebuffs with composure and decided to assume an attitude of indifference despite the boundless indignation that he felt. Charles's nature, alas, was less forgiving. He retired to Albano where he divided his time between hunting and drinking in an endeavour to blot out from his mind the remembrance of these insults and frustrations. The Cardinal did his best to induce his brother to lead a more reasonable existence and to realize that the measures adopted by the Holy See were guided by political expediency rather than by personal hostility, but he soon despaired of anything short of a miracle to check his brother's intemperance. In a letter written to a friend he unburdened himself on the ever recurring topic of the 'nasty bottle' which, as he asserts elsewhere, 'every now and then comes on by spurts' and could only lead to disaster.

'I have very little to say [he wrote] except to deplore the continuance of the bottle; that, I own to you, makes me despair of everything, and I am of opinion that it is impossible for my brother to live if he continues in this strain. You say he ought to be sensible of all I have endeavoured to do for his good; whether he is or not is more than I can tell, for he has never said anything of that kind to me. What is certain is, that he has a singular tenderness and regard for me and all that regards myself, and as singular an inflexibility and disregard for everything that regards his own good. I am seriously afflicted on his account, when I reflect on the dismal situation he puts himself under, which is a thousand times worse than the situation his enemies have endeavoured to place him in; but there is no remedy except a miracle, which may be kept at least for his eternal salvation, but surely nothing else.'

Having failed to gain the recognition on which he had set his heart the Cardinal realized that the only thing to do was to accept the situation with as good a grace as possible and hope that happier times might bring a more favourable opportunity for the acknowledgment of their legitimate claims. Acting on this principle he urged his brother to pay his respects to the Pope as a private nobleman so that he could frequent the society of Rome (for few people were prepared to meet him as King of England, so that unless he were ready to pass by some lesser title it would mean

The Fight for Recognition

that most doors would be closed to him) and at the same time show some respect to the Pope whose bounty he was not too proud to accept.

There was, as the Cardinal remarked, 'a good deal of battling upon very trifling circumstances', but eventually he succeeded in bringing a somewhat reluctant brother into the Papal presence, where he was introduced as the Count of Albany. On reaching the Quirinal the Prince had to wait while his brother passed at once into the audience room. Eventually a chamberlain appeared and requested 'the brother of the Cardinal of York' to come forward. Charles, not a little irritated by this description, was now conducted into the Pope's apartment. Here he fell on his knees to kiss the hand offered to him by Clement XIII and remained in this kneeling posture until the Pope asked him to rise. For the remainder of the audience, which lasted a quarter of an hour, the Count of Albany had to stand while his brother, as a Cardinal, enjoyed the privilege of being seated. Thus twice in the day he had seen his younger brother take precedence over him as a Prince of the Church. If this was intended to rectify the little matter of taking the place of honour on the Cardinal's right hand, no doubt the mortifying lesson went home, but the Pope, forgetting the past, received his guest with cordiality.

This was the first meeting between these two natural allies whom the exigencies of external political pressure had compelled to oppose each other. They must certainly have appeared to have had little in common as they exchanged platitudes and studiously avoided controversial topics. The Prince, for all the rumours of his violence and drunkenness, had still all the charm so characteristic of his race when he chose to use it. The Pope, on the other hand, was small in stature and a slight physical deformity caused him to carry one shoulder slightly higher than the other, while the cares and anxieties which were soon to cut short his life weighed visibly upon him. It must have been with a sigh of relief that he brought to a close this encounter with the man whose father he had caused to be buried with all the pomps of a reigning monarch but whom himself he could only receive as the brother of one of his Cardinals.

The Cardinal King

Sir Horace Mann took some delight in representing this audience as a further humiliation for the Prince, pointing out that the younger brother was ushered in first 'by right of his Hat' and that the Prince was kept kneeling until the Pope asked him to rise. In point of fact, considering the incognito observed, there was nothing extraordinary in either of these points, for a Cardinal always enjoys the right of direct access, though, after the incident of the carriage drives, the insistence on this privilege was not empty of significance. But as it was understood that Charles was being received as a private nobleman it was a natural courtesy on his part to remain kneeling until the Sovereign Pontiff begged him to stand. This point would have been lost on Mann who was considerably lacking in the finer points of conduct in any matter that concerned either the Stuarts or the Papacy.

The Cardinal Duke himself seemed satisfied that all had gone well, commenting, indeed, that 'the visit went much better than I expected; the Pope was extremely well satisfied, and my brother seemed well enough content, though I asked him very few questions, and so I hope to draw from it a great deal of good.' Certainly Charles himself would appear to have sensed no humiliation in the situation (and on this point he was sufficiently touchy) for shortly afterwards he waited on the Pope again when Clement presented him with a rosary of a sort that is usually given only to sovereigns, hoping, perhaps, to compensate by this gesture for the stern measures which necessity had forced him to take against the House of Stuart.

6

If the Cardinal Duke had hoped for a little peace and quiet after all these political manoeuvres he was mistaken. A new menace appeared in the person of the Countess of Alberstrof, otherwise known as Clementina Walkinshaw, who since leaving the Prince had been living under the protection of the Archbishop of Paris in the Convent of the Nuns of the Visitation. As Charles had abandoned her completely his father had provided for her upkeep, granting her an income of six thousand livres a year. At King James's death this allowance had ceased, and as the new king

The Fight for Recognition

flatly refused to have anything to do with the woman he had once lived with or with her daughter, Clementina's situation was critical. The Cardinal came to her rescue, but the allowance was cut down to five thousand livres. On this reduced income the Countess was compelled to remove herself and her daughter to the less fashionable and less expensive convent of Notre Dame at Meaux-en-Brie, protesting indignantly at her reduced circumstances. It never occurred to her that the Cardinal was under no obligation to support his brother's mistress or that he had many prior claims on his generosity.

Having provided for Clementina Walkinshaw's upkeep the Cardinal hoped he would hear no more of her, but once again his peace was shattered when early in 1767 he learnt to his horror that she was spreading rumours that a marriage had actually taken place between Prince Charles and herself. The Cardinal was outraged at the news of these reports and was not content until he had obtained a signed statement from the unfortunate Clementina in which she stated categorically that 'such a report of marriage, or anything relative to the least tendency of that kind, is void of all foundation; and that I never gave the least room, either by word or writing, to such a falsehood...'

Satisfied with this declaration the Cardinal was able to turn his mind once more to the ecclesiastical matters that were his chief interest and hope that for the future his brother's concerns would look after themselves, as nobody seemed less eager to look after them than Prince Charles himself.

7

Charles Edward, meanwhile, was beginning to go out into Roman society where he continued to be known as the Count of Albany, or to visit the Alban hills where he could enjoy the pleasures of the chase. Lady Anne Miller visited Rome at about this time and has left us a description of the Prince in the years just before his marriage.

'He is naturally above middle size but stoops excessively; he appears bloated and red in the face, his countenance heavy and

The Cardinal King

sleepy, which is attributed to his having given in to excess of drinking. His complexion is of the fair tint, his eyes blue, his hair light brown, and the contour of his face a long oval; he is by no means thin, has a noble presence, and a graceful manner. His dress was scarlet, laced with a broad gold lace; he wears the blue riband outside his coat, from which depends a cameo as large as the palm of my hand, and wears the same garter and motto as those of the Order of St. George in England. Upon the whole he has a melancholy, mortified appearance.'

Music continued to be one of his diversions and was greatly encouraged by the Cardinal as being less dangerous and alarming in its consequences than the 'nasty bottle', and also, no doubt, less likely to produce in its devotees the 'mortified appearance' which had so impressed itself upon Lady Anne Miller.

The bottle, none the less, continued to feature conspicuously, the more so as the Prince now often became violent under its influence, on one occasion pursuing his attendants with a drawn sword to their considerable peril. These disagreeable scenes reached a climax in 1768 when the Prince insisted on appearing in his box at the opera when completely drunk. His three gentlemen, Andrew Lumisden, Hay, and Urquhart, having been unable to dissuade their master from exhibiting himself in such a scandalous condition, finally refused flatly to accompany him. The Prince flew into a violent fury and dismissed them on the spot. A few days later Charles demanded their return to his service, but they refused, having first sought the advice of the Cardinal Duke, who gave them his support for he realized that their position had become intolerable. To Lumisden the Cardinal gave a gold snuff-box that had belonged to James III as a token of remembrance. Charles had now only two persons of British nationality left with him; Stuart, his valet, and Wagstaffe, the Protestant chaplain.

For all the loyalty and brotherly affection which Henry owed him he must have found his brother's presence in Rome a source of continual embarrassment. This morose, often drunken and sometimes violent brother whose claims to a kingdom were a matter of very little interest to the inhabitants of Rome, must often have caused the Cardinal to wish that his brother would take his

Prince Charles Edward Stuart in Middle Age

The Fight for Recognition

troubles elsewhere as he seemed incapable of settling down with any semblance of dignity in the palace where his father had lived and died. The Cardinal must, indeed, have been almost happy to escape for a while from what he described as Charles's 'most singular way of thinking and arguing which indeed passes anybody's comprehension' when the death of Clement XIII in February 1769 enabled him to retire into the immunity and comparative safety of the Conclave.

8

The Pope's death was unexpected. He died suddenly, sitting on the edge of his bed, while his attendants were pulling off his stockings. The post of Camerlengo, which changed hands with every Pontificate, was held by Cardinal Rezzonico, nephew of the late Pope, who now performed those traditional ceremonies which had fallen to the lot of the Cardinal Duke on the death of Benedict XIV.

Ten days after the death of the Pope the Conclave assembled. After a Votive Mass of the Holy Ghost the Cardinals entered the Vatican in solemn procession and remained there until a successor had been chosen. Each Cardinal was allotted a cubicle consisting of two small rooms. These were hung with green cloth except in the case of those occupied by the Cardinals created by the last Pope, in which case they were hung with purple. The Cardinal displayed his coat of arms over the door of his cubicle. As the conclave progressed there was much coming and going between these various cubicles as the Cardinals plotted and schemed between each scrutiny, which by tradition had to be held twice every day.

The process of election often took months as the ancient custom of reducing their Eminences' ration of food in proportion to the length of time they took to choose a Pope had long been abandoned. They now contrived to live with some degree of luxury even in the conclave, and processions of gilded coaches would arrive each day bringing the Cardinals' dinners from the kitchens of their palaces in Rome.

The Cardinal King

Once again the conclave divided itself between those who supported the Society of Jesus and those (chiefly the subjects of the Bourbon and Hapsburg courts which comprised the greater part of Catholic Europe) who were pledged to seek its disbandment as the price for nomination to the Tiara. Cardinal York, who wished to have in his own hands the direction of the Seminary at Frascati —which the Jesuits at present controlled—was prepared to side with the anti-Jesuits, but he hoped to make a more accommodating attitude to the House of Stuart a condition for his support.

While the Cardinals were busy deliberating over the chances of likely candidates the conclave was suddenly convulsed by an unexpected diversion in the form of a visit from the Emperor Joseph II of Austria (who also enjoyed the title of King of the Romans) who presented himself at the door of the conclave with his brother Leopold, Grand Duke of Tuscany, and begged leave to enter. The Cardinal Dean, hastily summoned, was a little nonplussed at a situation so utterly unprecedented but eventually the Emperor and his brother were allowed to enter after the former had offered to remove his sword. Once inside he asked his hosts to address him as Count Falkenheim so that complicated questions of etiquette would not add further confusion to the unusual circumstances of the occasion.

With his meticulous curiosity Joseph II asked innumerable questions and, we may assume, bestowed advice in all directions, while a meal was quickly prepared for his entertainment. Afterwards, that the imperial inquisitiveness should be fully satisfied, a sham election was held for the edification of his Imperial and Apostolic Majesty. The news of this pious masquerade greatly amused Horace Walpole when he heard about it from his friend at Florence: 'I delight in the mock election of a Pope made to amuse Caesar,' he wrote; 'how the Capitol must blush at such a Caesar and such an entertainment.'

After the departure of the Imperial couple the Cardinals returned to the main business of the conclave much refreshed by this unusual episode. If further diversion were needed it was provided soon afterwards when one of their Eminent colleagues, Cardinal delle Lanze, suddenly took leave of his senses and, imagining him-

The Fight for Recognition

self Pope, went about bestowing indulgences in all directions. In this deplorable condition he was removed discreetly from the Vatican.

The leading figure in this conclave was the French Cardinal François Joachim de Pierre de Bernis, Archbishop of Albi and soon to be French Ambassador in Rome, who owed his political and ecclesiastical advancement chiefly to the interest of Madame de Pompadour. Nicknamed *Babet la Bouquetière* by Monsieur de Voltaire he had been elected to the Académie Française when only twenty-nine largely on his reputation as an author of light verse. He had received the Red Hat while still in his early forties when Horace Mann had noted in his correspondence with Walpole: 'The Abbé Bernis is to be made a Cardinal soon, which will make him perter than ever.' This prelate, whose liaison with the Princess Santa Croce was soon to be the talk of Rome, now joined forces with the prim and morally irreproachable Cardinal of York in the business of finding a successor to St. Peter, for both had found a candidate suitable to their own ambitions in the person of Cardinal Ganganelli, a Franciscan friar of humble origin.

As a Franciscan, Ganganelli could be relied upon to harbour no love for the Jesuits; to Cardinal de Bernis, who was acting on the instructions of the Duc de Choiseul, he provided guarantees which were sufficient to satisfy Louis XV, and to the Cardinal Duke he managed to convey a feeling of benevolence for the cause of the Stuarts without actually committing himself to any promises. With the support of the anti-Jesuit party and the influential advocacy of the Cardinal of York his election to the Papacy was assured. He assumed the name of Clement XIV and being only in priest's orders was immediately consecrated Bishop of Rome by the Dean of the Sacred College.

9

The Cardinal Duke was soon disappointed in the new Pope as a supporter of the claims of his House, but as an adversary of the Society of Jesus he proved a more formidable, if somewhat reluctant, foe. It may have been to make up to the Cardinal Duke for his political disappointments that Clement XIV deprived the Jesuits of their College and Church at Frascati which, together with their other property there, he handed over to the Cardinal. He further appointed him a visitor to the Jesuit Seminary at Rome with powers to investigate into its spiritual and temporal affairs. These acts were preludes to the Bull *Dominus ac Redemptor* promulgated in July 1773 against the Society which was followed by a Decree which abolished the Jesuit Order. In the activities that led up to these decisions (which Pius VII was later to reverse) the Cardinal Duke could be relied upon to side with the Pope and the Cardinals who were subject to the Bourbon courts, being described by Freiherr von Pastor as a professed enemy of the Jesuits.

Disappointed once more in his hopes for recognition being granted to his brother the Cardinal turned his attention to the Seminary which had now been placed in his hands, and in the direction of this institution he found a new outlet for his administrative talents. Under his care and protection it soon became famous as a place of learning. 'Though he was not himself either learned or endowed with great abilities,' Cardinal Wiseman was later to write, 'he knew the value of both, engaged excellent professors for his seminary and brought men of genius round him. Hence his college was frequented not only by aspirants to the clerical state, but by youths of the best families, destined for secular professions.'

It was also about this time that the Cardinal appointed a new secretary in the person of the Canon Angelo Cesarini who remained with him for the rest of his life and was to become his most trusted friend. It was Cesarini, later Bishop of Milevi *in partibus*, who was to be the principal executor of the Cardinal's last will, and who now had the management of his affairs.

To the incomes from his ecclesiastical offices in Rome and Frascati the Cardinal Duke could add the revenues of the abbeys of Anchin and St. Amand which had been bestowed on him by Louis XV, while from Spain he enjoyed a considerable income derived from pensions charged on the bishoprics of Jaen, Malaga, Segovia and Cordova, and the prebends of Chinchilla, Moron,

The Fight for Recognition

Heurta de Olmos, Gaca, Hermedes, Puerta de Santa Maria, Seville, Utrera and Menco. His income from Spain alone amounted according to Sir William Hamilton to over nineteen thousand *scudi* a year. Thus despite the many people he supported on his brother's behalf, as well as his own large establishments, the Cardinal Duke of York was at this time still one of the richest prelates in Rome, and could escape from the vicissitudes of politics to the quiet of Frascati there to enjoy what one of his biographers has described without exaggeration as a life of 'splendid tranquillity'.

But tranquillity was never a characteristic of the elder Prince. Having suffered sufficient mortification at the hands of Clement XIII he decided to leave Rome when it became apparent that he was likely to fare no better from his successor. Early in 1770 he set out for Pisa, where he took a course of baths for his health, and soon afterwards was on his travels again, much to the alarm of Sir Horace Mann and the spies and agents of the British Government.

5

Splendid Tranquillity

I

Frascati always remained the Cardinal Duke's favourite home. It was here that he could live the peaceful, cultivated existence that he so much enjoyed, though he never allowed his love of entertaining and good living—in the arts of which he rivalled the splendid example of Cardinal de Bernis—to interfere with his pastoral and episcopal duties. In these last years of the *ancien régime* before the great upheaval that was to tear Europe to pieces had overturned men's unquestioned acceptance of the general benevolence of things no one thought any the worse of a Prince of the Church if he lived on a scale of magnificence more suitable to a temporal prince. Indeed they would have looked upon him as singularly lacking in a proper sense of his position had he failed to do so. It was, in fact, in the rectitude of his private life rather than in his splendour of living that Henry Stuart tended to differ from some of his colleagues in the Sacred College.

He took a direct personal interest in all that concerned the welfare of his clergy and flock. We have already seen how he called a Synod at Frascati and how he visited the outcasts at Molara; these acts were typical of his high conception of the episcopal office which one of his English biographers describes somewhat quaintly as being 'after the ideal of St. Paul and Ruskin'. Under his direction schools were built and orphanages opened; medicine and food were distributed to the poor, and doctors from Rome were brought to attend to the sick. Whenever the Cardinal's coach drove out of his palace gates a crowd of

Splendid Tranquillity

beggars would assemble in the assurance of receiving generous alms.

With the townsfolk of Frascati he lived on terms of great friendliness and mutual respect. That he had their interests at heart was shown in 1779 when an excited mob had had a brush with the Papal troops. It was only through the intervention of the Cardinal that the town was spared from vengeance and the ringleader saved from execution.

The situation, however, was not always so happy as this, and there was a curious incident in 1782 when the Cardinal Duke narrowly escaped with his life. At this period a person named Giacomo Merolli had applied for the post of corporal of Police at Frascati, but being something of a cripple his application had been unsuccessful and a certain Felice Giannuzzi had been appointed instead. Furious at his exclusion from the coveted office Merolli had tried to incite the police to revolt, but being quite as unsuccessful in this as in his aspiration for the post of corporal, he was banished from the town and diocese after he had given vent to threats and violence.

Merolli, however, was not content to let matters rest and managed to return to Frascati hidden in a load of hay. Disappointment must have unsettled his reason for his purpose in returning was to set fire to the city with the particular intention of roasting alive the Cardinal Bishop whom he accused of having robbed him of his bread. This dramatic plan was soon discovered and the would-be corporal again banished, only to reappear a few days later armed to the teeth and again demanding satisfaction from the Bishop who he considered had deprived him of his livelihood. This time evading detection, Merolli hid himself near the church of the Capuchins which the Cardinal generally visited every day. His excuse was that he wished to present a petition, but as he had taken up a position that covered the route taken by the Cardinal and was armed with a musket, this excuse did not carry much conviction.

By pure chance the Cardinal entered the church that day by another entrance while the unfortunate Merolli was caught in his compromising position by none other than his successful rival

The Cardinal King

Giannuzzi who had the satisfaction of knocking him down and taking him into custody. Had the Cardinal taken his usual road to the church, and had Merolli's skill as a marksman equalled his determination for revenge (an unlikely coincidence) the Cardinal Duke's career might have come to an untimely and abrupt conclusion.

2

Sir Max Beerbohm has observed that mankind is divisible into two great classes: hosts and guests. There can be no doubt that the Cardinal Duke of York belonged to the former of these two classes; he was never happier than when entertaining his friends in his palace at Frascati where the lavishness of his hospitality was proverbial. He may be said to have kept open table at La Rocca where his meals were chosen with great care and served with princely magnificence. In his stables he kept sixty horses and coaches would be dispatched to take his guests back and forth from Rome.

One of his great entertainments took place on the 23rd of September, 1775, when Cardinal Orsini was the guest of honour and the great dining hall of the palace was filled with an elegant and distinguished throng. Suddenly, at the height of the dinner, a terrible crash was heard and host, guests, servants, table, plate, food, all disappeared through the floor while clouds of thick dust rose to stifle the cries of alarm and terror, as the Cardinal and his companions were flung headlong into the coach-house beneath. The ancient beams had given way under the weight of guests and furniture and caused the floor to collapse with frightening suddenness.

News of the disaster brought people running to the Palace to search for the injured among the debris of rotten beams and floorboards. The Cardinal Duke, more fortunate than some of the others, had fallen on to the roof of his own coach where he was discovered by his servants in a faint, severely shaken and bruised, but otherwise unhurt. Cardinal Orsini also escaped with only minor injuries, but some of the other guests were less lucky and one, a certain Dr. Gandolfi, died a few days later as a result of the fall.

Splendid Tranquillity

After recovering from this calamity the Cardinal ordered the Palace of La Rocca to be completely renovated and it remained much as his restorations had left it until it fell a victim to bombardment in the second World War. While the repairs were in progress the Cardinal occupied two rooms in the Seminary where he lived in edifying simplicity much comforted by the assurance of solid flooring. The rejoicings of the people of Frascati were such when they heard of their Bishop's providential escape that they decided to hold a thanksgiving service each year on the anniversary of the event, a custom which survived until the Cardinal's death over thirty years later. It is to be hoped that among the singing of Te Deums a moment was found for a short prayer for the repose of the soul of the unfortunate Dr. Gandolfi.

3

The Seminary at Frascati had been in the hands of the Jesuits since 1701 until the Brief of Clement XIV *Ad Futuram Rei Memoriam* of February 12th, 1770 placed it under the care of the Cardinal Duke who at once undertook the reform of its curriculum, at the same time spending some twelve thousand crowns in restoring and enlarging its premises. He installed a printing press and also had a stage erected where the students could perform classical and modern dramas. The Cardinal delighted in these presentations, one of his favourite pieces being based on an episode in the career of Sancho Panza from Miguel de Cervantes's famous novel.

But the Cardinal's chief interest was centred in the Library of the Seminary, into which he removed his own collection of books, manuscripts and engravings from Rome. These he housed in a room of fine proportions with a ceiling painted in allegorical designs by Taddeo Cunnoz. As his pride and interest in the library was well known it was customary for people wishing to gain his favour to present him with some rare edition or finely-bound tome, so that by the time of the French Revolution (when the library as well as the Cardinal's private collection was plundered by invading troops) the Library at Frascati was one of the finest in the States of the Church and attracted scholars from all parts. Among its treasures were six codices bound in silk and velvet with clasps of silver-gilt that the Cardinal had inherited from his father; a Book of Hours richly illuminated that had once been the property of Catherine de Medici, Queen of France; and a History of Scotland illustrated with miniatures of all the Scottish monarchs from the Bruce to James VIII.

The course of studies was thoroughly revised and, as Cardinal Wiseman tells us, eminent scholars and professors were engaged to supervise the instruction. The entire course covered nine years, consisting of four years of secular and five of ecclesiastical studies. The former was divided between two years of Greek and Latin grammar and two years devoted to the study of classical authors, modern history and literature. The ecclesiastical course began with a year of philosophy and was concluded by four years of Dogmatic and Moral Theology, Scripture and Canon Law. As a light relief from these weighty sciences instruction was also given in the Gregorian Chant.

One of the most brilliant pupils of this Seminary was Ercole Consalvi, later to be Cardinal Secretary of State under Pius VII, in whose career Henry Stuart took a particular interest, often inviting him to stay at Frascati after he had left the Seminary in 1776 to join the Ecclesiastical Academy at Rome. The future diplomat, who was later to negotiate the Concordat with Napoleon in 1801 and to secure the restoration of the Papal States at the Congress of Vienna, was a man of wide culture and a liberal patron of the arts. With the Cardinal Duke (who was a member of the Academy of St. Cecilia) he also shared a love of music, numbering the composer Cimarosa among his close friends. He owed much of his early rise to fame to the influence and protection of the Cardinal who, the Comtesse de Boigne tells us, treated him as a dearly loved son. It was Henry who presented the Abbé Consalvi to Mesdames, the daughters of Louis XV, when these unfortunate princesses had taken refuge in Rome at the time of the flight of the French Royal Family to Varennes, and it was through their representations that he was made auditor of the Rota. Henry was later to see his protégé appointed to the office of Archpriest of St.

Splendid Tranquillity

Peter's, a post which he had himself once filled. Cardinal Consalvi, for whose abilities even Napoleon had a word of praise, was certainly the most celebrated pupil to emerge from the Seminary that the Cardinal Duke had been so eager to take over from the Society of Jesus.

4

In matters of dress the Cardinal Duke would not always wear the flowing robes of his office for the cassock did not become *de rigueur* on all occasions for the Roman clergy until the time of Pius IX. In the privacy of his palace at Frascati the Cardinal would sometimes wear a purple coat laced with gold with a plain gold episcopal cross on his breast, or else a black coat lined with scarlet silk, a scarlet waistcoat, breeches of black velvet with scarlet stockings, and black shoes with scarlet heels. With his slim, still youthful figure, and handsome face ('smooth, ruddy, without a wrinkle' even when he was well over seventy) the Cardinal must have cut an elegant figure in this costume of scarlet and black.

He was an early riser, getting up in summer at sunrise and in winter long before it was light. After his Mass he would often go and pray at an altar in his Cathedral or in some special church in the town such as the Capuchin church near which Merolli had waited for him with a loaded musket. After these devotions he would often spend the morning at the Seminary either conversing with the students or passing some hours in study in the library where, like James III, he would read the Fathers of the Church, among whom St. Augustine was his favourite; or perhaps he would himself write some tract or pamphlet like his short treatise on the Sins of the Drunkard, a subject to which he could bring a certain amount of experience from his own family circle. After the midday meal (at which there was as often as not some guest to be entertained) the Cardinal's coach and six would be brought round and he would gallop off at full speed towards Rome preceded by his running footmen or else visit some neighbouring abbey such as that of the Greek monks of the Rule of St. Basil at Grottaferrata or the Convent of the Passionists on the summit of Monte Cavo.

This latter monastery occupied the site where once had stood a temple to the Latin Jove said to have been built by Tarquin. It is one of the few blots on the career of the Cardinal Duke that he ordered this great relic of antiquity to be destroyed in order that the Passionist Convent should be built from its ruins. It is difficult to understand how a man of such culture as Henry Stuart could have given his consent to so gross an act of vandalism, especially as the period when ruins of antiquity were considered as of little value was long since past. It is more surprising still that this regrettable lapse should have been singled out for special praise in his funeral oration many years later when Don Marco Mastrofini, who delivered the panegyric, reminded his listeners how the Cardinal was responsible for 'laying on the brow of the Alban Hills the first stone of a church to the Unspeakable Trinity on a site where formerly rose the heathen shrine of the Jove of Latinum.' The epithet which the preacher applied to the Blessed Trinity is, alas, more applicable to the Cardinal's sadly unnecessary act of despoilation.

If the duties attached to his office of Vice-Chancellor caused him to visit Rome the Cardinal Duke might pass the night there in his palace of the Cancelleria where he had furnished magnificent apartments which were to be occupied for a time, as we shall see, by his sister-in-law the Countess of Albany, but he preferred to return to Frascati where he could pass the evening surrounded by the men of learning attached to the Seminary, by some important guests from Rome or perhaps with a favourite student such as the young Ercole Consalvi. These would praise the Cardinal's hospitality, for he was by no means averse to a little flattery, and would be careful to use the royal style in addressing him lest they should suffer the terrible displeasure that had fallen upon the Prince of Liechtenstein who had used neither Royal Highness nor Eminence but had simply addressed his host as Monseigneur, as though he were no more than a mere Archbishop. It was some time before the Cardinal had recovered from the shock and even old King James (who was still alive at the time when this deplorable

Splendid Tranquillity

solecism was committed) had been highly incensed when he heard of it.

5

Thus, in the twilight of the ancient régime, in a European society still symbolized by Versailles and Schoenbrunn, an age aristocratic, cultivated, exclusive, the 'splendid Cardinal of York', as Mr. Cecil Roberts has described him, 'urbane, handsome and widely beloved for his qualities of gentleness and generosity, moved regally through the papal Court. . . .' In an epoch heartless and selfish for all its superb splendour and captivating grace the Cardinal Duke stands out as a Prince who never lost sight of the responsibilities he owed to his position or the duties that accompanied the high offices and vast revenues he enjoyed. It is in the setting of his beloved Frascati, surrounded by his books and the works of art he loved to collect, diligent for the welfare of his flock and the discipline of his clergy, that we see him at his best.

This was the life he loved, and it was to this life that he returned with a sigh of relief when early in the reign of Clement XIV Prince Charles left Rome for Pisa and further travels. It was in 1772, while still enjoying this 'splendid tranquillity' that he heard, without any prior consultations or warning, that his brother had been married by proxy in Paris on March 28th to the Princess Louise Maximilienne of Stolberg-Gedern. Once again the Cardinal Duke returned to Rome to prepare for the reception of Charles and his bride in the old palace in the Piazza dei Santi Apostoli.

6

The Marriage of Prince Charles

I

The negotiations leading up to the marriage of Charles Edward Stuart were conducted with the connivance, if not with the open approval, of the Government of France which since 1763 had been eager to support any act that might result in the embarrassment of England—even to the extent of reviving interest in the lost cause of the Stuarts. For this reason the idea of a union which would produce 'a race of Pretenders that would never finish' naturally commended itself to the Ministers of Louis XV. The Duc de Fitz-James was therefore encouraged to suggest to his royal cousin that the French Government would be ready to offer Charles a substantial pension if he would be prepared to marry.

Charles at this time had left Pisa, where he had gone for the cure, and was at Siena when this interesting piece of intelligence reached him. On August 18th, 1771, he left the town with all the secrecy that had attended his famous departure from Rome many years before when as a handsome young Prince he had set out in search of a crown. Now, a middle-aged, irascible and portly prince, his departure in search of a bride was to cause similar, if less urgent, occasion for wild speculation among the enemies of his House.

It was generally supposed that he had gone to Poland, and it must have irritated Sir Horace Mann who was so used to being the first in the field with news of the Prince's movements to have to hear the true version from other sources. Walpole was even more wild in his guesses: 'To the dissidents in Poland, think you?'

The Marriage of Prince Charles

he wrote to his friend, 'why, they have not a cheese-paring left. I should think rather to Spain, to be wafted to Ireland.' As a comfort to the poor Envoy, who perhaps fretted at having let the prince slip away so inconveniently, Walpole added a note of encouragement: 'Should I guess right, you must positively come home: you prevented his receiving the crown of England at Rome, and must now keep him from receiving it at Dublin.'

It was, however, neither at Dublin nor Warsaw but at Paris that the Prince arrived on September 9th, and was waited upon the next day by the Duc de Fitz-James. It is sad to reflect that in the midst of these delicate discussions over which King Louis' Government was watching with benevolent interest the Prince's unfortunate habits should have asserted themselves with deplorable consequences. The Duc de Choiseul requested Prince Charles to visit him to discuss the possibility of an expedition under the leadership of the Prince himself and the Duc de Broglie. To this important interview Charles came so drunk that it was impossible for the Minister to have any discussion with him. This act of almost incredible discourtesy and folly did unspeakable harm to his cause and resulted in all sorts of wild rumours and reports of his insobriety circulating not only in Paris but in other European Courts; indeed, according to the Duc d'Aiguillon, he was drunk during the greater part of his stay in Paris and quite incapable of being trusted with any plans or secrets.

After one or two eligible princesses, among whom was the Princess Marie-Louise of Salm-Kyrburg and the Princess Isabella of Mansfeld, had been discussed the choice finally fell upon the eldest daughter of the Princess of Stolberg. This lady was the widow of Gustavus Adolphus of Stolberg-Gedern, Prince of the Holy Roman Empire, Knight of the Palatine Order of St. Hubert, Count of Konigstein, Rochefort and Hohenstein, a soldier who had fallen mortally wounded at the Battle of Leuthen fighting in the cause of the Queen-Empress Maria Theresa. He had left his widow with a young family, innumerable titles, and no money. Through the bounty of the Empress the Princess of Stolberg had been able to place her elder daughter as a Canoness in the Chapter of St. Wandru at Mons where she would receive an adequate

The Cardinal King

education and from which her only hope of escape lay in an acceptable offer of marriage.

To marry a daughter without a portion to a king without a throne may be considered a fair deal to both sides, for in all other respects the Princess Louise Maximilienne Caroline Emmanuele was of a rank almost the equal of her husband's, being descended herself on her mother's side from the Royal House of Scotland through her grandmother Lady Charlotte Bruce, daughter of the Earl of Elgin and Aylesbury, who had married Maximilien Emmanuel, Prince of Hornes. Louise's mother (who was to live to be over ninety and was to be twitted at that advanced age for thinking more about gowns than eternity) was only too glad to get her eldest daughter off her hands, having already betrothed her second daughter to the Marquis of Jamaica, son of the Duke of Berwick, a Stuart connection which probably decided the Duc de Fitz-James to suggest the elder daughter to Charles.

The only person immediately concerned who was not at all pleased at the forthcoming marriage was the Queen-Empress herself, upon whose charity the Stolberg princesses had been living. She was not long in hearing about it for the Abbess of the Chapter of St. Wandru was her own sister-in-law. Her rage was such when it was made known to her that the marriage negotiations had been undertaken without her consent (a marriage that might sadly strain her friendly relations with the House of Hanover) that she refused ever to see the old Princess of Stolberg again. It was only after she had been reminded of the Prince's sacrifice for her on the field of battle and after receiving the most humble apologies from the Princess herself that the Empress agreed, somewhat reluctantly, to relent.

2

Now that the question of the marriage was settled Charles returned to Rome with his secretary Lord Caryll. At Genoa, in October, his carriage encountered that of the Duke of Gloucester, brother of George III. They met 'full butt' in a narrow street where the Hanoverian Duke halted his carriage, lowered the glass, and bowed very politely to his distant cousin as he drove by. The

The Marriage of Prince Charles

de jure King was very touched by this mark of respect but as the Duke of Gloucester was at that time in disgrace for having married Lady Waldegrave his object in so marked a courtesy may have been intended more to spite his brother in London than to show any particular regard for the head of the House of Stuart.

The Princess Louise of Stolberg meanwhile was making her way to Paris and there, on March 28th, 1772, the proxy ceremony took place. 'The new Pretenderess is said to be but sixteen and a Lutheran,' wrote Horace Walpole. In point of fact she was nineteen and a Catholic. Her husband was her senior by thirty-two years.

Descriptions of the appearance of Louise tend to differ but all who saw her at this period seemed to be captivated by her lively charm. Karl-Victor von Bonstetten in his Memoirs tells us that she was 'of medium height, had dark blue eyes, a slightly turned-up nose and the complexion of an English girl. Her expression was bright and piquant, and at the same time so sympathetic, that she turned all heads', while Count Vittorio Alfieri comments with enthusiasm on her 'dark eyes with a sparkle in them, and the sweetest of expressions; in addition—that which one rarely sees in combination—to a very fair skin and light coloured hair' all of which, he assures us, 'gave a lustre to her beauty which was well-nigh irresistible.' He was certainly to find it irresistible himself. Even Mann later found words of praise, describing her as 'a beautiful woman, much beloved by those who know her, who universally describe her as lively, intelligent and agreeable.'

It should not be thought that because Louise had been brought up in the atmosphere of a Convent that she was lacking in knowledge of the world. Indeed, if anything, the opposite was the case. Chapters for Noble Ladies, like that of St. Wandru, were not particularly noted for their spiritual discipline but were rather retreats for unmarried daughters or spinster aunts who were thereby enabled to enjoy a pension provided by the foundation but otherwise mix in secular society as much as they wished. It is probable that Louise received a good education while at Mons (for she fancied herself as something of a blue-stocking), but as she also emerged from her convent with a very thorough knowledge of

The Cardinal King

the use of cosmetics we can conclude that her studies were not entirely directed towards spiritual ends.

From her own point of view she had much to gain from the marriage. With all her quarterings her chances of making a good marriage were not particularly bright when she had no other endowments to bring to a marriage settlement beyond her youth. To marry a man considerably older than oneself was by no means unusual at that time while Charles, if his royal claims were unacknowledged, was still a figure of considerable consequence and a royal House was none the less royal for being in exile. There is no doubt that the glamour of royalty was a great attraction to Louise who long after she had left her husband and was living openly with her lover in Paris affected a chair of state in her reception room under a canopy displaying the royal arms, and made her servants call her 'Your Majesty'. That she saw nothing ridiculous in this masquerade suggests a shallow temperament despite her reputation for wit and learning.

At the moment of the ceremony in Paris, however, we may be sure that Louise began her career as 'the Pretender's Queen' with no regrets whatsoever, and indeed was probably only too thankful to escape from the provincial life offered at Mons to a position where she could cut something of a figure in European society as the wife of the hero of the Forty-Five.

From Paris she began her long journey to meet her husband in Italy. Like Clementina Sobieska she was accompanied by an Irish officer, a Colonel Ryan, who went with her as far as Venice from where she took ship to Ancona. Charles, who had sent a special courier to inform the Cardinal Duke of these events of which he had, up to now, been kept in ignorance, journeyed north with Lord Caryll to Macerata where Cardinal Marefoschi's palace had been placed at his disposal. Here the bridal pair saw each other for the first time and here the second ceremony took place on the day of their meeting, April 17th, which happened to be Good Friday, a day of sufficient ill omen upon which to begin married life. The Prince signed the register as Charles III and made his wife also use the royal signature. On Easter Sunday the couple left for Rome.

The Marriage of Prince Charles

The Cardinal, having smothered any resentment he may have felt at being excluded from the marriage negotiations, despatched the Marchese Angelelli, his Maestro di Camera, to meet Charles and Louise on the outskirts of Rome where he had sent his state coach with its six horses and out-riders in scarlet livery to drive the bride and groom to their Roman palace with as great a flourish as circumstances would permit. In this gala coach, with the carriages of the suite following, the cavalcade made an impressive sight as it passed along the Corso where crowds of idlers had collected to see the beautiful young woman who would now be the mistress of the Muti Palace. It was from the situation of this palace in the Piazza dei Santi Apostoli that the Roman wits were to dub her 'Queen of the Apostles' as it was now imprudent to refer to her as Queen of anywhere else.

Charles, who had apparently learnt nothing from his previous experience of the Papal Court, had no sooner reached Rome than he sent a message to the Secretary of State announcing the arrival of their Majesties the King and Queen of England. To this message Cardinal Pallavicini replied somewhat crushingly that no such persons could possibly be in Rome.

3

The day after the royal pair had installed themselves in the Muti Palace the Cardinal Duke drove in from Frascati to pay his respects in person to his sister-in-law and to present his wedding gifts. These included a fine gold box on the lid of which the Cardinal's own portrait had been set with diamonds and also a court dress of the finest lace and gold thread. Inside the gold box was a more practical present in the form of a draft on his banker for forty-thousand scudi, a sum representing about ten thousand pounds sterling.

Whatever feelings the Cardinal Duke may have entertained towards his sister-in-law as he drove into Rome to meet her for the first time, his generous and simple heart was completely won over as soon as he set eyes on her. Her charm of manner and intellectual attainments delighted him and he returned to Frascati full of praise

The Cardinal King

for his new relation. No doubt Louise did her best to please her brother-in-law. The Cardinal was an influential figure in Rome (very much more so than his brother whose presence was merely an embarrassment to the Papal government) and if Louise wished to figure prominently in Roman society she was quick to realize that she could only do so with the protection and approval of the Cardinal Duke.

For a while happiness reigned at the Muti Palace despite its gloomy associations and unhappy memories. Charles was delighted with his young wife and in the pleasure of her society the 'nasty bottle' seemed to have been forgotten. The Cardinal was no less delighted in these signs of grace which he was ready to attribute to his sister-in-law's influence, but his distress returned when Charles began once more to importune the Papal Court for the recognition of his royal claims. The Cardinal had long realized that such requests would be fruitless despite the good will of the Holy See (Clement XIII had been moved to tears during an audience granted to Lord Elcho because he had 'so bitterly hurt the Prince by refusing to acknowledge him' and Clement XIV shared his predecessor's feelings), but the Cardinal knew that further demands could only result in loss of dignity for his brother and the cause. For this reason he had strongly advised Charles against insisting on Louise adopting the style of Queen, for he realized that it would make her position impossible in Rome, but Charles was adamant. 'I pay no regard to my brother or to any one else when the maintenance of the dignity due to me is concerned . . .' he wrote to Cardinal Marefoschi who now pressed his claims at the Vatican: 'It will be proper to say to the Pope that one of the first conditions of the marriage was that the Queen should be treated like the late Queen.'

Undaunted by the rebuffs he had received Charles now requested the restoration of the bodyguard of Papal troops that had attended his father despite the fact that Louise herself joined with the Cardinal Duke in urging him to modify his demands. When Clement XIV returned a polite but firm refusal to the claims made in the Prince's name by Marefoschi Charles gave vent to his feelings in a burst of anger:

The Marriage of Prince Charles

'I could not have believed [he wrote] that the Pope would have wished to make an event tragical, for which every good Catholic ought to have given his service to make it splendid and agreeable. Did they wish to perpetuate the family of Hanover, and to cut off the Legitimate Catholic race? Finally, did they wish to compel me to leave this country? How could they imagine that the Catholic courts would not be scandalized and chilled by such proceedings? It is for the Pope to go before them, showing them a good and not a bad example. The sheep usually follow their shepherd, and it is his duty not to disgust them by showing a path of brambles and thorns.'

The Pope was not to be moved by this outburst of moral indignation from a 'good Catholic' who had already once renounced his religion for political ends. Alas, few Catholic courts in 1772 would be either scandalized or chilled by the action of the Pope to which they would almost certainly have expressed their approval had their opinions been asked, while no wish was dearer to the heart of the hard-pressed Pope than that Charles Edward Stuart should leave his country.

4

Louise, meanwhile, was enjoying the society of Rome in which she had considerable success. It was at this time that Bonstetten saw her when her beauty, as he put it, 'turned all heads'. It certainly turned his, for the enthusiastic Swiss was soon referring to her as the Queen of Hearts, a title considerably more fitting than Queen of the Apostles, for there was little in Louise's nature to merit so evangelical an association. As Queen of Hearts she was to share her title with that other Stuart princess, Elizabeth, the 'Winter Queen' of Bohemia, from whom the Hanoverian dynasty was descended.

It was about this time also that a curious rumour reached England that the Cardinal Duke was dead. It is difficult to say what gave rise to this report beyond Henry's reputation for having delicate health and the English Government's over-eagerness to see the ancient dynasty extinguished—the more so now that

The Cardinal King

Prince Charles's marriage threatened the exact opposite—but whatever the cause in August 1772 Walpole was writing to Mann: 'It has been said in our newspapers that the Cardinal of York is dead; but your silence makes me conclude it is not true; which is probable, too, by its being in our papers, for they are absolutely nothing but magazines of lies, blunders, scandal, virulence, and absurdity.' In actual fact, as Louise enjoyed the flattering talk of Bonstetten or danced at a fancy dress ball with young Mr. Coke of Norfolk (to whom she gave a white cockade), Charles and the Cardinal, who was very much alive, were faced with a further source of mortification by the sudden arrival in Rome of Clementina Walkinshaw and her daughter Charlotte.

These two ladies made their unwelcome appearance in the course of the year 1773, having decided that the Prince's recent marriage was an excellent opportunity to apply for an increase in their allowance. As the Prince himself did not give them a penny they were more concerned to gain an interview with the Cardinal Duke as it was upon his charity that they depended. Henry considered that he had done quite enough for them already and looked upon their visit to Rome as little more than an impertinence. Miss Walkinshaw did not accept this interpretation of her conduct and preferred to adopt the attitude of a woman wronged, and when she could not prevail against the man who had really wronged her or the brother who had done no more wrong than provide for her support, she turned to the Cardinal Secretary of State. The Cardinal Pallavicini, who filled this office under Clement XIV, had had quite enough of the Prince's embarrassing demands without having to contend with those of his former mistress. He wrote to the Cardinal Duke's treasurer, the same Monsignor Lascaris who had once been in the service of King James, informing him of the futility of Clementina's remaining in Rome and telling him that if she refused to leave he must 'convince her of the uselessness of her resistance and of the worse position she will consequently be in'.

Both the Prince and the Cardinal Duke refused to see either of them. From the Cardinal's point of view there was no reason why he should receive the woman whose liaison with his brother he

The Marriage of Prince Charles

had always deplored, especially at a time when he had high hopes of the latter's restoration to a more sober and rational life as a result of his marriage. Clementina Walkinshaw's support was entirely his brother's responsibility and the fact that Charles refused to shoulder this responsibility, which he preferred to leave to the Cardinal Duke's generosity, did not give this woman or her rather pushing daughter the right to molest the Cardinal with endless letters and appeals. As for Charles himself, his conduct was less excusable; and the fact that he refused so much as to see his daughter is all the harder to forgive when one considers how later he was to depend upon her when he was himself in need of her companionship and support.

As soon as it became clear that they had nothing to gain financially as a result of their long and expensive journey the two women made preparations to return, but as a parting shot Charlotte sent a letter to the Cardinal Duke's secretary asking that His Royal Highness would not refuse her permission to change her convent at Meaux for one at Paris. To this submissive request she received the reply that His Royal Highness and Eminence was perfectly indifferent to her place of retirement provided that she remained always in a nunnery. On the receipt of this discouraging answer, which was as much as either lady could extract from their reluctant benefactor, they had no choice but to return empty-handed to France.

5

With the departure of Clementina Walkinshaw and her daughter a certain amount of peace came into the Cardinal's life though anxiety for his brother returned when towards the end of 1773 it became apparent that the bottle was not, after all, forgotten. The indifference of the Papal Court to Prince Charles's claims and the fact that his wife had showed no signs of presenting him with the heir he longed for all helped to undermine his resistance to the oblivion that alcohol offered him and in which he was soon again to take refuge.

The Cardinal Duke must have been sincerely thankful when Charles and his wife moved themselves to Tuscany in the next

The Cardinal King

year. Preparations were under way for the celebration of the forthcoming Jubilee in which Henry Stuart, in virtue of his ecclesiastical rank, would play a principal part. Charles had asked that a special royal tribune should be reserved for himself and his wife at the opening of the Holy Door of St. Peter's. When this request was refused he left Rome in a rage; but if he had hoped to spite the Pope by this action he was mistaken, for the Papal Court did not conceal its satisfaction at his departure.

The Pope himself, indeed, was beyond caring about anything. Since his Bull suppressing the Society of Jesus his fear of poison had become such an obsession that it had finally affected his reason. He would spend as long a time as possible at his villa at Castelgandolfo refusing to grant audiences and only seeing those whom he felt he could trust. Among these was the Cardinal Duke of York, his neighbour at Frascati, who often visited him during his fatal illness. This Pope who had once been noted for his vigorous health now became a prey to every sort of fear and hallucination and on his return to Rome ordered the strictest precautions for his safety, forbidding people to loiter in the courtyards of the Apostolic Palace, refusing admission to any person carrying a stick, and doubling the Swiss Guard. He would sit for hours with open, salivating mouth, gazing vacantly into space. Official business was brought almost to a standstill by the Pontiff's refusal to see anyone but his secretary Bontempi.

Cardinal de Bernis managed to secure an audience and tried to show Clement the absurdity of his fears of poison, but without avail. An attempt had recently been made on the life of the King of Naples and this had had the effect of completely demoralizing the Pope who was already in a low physical state due to the serious turn taken by an infection of the skin from which he had suffered intermittently for some years. When not lost in an almost imbecile stupor he would wander aimlessly about his apartment or spend the night pacing the corridors of the Palace. He was like one possessed, 'haunted' as Giulio Cordara wrote 'by the ghost of the dead Society of Jesus. . . . This distressing thought so raked him day and night that sometimes he would babble in sheer grief and seemed to be beside himself. Often in the night he thought he

The Marriage of Prince Charles

heard the bronze bell of the Jesuits, though no one had rung it.' This was the man who, in his prime, had received the Duke of Gloucester on his visit to Rome when that Prince had been so impressed with his personality that he had remarked with Hanoverian boisterousness that if Clement XIV had reigned in the time of Henry VIII England would never have seceded from the Roman obedience!

Clement made what was virtually his last public appearance on September 8th, 1774, the feast of the Nativity of the Blessed Virgin, when the Jubilee of the following year was proclaimed. He was so weak that he had to be carried up the steps of his throne and the service, through which he sat listless with exhaustion, had to be shortened. Two days later he left the Quirinal for further ceremonies connected with the Jubilee but fainted in his carriage so that the crowd, which had expected to see the Pope drive past in state, instead saw his unconscious body placed on a litter and hurried back into the Palace from which he was never again to emerge alive.

A curious circumstance of the Pope's last days concerns the visit of a mysterious Englishman who was said to have sold him a powerful elixir, supposed to be an antidote for poison, for the sum of two thousand *scudi*. A certain amount of mystery surrounds this strange episode, though a report was sent to the Marquis Tanucci, Prime Minister of Naples, that nightly visits were paid by this man to the demented and fast-dying Pope. Nothing more seems to be known about him but that his name was Menghin. Was he, perhaps, one of the impecunious hangers-on of the Jacobite Court who still lingered in Rome? Whoever he was his elixir was not powerful enough, for by September 22nd Clement XIV was dead.

The rumour that this Pope had been poisoned by the Jesuits was soon being discussed everywhere in Rome, no doubt encouraged by the enemies of the Society who would stop at nothing to see it discredited and to prevent a popular demonstration in its favour. Horace Mann provided Walpole with a lurid account of the autopsy in which no nauseating biological detail was spared and he had no hesitation in attributing the end to the work of poison. The body decomposed so rapidly that the funeral ceremonies had to be hurried through and the face of the corpse covered with a mask. As for the Sacred College of Cardinals, their attention was directed to the problem of who should succeed Clement XIV rather than to the question of by what means, fair or foul, he had met his end.

Earlier in the same year King Louis XV had died at Versailles, receiving the last Sacrament like a good Christian while the weeping Madame du Barry was discreetly ushered out of the Palace into compulsory retirement. His death was due to smallpox and the course of the disease was rapid despite the attention of six physicians, five surgeons and three apothecaries.

With the passing of this monarch, whom the young Henry Benedict had met during his visit to France at the time of the Forty-Five, the Stuarts lost one of their last royal friends. Only Charles III of Spain, who as a young Infante had been with Charles Edward at the siege of Gaeta when Henry was only nine years old, now remained of the monarchs who had reigned when Stuart hopes had run so high. Though Louis XV had long since ceased to give political support to their cause he was in essence a kind-hearted man whose chief fault lay in his easy-going laziness and the lack of decision he brought to the conduct of his public duties rather than in the concupiscence for which he is chiefly remembered, and he always gave to his Stuart cousins what help he could. It is probable that he would have supported the conduct of his Ambassador at the time of the death of James III had his political circumstances permitted him to do so. As it was, he had been a generous benefactor to the Cardinal Duke, who drew a large income from his French benefices, and he had agreed to a pension being paid to Prince Charles at the time of his marriage to Louise of Stolberg. But any further recognition he had long since been unable to give, for he realized that their cause was lost with the same disillusioned foresight with which he had predicted the deluge that was to follow his own reign.

Europe was now moving into a new age and the House of Bourbon was to be as much out of touch with the spirit of it as ever the House of Stuart had been, and was soon to share its

The Marriage of Prince Charles

fate. Little did the Cardinal of York think as he attended the requiems sung in Rome for the soul of Louis the Well-beloved that he would survive by nearly fifteen years the young prince of twenty who now ascended the throne of St. Louis; or that he would live to see the son of an obscure Corsican lawyer, now only five years old, rise from the chaos of revolution to be Emperor of the French.

6

All this remained hidden in the future. It was still in the recognizable world of the *ancien régime* that the Cardinal entered the Vatican to elect a new Pope. The doors of the conclave were closed on the evening of October 5th, 1774, but the difficulties of finding a successor to Clement XIV who would meet with the approval of the Catholic monarchies and at the same time be acceptable to those who still secretly supported the Jesuits or desired their restoration were such that the Church had to wait until February 15th, 1775, before the electors were able to announce a new Pope.

The anti-Jesuit party was again led by Cardinal de Bernis who had instructions only to favour the election of a Pope who would confirm Clement's Bull of 1773. To secure the necessary support he persuaded the Dean of the Sacred College, who was now Cardinal York's friend Giovanni Francesco Albani, to delay the scrutinies until the foreign Cardinals had arrived, as Clement XIV had left the College in a depleted condition with as many as fifteen vacancies at the time of his death—indeed only twenty-eight Cardinals were present when the conclave assembled in October. And so for some time their Eminences were immured in idleness within the Vatican while the Roman populace amused itself by reading the lampoons and pasquinades that were circulated about the venerable electors. One of the most scandalous of these found its way into the conclave when the outraged Dean gave orders for it to be burnt publicly in the Piazza Colonna.

The prospect of delay was particularly trying to the Cardinal de Bernis who was at this time at the height of his infatuation for the Princess Santa Croce. His desire to see her was such that he is

The Cardinal King

said to have knocked a hole in the wall of his cell through which he could escape from the claustrophobic atmosphere of the Vatican and the uninspiring company of his fellow prelates into the more congenial society of his inamorata. The use of this exit, conveniently veiled by tapestry, enabled the French Cardinal to endure the passing weeks with considerably more composure than his colleagues; indeed there is no knowing how long he might have gone on enjoying these clandestine visits had not the sudden illness of the Princess suspended his excursions and enabled him to give his mind to matters more urgent to the well-being of the Church.

When sufficient Cardinals had assembled there started the business of canvassing the various *Papabili*, as the most promising candidates for the Tiara were termed. Neither side could agree to anyone likely to secure the necessary majority and deadlock followed deadlock until it looked as though the conclave would last for ever. The courts of France and Vienna grew impatient and instructed their ambassadors to urge the electors to greater efforts. Eventually it was decided that both parties should select three candidates whose names should be submitted to an independent Cardinal who could ascertain their chances by secret questioning of the whole College. The Cardinal Duke was chosen for this duty as both sides could rely on his integrity while as a Roman prelate he was supposedly free from pressure from the Catholic sovereigns or other politically interested parties. His mission, however, was a failure, as none of the six names showed any signs of securing a two-thirds majority.

At length, after further fruitless negotiations, a choice was finally made in favour of Cardinal Giovanni Angelo Braschi after he had given an undertaking to govern in harmony with the Catholic courts and had satisfied Bernis and his party of his anti-Jesuit sentiments. Relieved at finding an acceptable candidate at last the Cardinals elected him unanimously (Braschi himself voting for the Cardinal Dean) on the two hundred and sixty-fifth day of the conclave. After wavering between the names of Clement and Benedict he finally decided to reign as Pius VI, a name that had not been used since the death of the saintly Michael Ghislieri

The Marriage of Prince Charles

two hundred years before. One of his first duties as Pope was to open the Holy Door of St. Peter's, a ceremony that had been postponed owing to the death of his predecessor.

The new Pope was a man of noble family but of little or no private fortune. Of blameless reputation in both his public and private life he had brought great zeal and ability to the offices he had previously held in the church. He was a man of commanding presence and if there was any blemish on his character it lay, perhaps, in the pride, amounting to vanity, that he took in his personal appearance. His curling white hair (which some said was a wig) was always dressed with excessive care while at his coronation, at which the allocution was preached by the Cardinal of York, people declared that he lifted aside his heavy robes to display a shapely foot for the admiration of the faithful. He was also to be accused of the more serious offence of nepotism.

7

While the conclave was in session Prince Charles announced that he expected to hear at any moment that his brother had been elected Pope; an opinion that would greatly have surprised the Cardinal Duke himself, for he never had any ambitions in that direction and would certainly never have been acceptable as a *Papabili* if only on account of the equivocal status of his family. The reason for the Prince's remark is difficult to find unless we accept the opinion of Sir Horace Mann that he 'probably was heated with wine (which is very often the case) when he said this'.

After wandering about Italy for some time following his departure from Rome he finally settled with his consort at Florence. This gave Mann an unequalled opportunity to continue his spying on the banished dynasty from close quarters and both his despatches to the Secretary of State and his private letters are full of descriptions, usually of a derogatory character, of the declining health of 'the Pretender' and the escapades of his pretty young wife.

As the Grand Duke Leopold (who was a younger son of the Empress Maria Theresa) was as adamant as the Pope in his refusal

The Cardinal King

to recognize King Charles III the Prince had now adopted permanently the incognito title of Count of Albany which he had used at his audience with Clement XIII and from henceforth he and his wife were always known as Count and Countess of Albany except to the members of their own household and visitors who were particularly eager to gain their favour from whom they would receive the title of Majesty. At first they lived in a palace lent to them by Prince Corsini, but about three years after they had settled in Florence Charles purchased the Palazzo Guadagni and here he spent the remainder of his time in the Tuscan capital. It is said that one room in the palace was decorated in the Royal Stuart tartan—a rather startling taste in interior decoration that was later to be favoured by Queen Victoria at Balmoral.

The position of an elderly, ailing husband with a young and attractive wife is a proverbially difficult one and tends as often as not to result in situations which are the stock in trade of the writers of *opéra bouffe*. The *ménage* at the Palazzo Guadagni was no exception. Charles had already shown the jealous side of his nature in the absurd episodes that had characterized his relationship with Clementina Walkinshaw and this trait soon reappeared with regard to his wife. 'He is jealous to such a degree' wrote Horace Mann, 'that neither there [at the Opera] or at home is she ever out of his sight. All the avenues to her room, excepting through his own, are barricaded. The reason he gives for this is, that the succession may never be dubious'.

Louise, for her part, soon began to find life with her gloomy invalid of a husband excessively dreary though she still managed to enjoy a fairly full social round with visits to the Opera, dinner parties, and excursions to the Casino dei Nobili. Her spare time she devoted to the study of mathematics, correspondence with her friends, and irritating her husband with sulks and petty squabbles which either drove him to bursts of anger or bouts of drink.

They would take walks together in the town where their appearance would be an occasion for curiosity to the English visitors who would stare with little respect for courtesy at the interesting couple, the red-faced, haggard-looking prince wearing

The Marriage of Prince Charles

the blue ribbon of the Garter and walking with some difficulty on his swollen legs, and the young princess whose youth and beauty were still fresh, though according to Mann these charms began to fade after some years at Florence. In 1779, after Charles and Louise had been five years his neighbours he sent Walpole an account which, even allowing for his usual malicious exaggeration where the Stuarts are concerned, paints a dismal picture of the state to which the Prince was reduced:

'The Pretender . . . is in a deplorable state of health. He has a declared Fistula, great sores in his legs, and is insupportable in stench and temper; neither of which he takes the least pains to disguise to his wife—whose beauty is vastly faded of late. She has paid dear for the dregs of Royalty. How will his brother be stiled when he succeeds to his Kingdom? He is already called at Rome *Sua Eminenza Reale*, but that will not do then. I dare say he has settled this already in his own mind.'

Mann's curiosity on the subject of the Cardinal Duke's royal title was never to be satisfied for despite all the ink he wasted in forecasting the death of Prince Charles he had the misfortune himself to die first, an eventuality he had not bargained for.

There were moments of consolation during this dreary existence at Florence as, for example, when the Prince met the Duke of Hamilton during one of his walks. Accustomed to the slights he had received from his fellow countrymen the Prince was prepared to be cut, but instead the Duke made a point of bowing respectfully in the direction of the Prince, and repeating this salutation when they met again. Acts such as this were balm to the wounded spirit of this forgotten King. His health was rapidly deteriorating; he continued to frequent the Opera rather than let his wife go alone but was so ill that he had to have a couch made for him in the box on which he slept during the greater part of the performance.

It was at this time that a new visitor presented himself at the Palazzo Guadagni in the person of Count Vittorio Alfieri with whose arrival the final humiliations of the Prince were to begin.

The Cardinal King

8

The squalid scenes which now characterized the life of Charles and Louise at Florence were in sharp contrast to the splendour that marked the opening of the new reign at Rome.

The Cardinal Duke was in his fiftieth year when the pontificate of Pius VI began, and he was then at the height of his power and influence. His wealth and magnificence made him an almost legendary figure to the masses of the people who thrilled at the sight of this handsome Prince of the Church with his fabulous diamond cross as he swept into Rome from Frascati in his state coach with its out-riders and running footmen in scarlet liveries. The townsfolk of Frascati were proud of their Royal Eminence whose love of spectacular ceremonial brought a note of pageantry to the town which had previously often known its Cardinal-bishop only from occasional visits of duty or necessity, while they benefited from his benevolent generosity and the prosperity which his presence there brought to the town.

The Italian temperament responds cordially to a brilliant display of wealth or splendour as it does with equal enthusiasm to manifestations of true art, and in the Cardinal of York the Italians found someone who was, for all his pride of British ancestry, as much Italian as themselves. 'There is no doubt what ever' wrote his biographer Vaughan, 'that the Cardinal Duke of York, albeit the grandson of a reigning British Monarch, was in reality a foreigner by birth, by training, by religious sympathy and by an uninterrupted residence abroad; for out of a long life exceeding eighty-two years, only twenty months were passed by him outside the borders of Italy. Nor can he be described merely as an Italian; he was essentially a Roman, who rarely crossed the frontiers of the Papal States and was bound by every tie of ecclesiastical duty and of natural affection to the capital of the Popes or its immediate neighbourhood.' Herein lay one of the major differences between the Cardinal Duke and his brother. When one considers that Prince Charles was also a Roman by birth and had spent so much of his life in Italy or in wandering over Europe it is surprising how

The Marriage of Prince Charles

English he always remained. The Cardinal, dilettante, art-loving, fond of good living and cultivated society, though he shared these tastes with such ancestors as James III of Scotland and Charles I of England, would have appeared irredeemably foreign to an English squire of the eighteenth century, while Charles shared all the prejudices of that class even to the extent of his fondness for heavy drinking. Charles was always waiting the call home, back to the Highlands or 'to speak to his subjects in Westminster Hall' while to Henry home was always Rome, or more especially his beloved Frascati whose good people he once told the Marquis d'Aubeterre 'in a flash of zeal' he considered as his true heirs.

As an Italian and Roman, as a lover of art and patron of scholarship, Henry Stuart must have shared to the full those ideals which guided Pope Pius VI in the first years of his reign in restoring to Rome some of the glories it had known at the time of Leo X. Once more the eternal city welcomed a host of scholars and artists from all parts of the civilized world. Pompeo Batoni (to whom both the Cardinal and Prince Charles had sat) was at the height of his career as a portrait painter while the young Antonio Canova was beginning to display his brilliant powers in the memorial to Clement XIII, one of his first major commissions. Jacques Louis David, the great French painter, came to Rome in 1775 where he remained for five years. From Germany came Raphael Mengs, Philipp Hackert the landscape painter, and Angelica Kauffmann. Goethe made two long stays in Rome at this time where, like royalty, he assumed an incognito, travelling under the name of Möller, merchant of Leipzig, though this did not prevent him from receiving, and refusing, an invitation from the Cardinal Secretary of State.

Royalty itself flocked to Rome in ever increasing numbers. Cardinal de Bernis was constantly complaining at the expense he was put to by having so often to entertain these distinguished visitors. The Emperor Joseph II, his brother the Archduke Maximilian and his sister the Archduchess Christine; Prince Leopold of Brunswick, Prince Augustus of Saxe-Gotha; King George III's brothers the Dukes of Gloucester and Cumberland and his son the Duke of Sussex; the Grand Duke Paul of Russia, the Dowager

The Cardinal King

Duchess of Weimar and the Duchess Maria Amelia of Parma; these, with countless lesser royalties, were rushing to Rome to visit the relics of Imperial times and to witness the magnificent ceremonies of the modern Papacy over which Pius VI presided with an actor's skill. Gustavus III was a welcome visitor to Rome for the sake of his reforms in Sweden which had given religious freedom to his Catholic subjects. He was received in audience by the Pope who gave him the Order of the Golden Spur. Another visitor, lavishly entertained by Cardinal de Bernis, was Louis-Philippe, Duc de Chartres, later Duc d'Orleans, and still later to be known as Philippe-Egalité, the regicide cousin of Louis XVI.

Under the patronage of Pius VI the Vatican Museum was considerably enlarged and its collection enriched by many new acquisitions. The Sacristy was added to the fabric of St. Peter's from the designs of Carlo Marchionne and in Rome itself three ancient obelisks which had been brought to the city from Egypt at the time of the Caesars were erected on new sites where they still stand, the most famous being that in front of the Quirinal flanked by the statues of Castor and Pollux, and the graceful obelisk outside the Trinita dei Monti at the top of the Spanish Steps.

In this world the Cardinal Duke moved with a calm serenity thinking, perhaps, as many others did, that the glory which Pius VI had brought to Rome was the dawn of a new age of peace and enlightenment and not the splendid sunset of a whole civilization. If he was spared a foreknowledge of the horrors that lay just over the horizon his tranquillity was not to remain undisturbed, for at the end of 1780 he received a letter from his sister-in-law which was to shatter his calm and send him rushing to the Pope for advice. The Countess of Albany's letter was to tell him that she had fled from her husband and taken refuge in the Convent of the White Nuns at Florence.

7

Poet and Princess

I

The official explanation of the Countess of Albany's escape into the Convent of the White Nuns was that she could no longer put up with her husband's brutal treatment and drunken habits, but to find the true cause for this apparently sudden action we must return to that day at the end of the summer of 1776 when Vittorio Alfieri, then at the beginning of his career as a dramatic poet, first presented himself in Florence where he had come to perfect his knowledge of the Tuscan dialect.

Count Vittorio Alfieri was a man of sufficiently extraordinary character quite apart from his reputation as a poet and dramatist. He was the prototype of the romantic brooding genius, the rôle that Lord Byron (who indeed acknowledged his debt to Alfieri) was later to play to perfection. He was born at Asti, a subject of the Piedmontese crown, in 1749, of a noble and influential family, and educated at Turin. His father had died while he was yet an infant and after his mother had married again he was brought up under the protection of an uncle, the Cavaliere Pellegrino Alfieri, later Viceroy of Sardinia. He first manifested his sense of the dramatic when, while still a child, having heard of the deadly powers of hemlock he had rushed into the garden and proceeded to devour all the flowers he could lay his hands on in the hope that this baneful weed might be among them. As a punishment for this unusual act, which resulted in violent retchings, he was confined to his room which, he tells us in his autobiography, 'afforded me an opportunity of brooding over my melancholy ideas'. He was seven or eight years old at the time.

As a child he was difficult and unmanageable and the only

punishment that had any effect on his proud spirit was one that made him look ridiculous in public, as when his tutor made him appear in church wearing a night-cap. At the school he attended at Turin he easily distinguished himself but it offered him little opportunity to discover his real talents and his masters managed to make very little impression beyond instilling in him a contempt for the type of education which was then considered sufficient for a Piedmontese nobleman. On leaving school all he seemed to have acquired was a taste for debauchery and a love of horses that was to last for the rest of his life.

The early years of his manhood were devoted entirely to travel. He visited France, England, Holland, Austria, Prussia, Sweden, Finland, Russia, Portugal and Spain, travelling with feverish haste and covering distances which even in these days would be considered remarkable. At Versailles he was presented to Louis XV who, he remarked, 'received with a cold and supercilious air those who were presented to him, surveying them from head to foot. It seemed as if on presenting a dwarf to a giant he should view him smiling, or perhaps say: "Ah! the little animal!"' Frederick II of Prussia he found even less to his liking than the King of France. 'On entering the states of the great Frederick, which appeared to me like a vast guard-house, my horror against this man of blood redoubled,' he writes, and when an official at Potsdam asked him why he was not in uniform (for at this time he held a commission in the Piedmontese army) he surveyed the soldier-filled ante-room in much the same way that he had himself been surveyed by Louis XV, and answered that he thought the court was already sufficiently crowded by uniforms. By the time he reached St. Petersburg he had had enough of courts and did not solicit an audience with the Empress; indeed, in Russia he found himself disgusted with all that he saw 'except their beards and their horses' both of which he considered impressive. Portugal fared no better from the point of view of this disillusioned traveller who wrote of Lisbon that 'everything in this city displeased me except the females, who are extremely voluptuous.' It goes without saying that Count Alfieri was a young man who was not easily satisfied.

While in Holland he became enamoured of a lady whose charms

Poet and Princess

so moved him that when the affair ended he again had ideas of suicide, though this time he did not choose hemlock as the fatal instrument. Having had to undergo a surgical bleeding he removed the bandages after the doctor had left in the hope of bleeding to death. In this rather half-hearted effort at self-destruction he was surprised by his valet who immediately restored the bandages to their proper place and refused to leave the room until his master was in a less desperate frame of mind.

Alfieri's fondness for the fair sex got him into further trouble during his visit to England where he soon fell under the spell of Lady Ligonier, the all too frail wife of the Viscount Ligonier, a nephew of the celebrated Field-Marshal. In the course of his secret visits to this lady, who returned his passion with an ardour based on a wider experience than her lover realized, the future poet managed to dislocate his shoulder in a fall from his horse and still had his left arm in a sling two nights later when the deceived husband entered his box at the Opera and demanded satisfaction. The secret visits had not been so secret after all and Lord Ligonier had received a full account from his servants of the nightly visits paid to his wife by the foreign Count while he himself was away on military duties. The two men retired to the Green Park where a duel was fought. Noticing that his opponent's arm was in a sling Lord Ligonier enquired whether this would prevent him from fighting. 'I replied in the negative', Alfieri tells us in his account of the affair, 'and thanking him for this mark of attention, immediately put myself on my guard. I was never a proficient in the use of the sword. I rushed on him contrary to all the rules of the art, like a mad man as I was, for in fact I wished to meet death at his hands.'

All that he did, in point of fact, meet at the hands of his challenger was a small wound in the arm between the elbow and the wrist. It was so slight that at first Alfieri did not notice it, but Ligonier, who knew more of his wife's character than her lover did, considered that honour was satisfied and left the field. Alfieri bound up his wound with a handkerchief, having to use his teeth to knot it owing to his useless left arm, and then returned to the Opera where he apologized for his absence by saying that he had suddenly remembered an appointment. He then sat down to enjoy the remainder of the Act.

Lord Ligonier immediately began proceedings for divorce, but with the same magnanimity he had shown on the field of honour he did not press for heavy damages against Alfieri. By then the unfortunate lover had discovered that the lady who had enjoyed his embrace had only just left the arms of her husband's groom, and torn between fury, humiliation and disgust, he left England almost at once. 'Even now, after the lapse of twenty years,' he tells us with disarming frankness in his autobiography, 'when I reflect on what I then suffered, my blood boils in my veins.'

It was on his return to Italy that Alfieri first felt the need to express his turbulent nature in artistic creation and began to make up for the deficiencies in his education with the same vehemence that he had previously devoted to the pursuit of travel, women and horses. For some time the calls of love greatly interfered with the demands of his Muse and it was, indeed, while watching by the sick bed of one of his lovers that he first jotted down on a sheet of paper some dialogues that suggested to him that he might have a talent for dramatic construction. Gradually the artistic instinct triumphed. He began to read the Italian classics as well as ancient authors and to perfect his still very imperfect knowledge of his native tongue. These studies he followed with characteristic violence. While reading Plutarch he was moved to such a degree of emotion, so he informs us, that 'I wept, raved, and fell into such a transport of fury, that if anyone had been in the adjoining chamber they must have pronounced me out of my senses.' On another occasion when the desire to meet his mistress was threatening to interfere with his work he cut off his red hair so that he could not appear in society and even made his valet tie him into his chair so that he would be prevented from rushing on an impulse into her arms.

This was the man who now arrived in Florence 'attended by a great train of horses and servants'. He had not intended to remain very long in the Tuscan capital, but Fate had decided otherwise. 'Scarcely had I arrived in that city', he writes, 'with the intention of remaining a month, or longer, as it should prove agreeable,

Poet and Princess

than an event occurred which induced me to take up my residence in it for several years.' The 'event' which caused this change of plan was his meeting with the Countess of Albany. At last he felt that he had found a worthy object for his love: 'Twenty-five years of age, possessing a taste for letters and the fine arts, an amiable character, an immense fortune, and placed in domestic circumstances of a very painful nature, how was it possible to escape where so many reasons existed for loving?'

2

Alfieri at first avoided the society of the Countess of Albany as his previous experience had taught him that love and study could not be combined without disaster to one or both and he was now determined to pursue literary fame at the cost of all else. For this purpose he gave up most of his fortune, which he handed over to his sister, so that he might be free from the restrictions on travel and the censorship of publications imposed on Piedmontese subjects by their King.

The allure of Louise was, however, to prove too strong for him to resist. He became a regular visitor at the Palazzo Guadagni, at the same time beginning work on his tragedy of *Maria Stuarda*, a subject he considered suitable to the new situation. Unlike his previous mistresses who had been a hindrance to his literary work, he found in Louise of Albany an inspiration which fired him to greater poetic efforts. 'I wrote also some amatory pieces,' he tells us, 'equally with the view of celebrating the mistress of my affections, and of dissipating the chagrin I felt on account of the domestic circumstances in which she was placed.' The lovers met often, but never alone, at the Guadagni Palace, and the fact that Prince Charles was always present was not the least trying of the 'domestic circumstances' which he complained of in a poem written in 1778.

> O Lady is my fear for thee displeasing,
> When my warm love is half compact of fear?
> Since I behold thee forced with grief unceasing
> The harsh yoke of an aged spouse to bear,

The Cardinal King

Like some trapped dove in vain for mercy pleading.
From hands so impious and from home so drear
I mean to snatch thee, my alarm increasing
With each foul act, with every falling tear . . .

But the moment for snatching had not yet come. Meanwhile Alfieri, who seems to have aroused the Count's jealousy less than one might expect, would read passages from his tragedy to the husband and wife. There were occasions when Charles's head would nod in sleep during the recitation; it would be ungallant to suggest that it was the tragedy which induced these slumbers, so we must assume that they resulted from the after-effects of a hearty dinner and a liberal ration of wine—but whatever the cause these precious moments were not wasted by the young couple. But the Prince was not nearly so somnolent as they wished. 'How have I offended thee, O Sleep, placid brother of Death,' cried the distracted poet, 'that thou dost no more return to shut the eye-lids of the worthy spouse?' Like everything that concerned Alfieri a note of the bizarre was introduced into this clandestine affair. It is said that on a visit to the Uffizi, Louise had admired a picture of Charles XII of Sweden. Alfieri at once had the costume of the king copied and clad in this fancy dress paraded himself outside the Stuart Palace.

For some time this amorous flirtation continued, the poet visiting his mistress when the occasion offered and devoting the remainder of his time to literary work or wild gallops over the countryside on one of his favourite horses. Charles seems to have been ignorant of what was going on under his very nose as his brother was later when the lovers had removed to Rome. This situation, as it continued until the year 1780, is described with some complacency by Alfieri in his autobiography.

'My days at that time glided away in an almost unruffled calm, which would have been uninterrupted but for the sympathetic feelings I experienced on account of my mistress, who was frequently treated in the most brutal and cruel manner by her old peevish and drunken husband. I participated in all her sufferings, and experienced all the bitterness of death. I could only see her in

Poet and Princess

the evening, or when dining at her house; but the husband was always either present or in an adjoining apartment: this, however, did not arise from him entertaining any greater jealousy of me than of others, for during the nine years that they had lived together as man and wife, they had never visited but in company with each other; a mode of life which even must have proved wearisome to two young lovers of the same age: I remained therefore the whole day in my study, only taking an airing in the morning on account of my health. I had indeed the happiness of seeing her in the evening; but this happiness was embittered by witnessing the sorrow which oppressed her.'

At the end of this year, however, the longed-for opportunity came. The 30th of November, the feast day of Scotland's patron Saint, was always an occasion of high emotional tension in the household of Prince Charles. In 1780 St. Andrew's Day had been celebrated with the usual heavy drinking. Urged on perhaps by jealousy or perhaps momentarily crazed by alcohol and the bitter memories that flooded in on him at this time the Prince burst into his wife's room and loaded her with abuse. Then in a final spasm of fury he flung himself on her and would have strangled her had not her screams brought members of the household running to her aid. Now really terrified for her life and in constant fear of another drunken attack Louise began to plot with Alfieri to escape from under her husband's roof.

In their scheme they were assisted by Geoghegan, a member of the household, and Madame Orlandini, an Irishwomen married to an Italian. Through this woman it was proposed that Louise should visit the Convent of the White Nuns, ostensibly to look at some embroidery, but once there that she should place herself under the protection of the Superior. Charles, who saw no cause for jealousy in a visit to a Convent, at once gave his consent to the plan. He accompanied her as far as the Convent and sat in his carriage to await her return. When, after some time, she made no sign of reappearing the Count rapped on the door and asked how much longer he was expected to wait. To his intense surprise and rage he was told by the Reverend Mother that his wife had taken refuge in the Convent and had no intention of returning to him.

The Cardinal King

He was further told that the Grand Duchess of Tuscany had given her protection to Louise, though Cornelia Knight would have us believe that this Princess had another motive for wishing to see the Countess of Albany safely in a Convent; her own husband, the Grand Duke Leopold, was a little too 'partial to the cause of the unfortunate lady.' Horace Mann was soon aware of these developments and wrote with some glee but with little taste to inform his friend at Strawberry Hill:

'The mould for any more casts of Royal Stuarts has been broke, or what is equivalent to it, is now shut up in a Convent of Nuns, under the double lock and key of the Pope and Cardinal York, out of reach of any Dabbler who might foister in any spurious copy. Historians may now close the lives of that family, unless the Cardinal should become Pope, and that would only produce a short scene of ridicule.'

Once inside the Convent Louise wrote to her brother-in-law telling him what she had done and giving as the reason her husband's brutal treatment which she declared she could no longer endure. Needless to say there was no mention of Count Vittorio Alfieri in the letter to the Cardinal Duke of York.

3

On receiving this letter the Cardinal had hurried into Rome to discuss the problem with Pope Pius VI. It should be remembered that he had not seen his sister-in-law since she had left Rome in 1774, a time when, as the *Diario* records, 'he was delighted to recognize in the young Princess all the good qualities that rumour had endowed her with' and that no rumours of any other sort had reached his retreat at Frascati. On the other hand he knew his brother's habits only too well, the drunkenness and the fits of violence which had caused such scandal at Rome when the Prince had returned there after his father's death. He therefore wrote at once to suggest that Louise should come to Rome where he had arranged for her to be received in the same Convent where his mother had once found a refuge when he was a child.

Poet and Princess

Frascati. Dec. 15, 1780.

MY VERY DEAR SISTER,

I cannot express to you the sorrow I have felt on reading your letter of the 9th of this month. Long ago I foresaw what has now happened, and your escape being made with the approval of the Court has fully justified your conduct. You may rely, my very dear Sister, on my kind feelings towards you, for up till now I have always sympathized with your position; on the other hand I beg you to recall that I had no share whatever in bringing about your indissoluble union with my brother beyond giving my formal consent to the marriage, of which I had received no previous notice. As to what happened afterwards, no one better than yourself can bear witness to the impossibility of my assisting you in the least degree during your subsequent troubles and difficulties.

Under the circumstances, nothing can be wiser or more convenient than for you to come to Rome and live in a convent; so I have not lost a moment's time in going into Rome expressly to serve you by arranging this matter with our very Holy Father, whose kindness towards yourself and me I cannot sufficiently describe. I have thought of everything that could suit your case, and I am glad to say that the Holy Father has approved of all my suggestions. You will reside in the convent where the Queen, my mother, remained some time; the King, my father, had a special regard for it. It is the least restricted convent in Rome. French is spoken there, and some of the nuns are highly distinguished.

Finally, my very dear Sister, remain calm and allow yourself to be guided by those who are attached to you; and above all never tell anyone that you do not intend to return to your husband. Do not fear that I should ever have the courage to advise such a step, unless a miracle were to take place. But in all probability God has permitted the past in order to induce you to lead a holy life, so that all the world may thereby perceive the purity of your aims and the reasonableness of your conduct; so also we may hope that by the same means He intended to convert my brother. . . . My dearest sister, be anxious about nothing. Monsignor Lascaris,

The Cardinal King

Cantini, and I shall arrange all that is necessary. I feel deeply for you.

      Your very affectionate brother,
           HENRY, *Cardinal*

It is obvious from this kindly and piously expressed letter that the Cardinal, in his simplicity, considered that Louise had no other object in flying to the Convent of the White Nuns than to escape from the cruelty of her husband, and he seems to assume that this young woman, not yet thirty years old, would be content to remain in virtuous seclusion until such a time as death freed her from her indissoluble union, in the arrangements for which, as the Cardinal rather unnecessarily and quite unhelpfully pointed out, he had taken no part. The Countess herself must have had very different ideas as she read the Cardinal's letter, and the thought of passing her days in a nunnery, be it ever so unrestricted, must have filled her with dread. However highly distinguished the nuns might be it was not to enjoy their conversation, in French or any other language, that the Countess had run the risk of separating herself from her husband and throwing herself on the mercy of the Pope and her narrow-minded but good-intentioned brother-in-law.

For the moment, however, she had no choice but to accept the Cardinal's suggestions with a good grace. A letter from the Pope followed in which the Holy Father gave her the necessary permission to enter the Ursuline Convent in the Via Vittoria, promising her also the use of a carriage, a hint, perhaps, that life might not be so cloistral after all. On December 30th she left Florence, Count Alfieri and Geoghegan accompanying her coach as far as the borders of the Grand Duchy where these two gallants, who had armed themselves with loaded pistols, took their leave, as it would hardly have been seemly for the Countess to enter His Holiness's dominions with her lover in such close attendance. Alfieri returned to Florence 'like a forsaken wretch' and after a month of anguish during which he admits with great frankness 'I became incapable of every occupation, and could devote myself to no serious study; nothing gave me pleasure, everything, even

Poet and Princess

glory and myself, were forgotten,' he removed to Naples until such a time as 'motives of decorum' would allow him to settle in Rome.

One reason why the poet chose Naples was that it would give him a legitimate excuse to pass through Rome on his journey there from Florence. Here he was able to catch a fleeting glimpse of his mistress who was now enjoying the company of the nuns in the Via Vittoria. Despite the lack of restrictions and the use of a carriage Alfieri speaks of her as though she had been walled up for life:

'At length I reached Rome—I saw her: my heart is yet lacerated when I reflect on it. I saw her behind a grate, less tormented it is true than she had been at Florence, but in other respects much more unhappy. We were separated, and who could say for how long a time. I shed many bitter tears, but I had at least the consolation of reflecting that her health would be re-established, that she might sleep in tranquillity, and was no longer subject to the caprice and sway of a cruel and drunken tyrant; in short, that she would exist!'

He had certainly found the right expression. It might be said of the Countess of Albany that as far as the ability to exist was concerned she had no rival but the Abbé Sieyès; for before her death at the age of seventy-one this woman, who was to live through the French Revolution and Empire and see the restoration of the Bourbons to their thrones, who was to meet Napoleon and be told by him that had she had a son he would have made him King of England, had so little respect for the memory of her husband that after his death she actually visited England and was received by King George III and Queen Charlotte and later, sitting at the foot of the throne, saw her husband's rival open Parliament in the House of Lords.

At the present moment, however, the Countess had only one motive in existence; to quit the Convent for which King James III had had such a special regard and find refuge in some place where she could enjoy greater liberty to receive her lover and take part in the social life of Rome. Alfieri, during the few days he spent in the city, did his best to ingratiate himself with the Car-

The Cardinal King

dinal Duke and the Papal government, which some years earlier he had roundly abused in a sonnet, before delicacy compelled him to continue his journey to Naples.

4

The strain of this second parting from her lover after the risks of her flight from Florence affected the Countess's health and for a while she was content to remain in the Convent until she had regained her strength. To the Cardinal she wrote in affectionate terms though in actual fact she was already planning to deceive him.

'If you could see me now these days, my dear Brother, you would think me bad tempered, but I am only out of spirits and have such headaches that I can hardly speak. So I hope you will rest thoroughly assured that I am very happy; indeed it would be impossible for me to feel otherwise with such a brother as yourself. So never believe that I am cross, I beg you. Farewell, my dear Brother, keep me in your good graces, and be always persuaded of my tender affection.'

Henry was completely taken in by his sister-in-law's expressions of 'tender affection'. It never occurred to him for one moment that she had any other wish in life than to remain in chaste seclusion from her husband. Living chiefly at Frascati away from the gossip and social activities of the Papal capital he was quite out of touch with what went on there outside the ecclesiastical circles in which he moved, while the genuine affection which he himself felt for Louise made him ready to grant her all the favours she might ask, and she was not to be slow in asking.

Living as he did chiefly at his episcopal seat outside Rome the great Palazzo della Cancelleria was rarely occupied except for official business, and it soon occurred to Louise that this magnificent palace would make a more fitting setting for her activities than the interior of a Convent. As soon as her health was restored she began to suggest such a move to the people most likely to influence the Cardinal in favour of her plan. She even appealed to the Pope. According to Sir Horace Mann, who missed nothing of

Poet and Princess

what went on in Rome, the meeting took place in the sacristy of a church. In this setting, reminiscent of Puccini's *Tosca*, the Countess used every argument except the true one to persuade the good-natured Pope that nothing but happiness could result from her removal from the Convent to the Palace. To her arguments, which can hardly have been very weighty, she added the inducement of tears and an expression of injured innocence which made a convert of the susceptible Pontiff on the spot. Of course the Countess should leave the Convent! He would speak to the Cardinal of York himself. The Cardinal, when approached, offered no resistance, and so, only a few months after her arrival as a fugitive in the city, the Countess of Albany was installed in a splendid apartment on the second floor of Bramante's sumptuous palace from where she was soon to reign as one of the leaders of Roman society.

It was useless for Prince Charles to protest, through his friend Prince Corsini, of the liberty now enjoyed by his runaway wife. The Papal Court had had enough of him and his protests fell on deaf ears. The Cardinal, whose ability only to see one side of a question was later to cause his sister-in-law much humiliation, was at present wholly on her side in the dispute with his brother, and took no notice of the letters which Prince Charles sent to him from Florence complaining bitterly of the conduct of his wife and the red-haired Piedmontese Count who, by May 1781, was back in Rome once more. When Charles protested at his presence there the Pope told Prince Corsini, who again spoke on behalf of the Count of Albany, that the great poet honoured Rome with his presence, and further ordered that half the pension allowed by the Apostolic Chamber to Prince Charles should in future be paid to the Countess.

Thus installed in a Palace of considerably more grandeur than the one she had occupied as a virtuous wife during her first visit to Rome, free to see her lover when circumstances should permit, and protected from scandal by the fact that she lived there with the full approval of her brother-in-law, the richest and most influential Cardinal in Rome, the Countess of Albany, in the words of H. M. Vaughan, 'at once took rank in Roman society as one of its most exalted leaders, yielding the palm alone in this respect to the haughty Princess Rezzonico, niece of Pope Clement XIII.' It was indeed good, in such circumstances, to exist.

5

Rome looked upon the association between the Countess and the poet with complacency. It was the age of the *cavaliere servente*, and if anyone chose to put a scandalous interpretation on their friendship it could be countered by the fact that the lady was living under the roof of her brother-in-law who was known to hold in horror any suggestion of immorality, who was, in fact, looked upon as something of a prude, and if he raised no objections to an affair which was the talk of all Rome then it was not for anyone else to question it. It probably occurred to no one that the Cardinal was completely ignorant of the romantic comedy that was being played out in the splendid setting of his Roman palace; his confidence in his sister-in-law was complete and as he never listened to gossip and anyway spent most of his time at Frascati there was little likelihood of his eyes being opened to what all Rome saw with amused indifference.

Alfieri admits that he went out of his way to make a good impression on the Cardinal for whom he had no more liking than he had for Prince Charles. Louise, who had made a study of flattering her brother-in-law, sent the poet out to Frascati with a gift which she knew would please the recipient and at the same time managed to suggest in the accompanying letter that her acquaintanceship with Alfieri was of a casual and purely literary nature.

May 15, 1781.

Since I had noticed, my dear Brother, that your fine library lacked a good copy of Virgil, and since I knew of a most beautiful example, I send you the very book; and I take the liberty of sending it to you by the hand of Count Alfieri, who has dined today at my house, and has told me he was going tomorrow to pay you his respects. I hope, my dear Brother, you will do me the honour of accepting my gift as a mark of my tender and sincere attachment

Poet and Princess

towards yourself. Would that I could give you proofs of it every hour of the day! But rest fully persuaded that I am as devoted to you as if I were your own sister, and accept the assurance of a boundless affection.

LOUISE.

If the Cardinal had had any doubts about the character or intentions of Alfieri his fears must have been allayed when he heard that the Count had been received in audience by the Pope. Pius VI received the man whose sonnet on Rome, written some years previously, had roundly condemned both the Pope and his government, with affability. 'He would not permit me to kiss his foot,' Alfieri wrote afterwards, 'but raising me from the humble posture into which I had thrown myself, he patted me on the cheek with a grace truly paternal. Notwithstanding the sonnet I had written on Rome, which stared me in the face, I replied to these compliments like a thoroughbred courtier. . . .' The Pope seemed highly satisfied with the encounter and would probably have been much surprised had he known that the poet was later to record that he 'entertained no very profound veneration for His Holiness as Pope, and still less for Braschi as a man of letters or the patron of literature, since I considered him as neither the one nor the other.' How different was this audience with its background of simulation and deceit from that granted by Clement XIII to Prince Charles sixteen years previously with the great question of recognition still an unsettled problem between them. The Prince had been dragged reluctantly to that sad and unprofitable audience; but on this occasion the republican-minded Count was only too willing to dance attendance on a Pope whom he despised so that he might continue unmolested his intrigue with the wife of the banished Stuart who but for his family's identification with the ancient faith might now be wearing a crown.

Such considerations did not trouble the mind of Alfieri. He rented the Villa Strozzi near the baths of Diocletian on the Esquiline Hill, that part of Rome where Virgil and Horace had once lived. In this retreat, sanctified by its association with these great poets, he could divide his time between literature and love. It is perhaps equally appropriate, if less romantic, that a man who spent so much of his life in foreign travel should elect to live near the spot where the principal railway station of Rome now stands. Once more the poet's life took on a familiar routine without the anxieties that had clouded his existence at Florence. 'The Villa Strozzi . . . afforded me a delightful retreat' he writes, 'where I passed my mornings in study, only riding for an hour or two through the vast solitudes which in the neighbourhood of Rome invite to melancholy, meditation, and poetry. In the evenings I proceeded to the city, and found a relaxation from study in the society of her who constituted the charm of my existence.'

In these rides across the 'vast solitudes' he was sometimes joined by the Countess, who was an intrepid horsewoman. These excursions were rare and secret owing to the scandal that would have arisen had they been discovered; a situation that would have been difficult to explain away to the Cardinal Duke. Such clandestine meetings were made easier by the fact that Elia, Alfieri's confidential servant and valet who, in the character of a Leporello, had accompanied his master on all his adventures since he was sixteen, was now installed in the Countess's household, and was a valuable go-between in arranging secret assignations between 'Psipsio' and 'Psipsia' as the lovers called each other, names which were supposed to represent the sound of a kiss.

It was a time of happiness and success for both of them, and even the Cardinal was happy in what he imagined to be the sincere affection in which he thought himself to be held by his sister-in-law. The Countess greatly enjoyed her freedom after the agonizing years of virtual confinement in the Palazzo Guadagni; and Alfieri basked contentedly in the fame which his reputation as a poet brought him, at the same time delighting in the love of his mistress. It was a time, also, of great social splendour in Rome and the Countess of Albany was to be seen at receptions and *conversazioni* in the palaces of the Roman nobility where her beauty, and the dazzling Stuart and Sobieska diamonds which she wore, made her a brilliant figure. She also enjoyed a reputation for wit, though those of her letters that remain to posterity show little trace of this though they are not lacking in the sort of spiteful malice that

Poet and Princess

sometimes passes for wit. She was a frequent visitor at the Palazzo de Carolis where the Cardinal de Bernis lived. Her coach would arrive at the grand entrance and at the cry of '*Torcie!*' two servants would appear, each holding a flaming torch, to light her up the marble staircase. This was the very palace where the Cardinal of York's footman had flung his torch under the prancing feet of the Princess Rezzonico's horses as both arrived at the same moment for the reception in honour of the birth of the Dauphin; but the Cardinal Duke only came on such official occasions and it would be rare indeed for him to meet his sister-in-law except when she went out to dine with him at Frascati.

The Palazzo Santa Croce, famous for its pictures and for the beauty of the Princess whose home it was, was another house that welcomed the Countess of Albany and was also a place where she could be certain that she would not encounter her brother-in-law. The Princess Santa Croce represented a section of society with which the Cardinal Duke did not mix and which, indeed, he viewed with some horror and dismay as can well be understood when it is remembered that it was this princess who remarked to her escort in St. Peter's while people were going up to kiss the relic of the True Cross on Good Friday: 'This is my fête, so you ought to kiss me!' This remark, says Cornelia Knight, was made in a voice 'loud enough to be heard by the whole congregation'. A society which tolerated comments in such taste would hardly scruple at the conduct of Louise and Vittorio Alfieri or care to move in the same circles as the pious Cardinal Duke of York.

The climax of their years in Rome came with the presentation of Alfieri's *Antigone* in the private theatre of the Spanish Ambassador, the Duke of Grimaldi, in his palace in the Piazza di Spagna. The poet himself played the part of Creon and the other rôles were divided between the Duke of Ceri, the Duchess of Zagorolo, and other amateurs who were fortunate enough to combine histrionic talent with nobility of birth. Prominent among the spectators, and splendidly decked out in the jewels belonging to the husband she had deserted, was the Countess of Albany, who openly shared with the author of the play the praise lavished on him by an audience in which was represented all the nobility of

The Cardinal King

Rome and a good proportion of the College of Cardinals. This sharing of the triumphs of the evening amounted almost to a public acknowledgement of their association and it appears incredible that the Cardinal of York, who never attended such performances (prefering the plays performed by the students of his Seminary at Frascati), did not hear any rumours of that evening's entertainment which might shatter his 'splendid tranquillity' or at least make him question the propriety of his sister-in-law's conduct.

But he heard nothing, perhaps because he wished to hear nothing, for having once taken his sister-in-law's part in her quarrel with his brother it took more than a mere concert in Rome or the report of idle gossips to undermine the tremendous obstinacy with which his opinions were held. He was also a man in whom a high sense of honour combined with a character singularly lacking in subtlety made it impossible for him to attribute dishonourable motives to others unless the proof was literally staring him in the face and then, as often happens with such people, he tended to react violently in the opposite direction. It was this sudden opening of his eyes which accounted for his ruthless treatment of Louise and Alfieri, for which he has often been blamed, when the truth of the situation was finally brought home to him.

6

It was not in Rome, but in Florence, that the Cardinal Duke learnt the truth which almost everyone else had known for the best part of three years. In March 1783 Prince Charles was taken seriously ill and his life was despaired of. Fearing the end he made a Will in which he recognized his long neglected daughter Charlotte, and on March 30th he had her legitimatized by an act of the French Parliament, bestowing upon her the title of Duchess of Albany. (To assure its legal validity, when the act was finally signed in the July of 1784, he so far forgot his unacknowledged kingship as to allow himself to be described simply as 'Charles Edward Stuart, grandson of James II, King of Great Britain'.) Seeking also a reconciliation with his brother he begged the

Poet and Princess

Cardinal to visit him, and Henry set off for Florence greatly wondering whether he would find his brother alive.

At Siena, where he rested on his journey, the Cardinal was surprised to hear that Charles had made a remarkable recovery, and on arriving at the Palazzo Guadagni he found him already convalescent and, to judge by the priests who thronged the place, also in an edifying state of religious resignation. The broken man greeted his brother with emotion and began at once to pour out the story of his wrongs. With mounting incredulity and amazement the Cardinal now heard for the first time the full account of the Alfieri affair from the Prince's point of view. He was at first reluctant to believe this story, exposing him, as it did, to the position of one who had unwittingly given his protection to the blossoming of the whole scandal, but the Prince's story was supported in every detail by the Archbishop of Florence, and the Cardinal's eyes were opened at last. He was filled with fury and indignation when he realized how he had been tricked by his sister-in-law whose troubles (as he had written to tell her) he had hoped would induce her to lead a holy life so that all the world might perceive the purity of her aims. The discovery of what all the world, except for himself, had in fact perceived was a shattering blow to the faith and trust he had placed in her, and he lost no time in rushing back to Rome determined to put a stop to this unsavoury situation at once. 'The tables are now turned. The cat, at last, is out of the bag,' wrote Horace Mann who, needless to say, was fully informed of all that happened in the Guadagni palace. 'The Cardinal of York's visit to his brother gave the latter an opportunity to undeceive him, by proving to him that the complaints laid to his charge of ill using [the Countess] were invented to cover a Plot formed by Count Alfieri who, by working up Tragedies, of which he has wrote many, is most expert, though he always kept behind the curtain, had imposed upon the Great Duke, the Pope, and the Cardinal, and all those who took part.'

Arrived in Rome he immediately despatched a curt note to the Countess forbidding her to receive Alfieri in his palace and at the same time asked the Pope to have the Count banished from Papal territory. Having swung from one extreme to the other with regard to his sister-in-law's conduct the Cardinal was now quite unable to contain himself in his fury and complained loudly about Louise to all who came near him, though we may consider as something of an exaggeration Cornelia Knight's claim in her autobiography that 'he told every postillion on the road from Florence to Rome the bad opinion he had of his sister-in-law and Count Alfieri, and he held the same discourse with all the shabby people about Frascati.' We can be sure that the Cardinal Duke with his great sense of personal dignity and the respect owed to him as a prince of the blood as well as of the Church would not discuss his family scandals with postilions or 'shabby people', but he probably complained pretty vociferously to his intimates and fellow ecclesiastics, and these people would hardly be able to resist passing on so delectable a morsel of gossip.

Pius VI, while not wishing to offend the Cardinal by refusing his request, did his best to tone down the order of banishment so that Alfieri could quit Rome without too much loss of face, while from Louise he received a letter in which she protested her complete innocence; a letter which His Holiness very probably read without much conviction. He had, however, no wish for an open scandal, and brushed aside the Cardinal's request that the Countess should return to the Convent in the Via Vittoria. Henry's outspoken indignation was already resulting in a reaction in favour of the chastened lovers, so that Louise, when she wrote (still protesting her innocence) to inform the Cardinal that his wishes were fulfilled, was even able to introduce a slight note of reproach into a letter in which hurt pride, moral indignation, flattery and hypocrisy were ingeniously and wonderfully combined.

'According to the advice you gave me, my Brother, for which I thanked you at the time, because I believed that the matter was quite private, I have induced Monsieur le Comte d'Alfieri to leave Rome. He went this morning. I should have sought to hasten his departure, but after serious meditation and after consulting with the most sensible of my friends I concluded that an abrupt and apparently enforced exit would have given colour to those disagreeable but ill-founded rumours on my conduct, that are only too prevalent. Well, in any case, your wish is fulfilled and your advice followed. The only grievance I feel is that the matter has aroused gossip which injures my reputation and my sense of honour. See what unpleasantness you would have spared me, if (as we had originally agreed) you had confided your views of the matter to myself alone, and had not most unnecessarily informed the Pope; in short, if you had not allowed yourself in your first excitement to follow a course of action (and in this I appeal to your kind heart), which you must now perceive was most distressing to myself, not only because I am your sister-in-law, but because I am a woman. Do not, however, dread that from this time onward I am going to load you with reproaches; for I shall avoid doing so. I shall only recall the marks of affection I have received from you in the past, whereof I shall always retain the warmest recollection. In spite of all that is just past, I feel a devotion no less sincere, of which I entreat you, my Brother, to accept the assurance.

'Your very humble and obedient Servant and Sister,
'LOUISE'

Alfieri took a more disarming line in excusing his conduct and endeavouring to turn the tables on his priestly accusers. 'Justice . . .' he writes, 'compels me to confess that the husband, the brother-in-law, and the priests, had reason to complain of my frequent visits (to the Countess) . . . I am only sorry that the zeal of these priests, who were the sole promoters of this cabal, was neither evangelical nor exempt from secondary views, since the example of many of them afforded an ample apology for our conduct.'

Count Alfieri left Rome on the 4th of May, 1783, suggesting, in his autobiography, that he did so not because of the order of banishment or to please that 'violent and inconsiderate man' the Cardinal, but simply because he was too much interested in the 'honour, the fame, and the tranquillity of the worthy and respectable female' who was the object of the calumnies not to adopt every means in his power 'to put an end to such unmerited clamour.' That the clamour was unmerited is an opinion that we need not feel ourselves obliged to share. Louise and Alfieri had acted with great indiscretion, especially when it is remembered that Louise had arrived in Rome in the character of a wronged and ill-treated wife fleeing for refuge and protection. The Cardinal Duke, if he had possessed more worldly wisdom, might have dealt with the situation with more tact had not his judgement been distorted by the resentment he felt at the thought of the deception to which he had been subjected by the sister-in-law he had gone out of his way to please and to protect. It was an ill return for all his kindness. But he bore her no malice for the ridicule to which her conduct in Rome had laid him open, for, as Mann comments, his violent reaction to the scandal only succeeded in exasperating the Roman nobility against him. 'Instead of considering the delinquency of the parties,' he wrote, 'their wrath is turned against the Publisher of the Scandal; and they compassionate the situation of the disconsolate Lady who, I really believe, will marry the Count a week after she becomes a widow.' As for Louise herself, she never forgave the Cardinal, though she continued to write to him in flattering terms so long as it served her purpose.

7

This unpleasant family quarrel was a source of great irritation and distress to the Cardinal who wished for nothing more than to live in peace and fulfil the duties of his chosen career. The period of the Countess of Albany's stay in Rome saw him at the height of his influence and prestige as a prince of the Church. This was the time when the ecclesiastical policy of the Emperor Joseph II was causing so much anxiety to the Papal curia. The action of this voluble but narrow-minded liberal in suppressing seven hundred convents, halving the number of secular priests, and forbidding the publication of papal bulls in his dominions was hardly the sort of conduct expected in one who enjoyed the title of Apostolic Majesty, and in 1781 Pius VI had made the journey to Vienna in order to expostulate in person with the Holy Roman Emperor. During his absence on this unsuccessful mission much of the government of Rome was in the hands of the Cardinal Duke in virtue of his office of Vice-Chancellor. From these duties connected with his ecclesiastical life he must have turned with reluctance to the sordid intrigues of his sister-in-law and the pathetic protests of his brother in Florence.

After the departure of Alfieri, Louise again gave way to dejection and nervous depression. The Cardinal, who still retained an affection for her, suggested that she should spend some time at a villa of his in the Alban Hills. Here she divided her time between playing the harp and writing a series of hysterical letters to Francesco Gori, a friend of Alfieri's. 'Music alone deadens my grief somewhat,' she told him, 'and I spend my whole day playing on the harp, and that because I know the Friend would be pleased if I learned to play well. If you could only guess at the horrible thoughts that cross my mind. . . . If this state of things is not brought to a speedy end, I shall have to take some violent action.'

Charles, meanwhile, had again been seriously ill. On January 24th, 1784, he had an apoplectic seizure and for two days lay speechless. The Cardinal, sure that the end was near, actually went so far as to prepare a protest to be circulated to the European Courts announcing his right of succession to the empty title of King, while Mann expressed his own opinion on the subject in a letter to Horace Walpole dated the day of the Prince's stroke. 'It will be a singular circumstance to see a King-Cardinal. The Emperor Maximilian wanted to be one, in order to become Pope, and then a Saint, that his daughter might pray to him; but his ambition was disappointed by his not getting money enough to bribe His Holiness and his Sacred College.' But the time for the succession of the King-Cardinal had not yet come, for again the Prince's remarkable constitution withstood the attack though John Stuart, his confidential servant, who had kept the Cardinal informed on the progress of the illness, took the precaution to lock up all valuable papers and possessions as he could no longer trust the people the Prince had about him.

During this winter a visitor had arrived in Florence who was destined to settle the deadlock between the Prince and his wife by arranging for a legal separation between them. The person who undertook these delicate negotiations was King Gustavus III of

The Cardinal King

Sweden who, accompanied among others by Count Axel Fersen, was travelling in Italy under the name of Count Haga. Remarkable among kings as a monarch whose writings occupy a genuine place in his country's literature on account of their own merit, Gustavus brought the same wisdom he had displayed in settling the problem of the factions known in Sweden as the Hats and the Caps to the less important but no less complicated business of Charles and Louise. The Countess, anxious for her freedom, put few obstacles in the way of a settlement and agreed to surrender her pin-money and those of the Sobieska diamonds and rubies which she had taken with her to Rome. She retained, however, the pension of sixty thousand *livres* settled on her by the French court at the time of her marriage. Once again the Cardinal Duke was kept in the dark about these negotiations until they were almost complete, when a letter from Louise on the subject caused him to give vent to another outburst of indignation. In this letter the Countess told him with some smugness that she was 'very far from seizing on the fortune of your Brother, as he declares, and it is without any regret that I now restore him not only the 1,000 écus that you pay me, but also the 3,000 which by my marriage settlement constitute my own pin-money.'

The Cardinal was far from satisfied by this settlement of money, a large amount of which came out of his own pocket, and busy though he was in preparation for the ceremonies of Easter, he lost little time in telling the Countess just what he thought about the whole thing. Not only did he disapprove of the idea of a separation, but he considered that Louise was taking a great liberty in passing on to his brother money which she received from himself. His reply was expressed in unusually irascible terms and had none of the conventional terms of affection which Louise, in view of his great wealth and influence, still hoped to receive from him.

My Very Dear Sister,

I am so busy these days, that I have scarcely the time to reply to your letter, and therefore I confine myself to assuring you that nobody in the world ought to desire a settlement between yourself and your husband more than I; but I can never approve of a separation, whose sole aim is interest.

I cannot, and ought not, to interfere in any arrangements you two may devise together, but I bid you remember that everything you have received from Cantini (my steward) since you have resided in my palace of the Cancelleria has come from *myself*; and that the said Cantini has my orders to pay it to you so long as you live with me. It is a piece of insolence therefore on my brother's part, this disposing of money which is mine, as though it were his own, and without my knowledge, so that I feel compelled to acquaint him with my own opinion of his conduct in this matter. And I beg you once for all, my very dear Sister, not to annoy me further on this point, for really it quite upsets my health, to have my brother expecting me to carry out every scheme that comes into his head, by force of abuse and without any acknowledgement of his obligation.

I wish you a very happy Easter, my very dear Sister,

HENRY, *Cardinal.*

The abrupt tone of this letter must have alarmed Louise, for she had no wish to offend so rich a relation, and in her reply, which was full of flattering appeals to his 'gentle heart' and 'ingrained sense of justice', she pleaded her husband's straightened circumstances in support of her plans, thus making herself appear in an edifyingly self-sacrificing light and at the same time carrying the hint that the Cardinal's attitude was really rather a mean one.

MY DEAR BROTHER,

I hasten to send you an exact copy of the mutual arrangement concerning our separation, which is based wholly upon the conviction we both hold as to the impossibility of living together, owing to our incompatibility of temper, and with the example before us of other persons no less distinguished than my Husband and myself, who have been placed in similar circumstances. You see now that your unhappy Brother is only obeying reason and not interest (as you suggest); and that he is not dealing with what is yours, since it is of my own motion and with full knowledge of his needs that I surrender back to him what he promised me

The Cardinal King

for my pin-money and you told me should be paid here in Rome.

I repeat, it is a sacrifice that I am making, and one which I believe I ought to have made earlier save for certain objections. Be assured, my Brother, the King is in need, and I should feel ashamed not to aid him. Stuart will be able to tell you that during his last illness he had not the wherewithal to pay for the Masses said on his behalf, and when Stuart wrote to you, there was but six sequins in the house. I assure you my Brother, that without the pension from the Apostolic Chamber in addition to the fifty-thousand *livres* from France he cannot possibly exist. I used to imagine he was hoarding, but I have examined the bankers' accounts, and I have seen that he was speaking the truth, so that I felt myself bound to assist him. You know, my Dear Brother, that I thought the same thing, when you suggested to me to keep the diamonds over which I have certain claims (all except the large stones you possess equally with your brother). But I never could have done a thing which would have made everybody exclaim, and being bound in conscience and in honour I cannot refuse him his request any more than can you yourself.

How is it possible, my dear Brother, that with your gentle heart and with your ingrained sense of justice and integrity, you cannot realize it is better for us to be separated on proper terms? Have you no satisfaction in my generosity towards your Brother (seeing that it is a proof of my own forgiveness of his evil conduct towards myself), or in my efforts to render him happy, by surrendering this money? It is an excess of attention on my part to have informed you at all, for you would never have found it out; and is it not better for him to live comfortably during the brief remainder of his life, and for you to be left in peace and myself also? What need then to irritate him by writing to tell him that he is disposing of *your* money, since it is I who am dealing with my own property and am bestowing it of my own free will?

Farewell, my dear brother, I beg you to be convinced of my tender attachment, which I shall always preserve.

Your Sister,
Louise.

Poet and Princess

It is hardly necessary to point out that Louise, who talks so grandly of her own property, did not have a penny to call her own before she married the Prince towards whom she now pretends to be acting with such noble generosity. As to her hypocritical references to his being able to live comfortably during the brief remainder of his life, there can be no doubt that these lines were written to touch the Cardinal's heart, for he could not know that only a short time before she had written to Francesco Gori: 'Who knows what will be the end of this man? This man in Florence who has been ill so long a time, he seems to me to be formed of iron to destroy us. You will tell me, to reassure me, that he cannot last long; but I see matters clearly. I don't suppose this last illness has given him a new lease of life, but I do think he can hold out very easily for a year or two longer. Of course he may at any moment succumb to the gout in his chest. What a brutal thing it is to expect one's happiness through another's death! O God, how it degrades the soul! Yet none the less I cannot refrain from this desire.' Despite the scandal over Alfieri the Cardinal still considered Louise as a fundamentally honourable woman, and he was convinced that she would be content not to see her lover again. That she was capable of such double dealing as is shown by comparing her letter to him with the one to Gori would have astounded him. It was only after the arrival at Florence of Charlotte Stuart, now Duchess of Albany, that the full truth about his sister-in-law was brought home to him.

Meanwhile the King of Sweden contrived to wrest some sort of agreement out of the Cardinal that satisfied the husband and wife and somehow set Henry's fears and suspicions at rest, and the deed of separation was finally signed. When all was done the King wrote to Louise from Paris a letter which she must have received with considerable relief.

Paris. June 13, 1784.

MADAME LA COMTESSE,

I have just received on my arrival in Paris the letter you have kindly addressed me from Rome, and I was greatly pleased with your gift of the rare and interesting medals struck at the time of your wedding. I shall deem myself happy, if I have been of any

The Cardinal King

service in softening your lot. I consider you can rest quite easy, Madame, as to your brother-in-law's attitude in this affair. Matters are now well advanced, and they cannot be put back. I shall not cease my own efforts to uphold the terms of separation I have already drawn up, but I believe all is well, and financial arrangements are alone likely to cause any trouble. I also expect that the Cardinal Duke's visit to Florence will only result in increasing bitterness of feeling between the two brothers. I trust the waters will benefit your health, and I look forward to our next meeting, when I hope to prove to you the warm friendship wherewith I have the honour to be,

    Madame la Comtesse,
        your good friend,
           GUSTAVUS.

One can only say that Louise's gift of medals commemorating her marriage was hardly a tactful present to the man who was virtually responsible for dissolving it. As for the Swedish King, he was destined eight years later to be shot during a masked ball at Stockholm. This tragedy, which deprived Sweden of its last great king before the succession of Bernadotte, was to provide Verdi with the subject for one of his operas.

8

When the Deed of Separation was signed Prince Charles issued the last proclamation in which he used all the forms customary to a reigning sovereign.

'We, Charles, legitimate King of Great Britain, on the representations made to Us by Louise-Caroline-Maximilienne-Emmanuele, Princess of Stolberg, that for sound reasons she wishes to reside at a distance separated from Our person: that circumstances as well as Our common misfortunes have rendered this event useful and necessary for Us both; and in consideration of all the arguments she has adduced to Us, We declare by these presents that We freely and voluntarily give Our consent to this separation, and that We do permit her to live from henceforth in Rome, or in any town she may consider most convenient, such being Our pleasure. Given and sealed with the seal of Our arms in Our Palace at Florence, April 3, 1784.'

At the bottom of this pathetic document he added in his own shaking handwriting the words, 'We approve the writing and all contained therein. C.R.'

Louise left Italy for Colmar on the Rhine where she was soon joined by her lover. The Cardinal was able to devote himself once more to the business of the Church and the welfare of his beloved flock at Frascati. It is always sad when great historical names are involved in situations that are worthy only for the plots of comic operas. All that can be said of the whole unfortunate affair is that it showed up all the parties in their worst light: Prince Charles as violent, drunken and sulky; Louise as shallow, deceitful and pleasure-loving; Alfieri as vain and self-centred; and the Cardinal Duke as blind, obstinate and not a little stupid.

8

The Royal Niece

1

After the legal separation between Prince Charles and his wife had taken effect the Cardinal Duke sincerely believed that his sister-in-law would have nothing more to do with the romantic red-haired poet who had been the cause of all the trouble. This belief did not arise merely from his own simplicity of character but was deliberately fostered by Louise herself who was careful never to mention the name of Alfieri in her letters, which she continued to address to the Cardinal with many expressions of affection. She also distracted attention from her own activities by ridiculing the events in Florence where her place as mistress of the Palazzo Guadagni had been taken by the Prince's natural daughter Charlotte, legitimatized and now, after thirty years of obscurity, enjoying full recognition by her father under the title of Duchess of Albany to which he also added the distinction of Royal Highness. The Cardinal's resentment at these honours, which he considered with rising indignation that his illegitimate niece had no right to bear, made him all the more ready to believe in the sincerity of the affection in which Louise professed to hold him, and brother and sister-in-law were again leagued together against the unhappy old invalid at Florence. Rarely had relations between the royal brothers been so strained.

2

Charlotte Stuart reached Florence at the beginning of October 1784. Before leaving Paris she had been received by Queen Marie Antoinette and had been granted the *droit du tabouret*, the coveted

The Royal Niece

right to sit in the presence of royalty which at the French court, where the type of chair or stool one was permitted to sit on was a question of the most complicated etiquette, was conceded only to the very highest nobility and to princes of the blood. To the woman who had languished all her life so far in dreary convents, entirely neglected by her father and only grudgingly supported by her uncle, who disapproved of her very existence, this must indeed have marked the beginning of a new era. But if a new life was beginning for Charlotte Stuart this was certainly not the case for her mother, Clementina Walkinshaw, who had to be content to remain in Paris. (Horace Walpole, relating these events to Lady Ossory, wrongly states that Clementina had died a year or two before her daughter's journey to Florence.) Though Charles now badly needed his daughter's presence this did not in any way dispose him to be reconciled to Clementina. 'Her mother was not allowed to accompany her,' Mann comments dryly on Charlotte's arrival, 'lest she should disgrace her.' It is, however, plain from the many letters written by Charlotte to her mother that she had a great affection for her, an affection which she was never able to feel for her father (with good reason) though she was obviously proud to be his daughter and glad for the change of circumstances which resulted from his belated recognition of her.

The arrival of the newly created Duchess of Albany caused some stir in the Tuscan capital, and beyond. In a despatch dated October 9th, 1784, the British Minister reported her presence to the Secretary of State in London:

'On the 5th instant Count Albany's daughter arrived here. She was attended by Madame O'Donnel who I am told is a French woman married to an Irish Officer of that name in the French service, and is to remain here in quality of *Dame de Compagnie*. She had likewise with her a Scotch gentleman named Nairn whom they call My Lord. She has appeared every evening since with her Father at the Theatres very richly adorned with the jewels that the Pretender had lately received from Rome. He had asked leave to put a canopy over his boxes with a cloth of State, but was refused; he obtained permission however to ornament them within as he pleased. One is hung with red damask and another of yellow, with velvet cushions to each, laced with gold, but of the common size with those of all the other boxes. All the ladies and gentlemen of the country leave tickets of visit at her door, which she is to return. The Pretender has wrote letters to the Pope, to the Cardinal his brother, to the courts of France and Spain and probably to many others, to announce the arrival of his daughter here; they are wrote by her and signed by him. Some attempts have been made for her being presented to the Great Duchess, but as she has not brought a letter of recommendation from the Queen of France to Her Royal Highness, it has been evaded by alleging that being in the country and far advanced in her pregnancy she did not receive anybody.'

To Horace Walpole Mann wrote a more detailed description of the Duchess from which we get a picture of a pleasant and lively creature who was not so foolish or so proud as to make the mistake of Louise who had, by insisting on the prerogative of royalty in not returning calls, found herself shut off from a large section of Florentine society.

'The arrival of the Lady Charlotte Stuart has caused some little bustle in the town. A French lady, who for thirty years had been totally neglected, but on a sudden transformed into a duchess, was an object that excited the curiosity of both sexes—the men to see her figure; the ladies scrupulously to examine that and the new modes she has brought from Paris: the result of all which is that she is allowed to be a good figure, tall and well made, but that the features of her face resemble too much those of her father to be handsome. She is gay, lively, and very affable, and has the behaviour of a well-bred French woman, without assuming the least distinction among our ladies on account of her new dignity. They flock to her door, and leave their cards, which she is to return; though the countess, her step-mother, did not. . . . The new duchess had appeared at the theatres, which were crowded on her account, with all her father's jewels, which are very fine.'

The Duchess, however, did not mean to spend her time entirely in visits to the theatre and a gay social round; she was a woman of forceful character who had come to Florence determined to make the best of the opportunities which her new situation in life

Charlotte Stuart, Duchess of Albany

The Royal Niece

opened to her. She had three main objectives in view; to clear up her father's chaotic financial affairs, to expose Louise of Stolberg to the Cardinal and finally, by so doing, to reconcile the two brothers. It is with the last two of these aims that we are primarily concerned here, but that she managed to succeed in all three is a measure of her ability and strength of purpose. It is not surprising that she seemed at times to be pushing, rather overbearing, and capable of remarkable changes of front when it suited her purpose, especially in her first exchanges with the Cardinal. To her credit it may be said that she made the last years of her father's life as peaceful and happy as his rapidly declining health and irritable temper would allow. That she always had an eye to the main chance is understandable in one whose life had up till now been spent in such neglect, and it is indeed a tragedy that when she had finally achieved the goal of wealth, recognition and freedom she should have been struck down in the very prime of life by a fatal disease.

3

The Duchess of Albany's first attempt to win over her uncle was completely unsuccessful. In the first flush of her new honours she wrote a gushing letter to the Cardinal Duke announcing her newly bestowed dignities and emphasizing the close relationship in which they stood to each other. It would have been almost impossible to pick on any theme more likely to exasperate his Royal Eminence than that of their relationship which only succeeded in reminding him of the irregular circumstances of her birth, an episode in his brother's life which the Cardinal had no wish to remember.

October 7th, 1784.

MONSEIGNEUR,

I should consider myself lacking in respect both to your Royal Highness and to myself, were I not to acquaint you with the news of my arrival in Florence. The kindness with which you have treated me up to the present moment appears to me a sure guarantee of your pleasure in receiving such news, and in sharing the joy and happiness with which my mind is filled today.

The Cardinal King

The King, my Father, by an authentic Act has now acknowledged me as his legitimate daughter; and he has sent this Act to the King of France, who has promised to place it on record, and consequently to grant me Letters Patent registered in the Parliament; so behold me today rejoicing in the good fortune of now approaching very closely to your Royal Highness, as well as being able to give all my attention to the nursing of a beloved Father, whose strength and health I shall bring back, if possible. I want him to share my own good health, and to free him from all troubles that Fortune has imposed upon him.

I have now, my very dear Uncle, to thank you for all the kindnesses you have heaped upon me since King James's death. The recollection of them lies deep in my heart. . . . Ever since I had the misfortune to lose my grandfather, King James, your Royal Highness has generously made my mother and myself an allowance of 5,000 *livres*. I have now the honour to renew my respectful thanks for the past, and to entreat you for the future to continue the annuity to my mother, who is penniless today; I regard her as a Second Self, if I may dare use such an expression. I feel sure you will not refuse me this service, for you understand my Father's position, and know how the wreck of his fortune has left him poorer than ever. All circumstances compel me to rely on your kind heart. The King, my Father, joins me in imploring this favour of your Royal Highness, and he begs me to assure you of his constant affection. I ask you, Monseigneur, not to mistake the feelings of devotion and of respect with which I shall always remain your Royal Highness's very humble and very obedient servant,

CHARLOTTE STUART,
Duchess of Albany.

This very tactless letter caused the Cardinal Duke immense annoyance. He was already very sceptical of letters that were full of affection and devotion but whose real purpose was only to get money out of him. He was, in fact, far from sharing the joy and happiness that filled his niece's mind when she wrote to him. He had always disapproved of his brother's association with Clementina Walkinshaw, and now to be treated with such familiarity by the offspring of this highly regrettable union was more than he could stomach. He refused to answer the letter but instead stopped the payment of Charlotte's allowance on the grounds that she was only entitled to it if she continued to live in France. Not only did the Act of legitimization anger the Cardinal (for it looked like an attack on his own rights as heir of the royal house), but he also strongly resented the bestowal of the title of Albany as this honour had always by tradition been borne by the second son of the King of Scots, and was therefore his by right though it had never actually been conferred on him. It was, however, the title under which he had been received by Louis XV, and the French court had always referred to him as Duke of Albany prior to his becoming a Cardinal. His refusal to acknowledge his niece brought an angry note from the Prince a month later. It was written in French in his own hand.

MY VERY DEAR BROTHER . . .

I am very happy to be able to tell you myself of my very dear Daughter's recognition by Me, by France and by the Pope; henceforward she is therefore Royal Highness for yourself on every occasion. I in no wise dispute your own rights. They are already established, since you are my Brother, but at the same time I beg of you not to dispute those of my very dear Daughter, whose title must be sacred to you.

I am your affectionate Brother,

CHARLES R.

It was true that the Pope had recognized Charlotte in the title of Duchess of Albany and had written to welcome her to Florence. No doubt the good natured Pius VI had done this to please the sick old Prince whom he could not otherwise acknowledge, and because he considered that no harm could come from such a gesture. This generous act greatly delighted Horace Walpole who wrote to Mann the following January: 'The pantomime carrying on at Florence and Rome is entertaining. So the Pope, who would not grant the title of king to the pretender allows his no-majesty

The Cardinal King

to have created a duchess; and the Cardinal of York, who is but a rag of the papacy, and who must think his brother a king, will not allow her title.' It was, indeed, an absurd situation.

As both father and daughter's letters produced no reply from the Cardinal Duke, Charlotte wrote again adopting a high-handed and haughty tone which must have infuriated her uncle more than ever and, when we remember how his sister-in-law's rebukes affected his health, probably caused him to take to his bed from sheer rage. 'I think that the highest pleasure you can bestow on the King, your Brother,' she told him, 'is to speak of me by the title that he desires you to accord me. Also it would be an immense service to all of us if henceforward you would allow all correspondence to pass through my hands, in order to save him further fatigue.'

If Charlotte had hoped to win over her uncle by such tactics as these she was soon to realize her mistake, for all her letter did was to sting the Cardinal into issuing a long Protest, which was forwarded to Florence and also laid at the feet of the Pope, in which he expressed his reasons for refusing to accord his niece the recognition demanded by her father. It was an opportunity to unburden himself of all the wrongs that he felt he had suffered at his brother's hands during the past few years; of the Prince's habit of keeping him in ignorance of his plans until they were already acted upon; of expecting the Cardinal himself to discharge his brother's financial obligations towards 'this person' (as the Protest describes the Duchess of Albany); and also, not least, for him to display a better knowledge of the constitutional law of the kingdom than his brother, to judge by his recent acts, appeared to possess. Written in the third person the Protest makes clear beyond any shadow of doubt the burning indignation felt by the Cardinal Duke on this occasion.

'The Cardinal Duke of York cannot do less than complain strongly of the proceeding of his Royal Brother concerning the irregular and improper action taken in summoning a natural daughter of his to live with him in so much publicity. It will easily be perceived on what grounds he may complain, if it is considered in the first place, what an indecent uproar was made some time ago about supposed poverty and destitution, when it was pretended his Royal Brother had not enough to live upon, and the burden was thrown upon the shoulders of the Cardinal Duke, against all justice; who is now informed in the most outrageously pompous manner, that he has taken upon himself an expense which will naturally exceed the maintenance of his own consort; an action which is in manifest contradiction to the former exaggerated statement.

'In the second place, the Cardinal Duke represents the situation in which he finds himself, on seeing follow immediately after a feigned reconciliation by means of autograph letters from his Royal Brother, a public proceeding of this description, as to which he has no information, and to which his consent was not asked.

'In the third place, he represents the irregularity of this pretended legitimation, which was not necessary to enable his brother to to give to this person a fair subsistence, which he had already been bound in conscience to do for thirty years past. As he did not do it, the Cardinal Duke, touched by pure compassion supplied the money privately. But it was not necessary to give her those titles, and to place her in a position for which there can be no explanation to the mind of any intelligent person, aware of the facts and of present circumstances except the intention of putting a public slight upon the Cardinal Duke and his sister-in-law.

'And here is reached the fourth point raised by the Cardinal Duke: that the said legitimation, as it seems to be intended, goes very much farther than has been the invariable custom in similar cases, and as in the recent example of James II in the person of the Duke of Berwick, since it reaches the very height of presumption to pretend to have the lady recognized as of the stem of the royal house, by granting her titles which would be most justly contested if he were in actual possession of his lawful right. Nor in that case would his Royal Brother, according to the law of the Kingdom, have the faculty thus to habilitate a natural child, and place her in the succession to the throne; a case utterly without precedent. In this state of things, the Cardinal Duke flatters himself that all his friends will accept his statement, convinced of its justice with regard to this business, so disgusting to him; which

The Cardinal King

he protests for his part to regard as null and void: in short, to ignore it so long as God gives him life.'

There was much to be said for the Cardinal Duke's point of view. He had, after all, provided for Charlotte and her mother during all the long years when Charles refused to have anything to do with them, and now she was threatening his very position as heir presumptive. It was not so much against 'this person' (whom he had never seen) as against his brother's selfishness and bleak ingratitude that the Cardinal protested. The woman, whose sudden appearance in Rome at the time of Prince Charles's marriage had caused them both such acute embarrassment, was now to be preferred above him by the brother whose rights and claims the Cardinal had upheld on all occasions, often at the risk of offending his ecclesiastical superiors and prejudicing his position, so very dear to him, as a prince of the Church. It is understandable that his resentment was so strong.

Whatever the Pope thought of the Protest there is little indication that it had much effect on Prince Charles who spent his time, so Mann tells us, in abusing the Cardinal for ill-treating his daughter. But on Charlotte herself, it had a more sobering effect. She was no fool, and seeing that her father's life could not last very much longer even with the healthier *régime* which her arrival in Florence had introduced (there is no mention of drunkenness after the Duchess of Albany took over the management of her father's household) she realized that it was essential for her to be on good terms with her uncle and resolved to adopt a more appeasing line in her next attempt to win him over.

Meanwhile her father, to show his confidence in her, invested her with the Order of the Thistle during the festivities, more sober than of yore, in honour of St. Andrew's Day, 1784. Seated in a Chair of State he had touched her on the shoulder with his sword after which his daughter, greatly delighted with her new honour, had gone round the company repeatedly saying '*Je suis Chevalier*', while favours made up to represent a thistle were distributed among the guests. When Louise of Stolberg heard of this she wrote angrily to the Cardinal, with whom she was still on tolerable terms, 'The King continues to be guilty of a thousand follies

The Royal Niece

at Florence. He can no longer walk. He is carried from one room to another on account of the size of his legs; but that did not prevent him presenting the Order of St. Andrew, at the end of dinner, to his daughter and to a certain Lord who is with him. It all seems very strange.'

4

The Cardinal's Protest opened Charlotte's eyes to the danger of her position, for should her father die this uncle was the only person upon whom she could rely for help and protection. It was essential for her to be friends with him and if possible to bring about a reconciliation between the brothers. She was about to leave for Pisa where Charles insisted, despite ill health, on going for the Carnival, but found time to send a note of abject apology to the Cardinal for having incurred his displeasure. 'Let me place at the feet of your Royal Highness', she now wrote in a very much more subdued key, 'my regrets and the very sincere sorrow I feel at having offended you. My grief is unbearable. I see my happiness has proved to be only a dream. . . . One favourable word will restore my courage and fulfil my wishes. Deign, Monseigneur, to say this word.' This meek message was simply signed 'Charlotte Stuart' without any flourish of offensive titles.

The letter, so submissive after the previous arrogant demands, touched the kind heart of the Cardinal Duke and produced, as it was intended to, a reply which must have raised the hopes of the Duchess once more. The Cardinal's resistance broke down at the thought of his niece's unhappiness, for though he disputed her claims he had no personal animosity towards her. Perhaps, too, he had heard how good an influence she exercised over his brother, for about this time the Pope had written to congratulate him on the Prince's improved spiritual condition, a happy circumstance which the Holy Father attributed unhesitatingly to 'the powerful hand of God, who has called your Royal Brother from the principles of darkness, in which he had previously walked, to those of the true light.' That the hand of Charlotte Stuart had also had some part in this reformation must have occurred to the Cardinal as he read the Pope's words. So it was that he at last replied to his

The Cardinal King

brother's daughter and encouraged a hope that the correspondence between them might continue, but even now he could not bring himself to address her as his niece, though he managed to acknowledge their relationship so far as to address her as cousin.

MY COUSIN,

I do not lose an instant in expressing my regret for having caused you trouble through my last letter.... Moreover, I beg you to understand that after some reflection I have become convinced of the uprightness of your intentions, and so certain am I of this, that I esteem you the more for them. And since you appear so anxious to obtain my friendship and my confidence (which pleases me much), I can assure you frankly that you have lost nothing of either of them, and that in the continuance of our correspondence I am certain that we shall grow to appreciate each other, since in whatever I do I hope you will recognize my sincere interest and my good faith in all that affects you. I beg you to inform me that you are quite pacified. Give me all the news you can of my Brother's health, for I dread the idea of his travelling to Pisa...

To this letter Charlotte replied expressing the 'equal joy and gratitude' with which she had received it, and went on to give an account of her father's health, which was far from good. The journey to Pisa had made his legs swell again but despite this he would miss nothing of the festivities. 'I fear terribly that the fêtes, at which my august father never fails to assist without missing any, will have a bad effect on the precious preservation of his life.' She then indulges in a little attack on her step-mother, the Countess of Albany who is always described in her letters simply as 'Madame', and her continued association with Alfieri to which, in a previous letter to the Cardinal, she had referred when she wrote that 'doubtless nothing, Monseigneur, could more shock your delicacy, your principles, and the glory of your house than the conduct of Monsieur Alfieri and his influence over Madame.' Thus gradually she would undermine what little confidence the Cardinal still had in his sister-in-law.

Prince Charles, too, wrote to his brother to express his delight

The Royal Niece

at the improved relationship between uncle and niece. 'Your letter . . . has been balm to my heart, since it assures me of your affection towards Myself, and towards a Second Self which I venture to state fully merits your generosity and esteem by her excellent virtues. I cannot describe to you, my very dear Brother, the happiness I feel in expecting that some day you will play the part of a father to a daughter that I have every reason to love tenderly.' The first step towards a full reconciliation between the Cardinal and the King had been taken.

5

The visit to Pisa offered Charlotte an opportunity to explain to the Grand Duchess of Tuscany (who had at last received her) that the Cardinal was no longer so warm in the support of his sister-in-law as he had been. She chose her moment to do this with diplomatic skill, for the Grand Duchess had the King and Queen of Naples with her, and the Queen, Maria Carolina, was sister to Marie Antoinette of France from whom 'Madame' was now trying to secure an increase of pension. Once the Queen of Naples could be persuaded of the wickedness of Louise no doubt the information would be passed on to Versailles, and Charlotte was soon able to secure from the royal ladies their condemnation and dislike for 'the proceedings of a person who had lost the memory of everything she owed to the illustrious name she bears'. For Louise was not only having trouble in money matters; her affair with the poet was also passing through a stormy phase the details of which Charlotte was not slow in passing on to her uncle. Once more back in Florence she wrote to the Cardinal on June 4th, 1785:

'Alfieri is, I am assured, totally out of himself against Madame because of jealousy: he reproaches her for having preferred to him a certain Elyat. However, this valet de chambre [perhaps Alfieri's own man Elia?] has been sent away, for yet other motives of the same sort. In a word, it is stated here there is a German named Count Proly who followed her to Paris. Alfieri does not hide his resentment from anyone, and says all the evil he can. That which is so revolting is that this man has taken a house here for

The Cardinal King

four months, and continually the King is liable to meet him, which is an object of trouble and disquiet to him—the more so because this bad character appears to be infinitely shameless, and that he affects to set defiance at my august father . . .'

Alfieri did not, after all, take a house in Florence, so the Prince was saved the humiliation of meeting him face to face in the street. But these revelations in the Duchess's letters had fulfilled their purpose and the Cardinal had now completely thrown over his sister-in-law who had deceived him on so many occasions. He was able to tell his brother that all communication between himself and Louise was now at an end.

'I conjure you to do what in you lies [wrote the Cardinal] to prevent a *quidam* like Alfieri from gaining his ends by a union so offensive to our family. It makes me furious, and it is well that you should know they are in constant communication by letter, and that it is no doubt that it is he who governs madame in all these proceedings. She has deliberately broken her word to me on this matter, and I broke off all communication with her several months ago. I am greatly obliged to your daughter for interesting herself so with you on my behalf. It proves the kindness of her heart, to which everyone bears witness . . .'

Charlotte must have triumphed in this victory over 'Madame', but knowing the vulnerability of her uncle's kind heart she kept him posted on all that passed between Louise and Alfieri lest he should relent and once more forgive his erring sister-in-law. In July she writes to tell him that Alfieri is at Pisa, but was to go on to Alsace in September. 'I was told yesterday that a horse that he loved took vengeance upon him, and threw him. It was thought he was killed, which would be a great loss to his horses.' Louise, meanwhile, is hoping to proceed to England. 'Madame, I am informed from Paris, has conceived the plan of several journeys which combat with each other. The hope of obtaining a pension from England made her decide to go there next year; but Alsace offers her sweeter pastimes . . .' Presumably the jealousies over the *valet de chambre* and Count Proly were now finished with. Charlotte could report that her interview with the Queen of Naples had born fruit, for when 'Madame' went to Versailles 'the

The Royal Niece

Queen refused to accord her an audience, and she was told that the sooner she went the better.' The reader will not be surprised to learn, as Charlotte admits, that the discomforted Louise 'does not fail to make the most perfidious suggestions regarding all of us.' One can hardly blame her.

Charlotte had certainly succeeded in her scheme for turning the Cardinal Duke against Louise of Stolberg, and had thus opened the door for a complete reconciliation between the two brothers. These letters to the Cardinal which cover the years 1784-5 display the hard, calculating side of her disposition which came from those long years of neglect and obscurity in France. The impression they give is of a determined, pushing individual entirely out for her own ends. It is pleasant to be able to record another impression, from an independent witness, which discovers a more agreeable side to the Duchess's personality. In 1785 the Abbé Dupaty visited Florence and left this impression of Charlotte Stuart:

'If benevolence of heart alone were necessary to entitle her to the throne of her ancestors she would soon ascend it. The Duchess showed me the presents made by Louis XIV to James II on his arrival in France—she showed me the gold toilet set the Queen found in her apartments the evening of her arrival. *Times are greatly changed* she said to me. She said no more. I mistake; she smiled. Her attention to her father is extremely affecting. When this old man calls to mind that his family has reigned, his tears flow not alone. The duchess weeps with him.'

The Duchess's attentions to her father were all the more praiseworthy in so far as they did not spring from affection. Her letters to her mother leave us in no doubt that she never came to love him, and indeed often found him both irritating and trying, for his ill health and disappointments had made him selfish and hard to please. But she had a strong sense of duty and was determined to do all that was necessary to bring him a little peace and dignity in his last years. Charles could count himself lucky to receive this care from a daughter whom he had so cruelly neglected for so many years, and there is no doubt that for his part he came to love her very dearly and to be entirely dependent upon her. By the middle of 1785 she was securely placed at the head of her father's household, had victoriously routed 'Madame', and could now turn her attention to the question of a meeting with her uncle the Cardinal Duke of York.

6

Prince Charles hoped that his brother would undertake the journey from Rome to Florence and wrote to ask him to come after the celebrations in honour of the feast of St. Peter and St. Paul on June 29th. For some obscure reason, however, the Cardinal Duke declared himself unwilling to enter the territory of the Grand Duke of Tuscany, and suggested as an alternative that the Duchess should visit him. To this Charles only agreed with the greatest reluctance as he now hated the idea of being parted from his beloved daughter. 'Without being at all importunate', he told his brother, 'she has gained my complete confidence, and consequently the days when I shall be deprived of her presence must prove very long and dull. . . . But in this anxiety she shows to pay you her duty I recognize her goodness of heart, and I cannot refuse to satisfy her in this request.' Charlotte also wrote to her uncle to express her happiness at the thought of meeting him but hoped that he would keep the place of meeting a secret from her father as the indefatigable old prince was quite capable—despite the deplorable state of his legs—of insisting upon coming with her.

Notwithstanding the fact that the Prince had agreed in principle to the idea of his daughter leaving him for the purpose of this visit he was still most reluctant to let her go and welcomed any incident that might delay her departure. The hot weather affected his health and more than once he was compelled to take to his bed, which made his daughter's presence at his bed side all the more necessary. Charlotte hoped that the Prince's old friend the Duchess of Attry-Salviati, who had great influence over him, would help to reconcile him to the parting, but unfortunately this useful lady decided instead to go away herself to Pisa where she found a more pleasant occupation in taking the waters than in persuading an obstinate old prince to act against his will. Furthermore the Cardinal himself was taken ill with influenza and received a letter of condolence from his niece in which she recommended some inhalations which had greatly benefited her when suffering from the same complaint. It looked at times as though there would never be a moment when one brother would be well enough to let her go and the other well enough to receive her, but the Cardinal recovered from his attack and in October, when he had to make a tour of several towns in the Papal States on official ecclesiastical business, agreed to meet the Duchess of Albany at Monte Freddo, near Perugia.

The Duchess must have felt some trepidation as she set out to meet this uncle whose opposition to her claims and pretensions she had only recently succeeded in combating, and who still found the word 'cousin' a more suitable form of greeting than 'niece'. But she was never lacking in self-confidence, and if she had any misgivings they cannot have long survived the first meeting. Charlotte must have been struck by the different appearance of the two brothers as she knelt to kiss the emerald ring held out to her by the stately and dignified prince who received her at Monte Freddo. The poor, sick wreck of a man she had left at Florence, his body wasted by disease and dissipation and his mind clouded by long years of frustration and misfortune was a poor figure now in comparison with Henry, Cardinal of York, a proud and handsome man, still slim and young looking despite his sixty years. But whatever her own thoughts and feelings may have been her royal uncle was instantly won over by her charm and by the qualities of character she displayed. Possibly also the marked likeness she bore to her father reminded the Cardinal of that prince as a young man and brought back memories of the distant times when they had been so united in affection and so hopeful for the future. It is also true, when we remember how easily Louise of Stolberg had been able to win his heart, that the Cardinal was no match for feminine charms when the intention was to please and flatter him, which both the Countess and the Duchess had every intention of doing.

The meeting between uncle and niece was a complete success, and another triumph for Charlotte who so impressed her uncle that as soon as he returned to Rome he wrote to Pius VI to tell the Pope of his final conviction of his niece's goodness and force

The Cardinal King

of character. In this way he probably intended to make amends for the harsh terms he had used in his Protest of the previous year. Charlotte took the opportunity to enlighten her uncle yet once more on the theme of Louise's continued association with Count Alfieri, though by now the Cardinal was quite convinced of the nature of his sister-in-law's behaviour in that respect, and hardly needed any more prodding from Louise's determined opponent. As a result of the Duchess's labours a letter was prepared later in the year which was signed by both the brothers and sent to the French court in which their case against the Countess of Albany was fully expressed and the request made that on account of the scandal her pension should be withdrawn.

It was also agreed that Charlotte should open a correspondence with the Cardinal's secretary, Canon Cesarini, to save Henry himself the fatigue of dealing with matters of business concerning the affairs of his brother and niece. Finally, before the Duchess returned to Florence, it was arranged that she should bring her father to Rome as soon as his health would permit him to undertake so arduous a journey, so that he might pass his last years near his brother in the old palace in the Piazza dei Santi Apostoli where he had been born. The Cardinal generously promised to furnish the palace and prepare it for his brother's arrival. The Cardinal returned to Frascati and Charlotte to Florence both highly satisfied with their first encounter.

Soon after his return to Rome Henry received a letter from his brother in a very different tone from that peremptory note which had demanded his recognition of the Duchess of Albany in November 1784. This time the letter, written in Italian by a secretary with a scarcely legible signature in the Prince's own hand, is full of affection and concern for the Cardinal and contains a pathetic account of the Prince's own health.

Florence. 29th October, 1785.

DEAREST BROTHER,

With infinite pleasure and deepest satisfaction I have heard of your safe arrival in Rome, and with equal content the kindness and solicitude you have displayed in furnishing my palace. I offer you my greatest thanks. I desire with all my heart, the moment I shall arrive, to express to you in person my affection and attachment in Rome itself. I must not keep concealed from you the fact that on my journey and during all my stay in Rome, I particularly desire to observe a complete incognito, and to be known by the title of Count of Albany, and my beloved daughter will be called Duchess of Albany. For some days I have been kept to my room and my bed, suffering much agony and terrible pain, due to the severe attack in the legs, but I hope to find ease and relief shortly. Meanwhile I beg you to acquaint His Holiness of my intention to visit Rome, and to render him my profound reverence, and to pay him my court, with a thousand other matters that I leave you to arrange in my name.

I embrace you dearly,

C. R.

Weary at last of the long struggle for the acknowledgement of his kingship the Prince was now content to be accepted in Rome by the title in which he had been known since he came to live in Florence eleven years before—yet even so it must be considered merely as a title of incognito. His daughter would be spared the slights which his wife had had to contend with when she first came to Rome as a bride. The Cardinal, remembering the fruitless and undignified proceedings at the time of his brother's succession, must have read this letter with a sigh of relief, and been all the more thankful for the calm influence of his valuable new friend the Duchess of Albany.

7

Illness again prevented the Prince from starting at once on his journey to Rome. He was taken ill shortly after his daughter's return and had to remain in bed, so she informed Canon Cesarini, for a month or six weeks. His condition was not improved by his physician who applied a 'violent remedy' to the invalid which did him more harm than good. 'My august Father', the somewhat exasperated Duchess explained to her uncle in a letter of November 5th, 1785, 'has the most blind confidence in his doctor, who is a young man without experience.' His iron constitution once again stood him in good stead, and despite the attack and the remedy Charlotte is able to say in the same letter that 'God be praised, the King is actually as well as can be: he eats, digests and sleeps well enough.' The Prince, now all piety and resignation, requests his daughter to 'say the most tender things to your Royal Highness, and begs him not to forget him in his prayers.' By November 12th she is able to say that her father is 'rejuvenated and ever ready to start, if his legs would not refuse him a little service', and hopes to be able to leave in about a month.

The thought of the Prince celebrating another St. Andrew's Day in Florence must have caused the Cardinal Duke some alarm for a reassuring note from the Duchess tells him that he need have no worries: 'The St. Andrew's Feast would have had, perhaps, its dangers in the past, but we shall keep the Saint's festival here; moreover, the King is still convalescent, and has been on a strict *régime* for a long time.' The Cardinal could banish his fears.

Eventually the Prince was considered well enough to set out, though it was decided that they should spend eight days on the road from Florence to Rome so as to spare the invalid as much fatigue as possible. The departure of the Prince and his daughter was duly reported to the Foreign Secretary in London by Sir Horace Mann.

'Count Albany set out from hence on the 2nd instant for Rome, but was not arrived there at the departure of the last letters, though he was expected a few hours after.'

The British Envoy, who had spied on the royal exiles since his appointment to Florence in 1740, was never to set eyes on his distinguished enemy again, for he died the next year after what must have been one of the longest tenures of a post in the history of diplomacy. He never ceased to pride himself on the way he had triumphed over the French Ambassador and the Papal Curia in preventing the Prince from being recognized as King after the death of James III in 1766, an act which had received the commendation of King George. He died, still British Envoy at Florence, in November 1786.

While Mann was writing his despatch the Cardinal Duke, who

The Royal Niece

had made all the preparations for the reception of his brother at the Palazzo Muti, was riding out to Viterbo to meet the cavalcade, and here the two princes greeted each other with considerable emotion. As Charlotte watched the two brothers embrace she must have felt that her work had been well done. Shortly afterwards the Duchess of Albany entered for the first time the palace where her father and uncle had been born and where her grandfather had died. For the Prince it must have been a homecoming full of sad memories.

9

King Henry the Ninth

1

We may be sure that the Cardinal Duke was glad to welcome his brother back to Rome when the royal exile returned to the Muti Palace on the 8th of December 1785. The eighteenth century liked a tidy ending to its dramas and nothing could have been more fitting than that the dying Prince should return to the place of his birth and be fully reconciled once more with his brother for the remaining two years of his existence. The storm of life was now over and he sank gradually into the tomb protected by the care and devotion of his daughter who herself began to notice the first symptoms of her own fatal disease during these years in the Piazza dei Santi Apostoli. Though she continued her brisk management of affairs she became increasingly subject to attacks of ill-health which were finally diagnosed as a cancer of the liver, the same malady from which her great-grandmother Mary of Modena had died, and which was to prove fatal to Charlotte Stuart within four years of her arrival in Rome.

The Duchess did her best to dispel the gloom which somehow seemed inseparable from the Stuart Palace which had been associated since the early years of the century with this family and its misfortunes. Here James III had taken refuge after the failure of the Fifteen and here he had heard the tragic news of Culloden; and now the Prince, whose birth in 1720 had been the one bright incident in the sad history of the palace, had come to die in it with his hopes all unfulfilled. He must often have recalled how he had set out from this very place in 1744 to win the three crowns and how he had taken leave of his father with the words: 'If I fail your next sight of me shall be in my coffin.' Now, on the edge of the grave and back in that same palace he had hoped never to see again, he must often have reflected on that question asked him long ago by a loyal adherent: 'What has your family done, sir, thus to draw down the vengeance of Heaven on every branch of it, through so many ages?'

To keep her father from brooding on his misfortunes the Duchess entertained lavishly, giving dinners and receptions to the leading members of Roman society and inviting the many distinguished foreigners who frequented Rome at this period. The future Lord Stanley of Alderley visited the Muti Palace in 1787 and wrote to tell his wife: 'I have been presented to the Count of Albany, styled still by his servants King of England. He wore the Order of the Garter, but permitted himself to be addressed as count, and as to such I was presented to him. The old man receives a great deal of company in his house since he had his daughter with him. It is one of the gayest in Rome. . . . Poor old man! he is interesting from what he was but he is now in a second childhood.' The gaiety which Lord Stanley of Alderley observed was on the surface only; behind this fragile façade lurked the melancholy of a broken old invalid and the grim determination of a young woman to conceal her own sufferings from him.

During the hot weather they removed to Albano where the villa once occupied by King James was again placed at their disposal, though the Prince was now too sick a man to enjoy the hunting which had been one of his chief pleasures in former times. The Cardinal, too, often invited his brother and niece to Frascati where his hospitality was proverbial. It was fifteen years since Charles had set foot in his brother's house, so his first visit there after the return to Rome was an occasion for rejoicing; as the Prince and Duchess alighted from their carriages before the episcopal palace their arrival was heralded with superb music provided by the Cardinal's band. Henry's visits to his brother were equally frequent, in fact a bit too much so for the practically-minded Charlotte who found his constant presence something of a bore—especially when he came empty-handed. To her mother she wrote: 'My sainted uncle comes to see me three times a week

The Cardinal King

and leaves me no time to breathe. He came for the fête of St. Charles but brought no present.' The Cardinal himself was so satisfied with his niece that she was no longer simply 'my cousin' but in the pages of the *Diario* appears always now as '*La reale nipote.*'

The efforts to divert the mind of the Prince were not always successful, as when the young Comte de Vaudreuil (the son of the officer who had arrested Prince Charles outside the Paris Opera in 1748) was presented to him by the Duchess. The Prince, uncertain of the identity of the young man, was struck with horror when his eyes fell on the face which bore a striking resemblance to that of the elder Vaudreuil. Memories of the humiliating scene in Paris nearly forty years before came flooding into his mind, and with a groan he fell fainting to the floor. A similar scene also occurred when a tactless English visitor, a certain Mr. Greathead, had pressed him with questions about his activities during the Forty-Five. Ewald has described the scene in a famous passage:

'His eyes brightened, he half rose from his chair, his face became lit up with unwonted animation, and he began the narrative of his campaign. He spoke with fiery energy of his marches, his victories, the loyalty of his Highland followers, his retreat from Derby, the defeat at Culloden, his escape, and then passionately entered upon the awful penalties so many had been called upon to pay for their devotion to his cause. But the recollection of so much bitter suffering—the butchery around Inverness, the executions at Carlisle and London, the scenes on Kennington Common and Tower Hill—was stronger than his strength could bear. His voice died in his throat, his eyes became fixed, and he sank upon the floor in convulsions. Alarmed at the noise his daughter rushed into the room, "Oh! Sir," she cried to Mr. Greathead, "what is this? You must have been speaking to my father about Scotland and the Highlanders! No one dares to mention those subjects in his presence." '

Thus the years passed from the end of 1785 to the beginning of 1788; the Prince gradually sinking but still, when his strength allowed, occasionally visiting theatres and showing himself in public as he delighted to do; the Duchess managing his affairs and caring for his health, presiding at his table in brilliant jewels, for the Cardinal had now given her his share of the Stuart and Sobieski diamonds, and concealing from her father the attacks of pain from which she increasingly suffered; the Cardinal peacefully employed in the pastoral duties of his See or in the official business of the Church at Rome, a constant visitor at the Muti Palace where harmony now reigned.

2

On January 11th, 1788, the Cardinal Duke had just finished his dinner when he was interrupted by the arrival of a messenger from the Duchess with an alarming account of the Prince's health. The Duchess was in some distress for she had herself been ill and until the moment of sending the messenger off to Frascati her father's plight had been kept a secret from her. The Cardinal's first reaction to this news was to leave for Rome at once, but as it was nearly half-past ten at night, the weather severe, and his own health none too good, he was persuaded to delay his departure until early the next morning, and had to content himself with despatching a courier with a message announcing his arrival.

The Cardinal left Frascati after his Mass the next morning and travelling at his usual great speed was soon galloping towards Rome. At the Muti Palace he was met by the Abbé Consalvi and was given the latest news of the invalids before he had so much as alighted from his carriage, and was greatly relieved to hear a better account of his brother. He then went up by a little secret staircase to the Prince's apartment where a full account was given to him by the physicians Saliceti and Mora. These worthy doctors had attempted to bleed their royal patient the day before but this operation the Prince had resisted 'remembering what he and others had gone through in former times.' The Cardinal was perhaps more interested to learn that the Prince had made his confession and spoken to Father O'Kelly, his Dominican confessor, about spiritual things. He then passed into the chamber of the sick man himself where, as the report of these events in the *Diario* tells us, he was 'much comforted at seeing his brother again. His Royal

The Cardinal King

Highness comforted him, encouraged him to suffer patiently, and they had a short, affectionate conversation together.'

The Cardinal then went to see his 'royal niece' who was in bed suffering severe pains, her anxiety considerably increased by her inability to attend to her father. The true cause of her illness had not yet been determined and it was thought by the physicians that it was due to 'the fact of the floor of her room having been remade last September while they were in the country at Albano, and that it had not dried sufficiently when she came back . . . on her return from the country.' The Cardinal had other thoughts in his mind about his niece as well as her physical health. In view of the Prince's serious condition he wished to be sure that proper provision had been made for the Duchess in his brother's will, and his efforts to see to this were duly recorded in the *Diario*:

'It is known that His Majesty, since his other serious illness in Florence, had made a will, but His Highness having found out from that time that it was largely in favour of John Stuart, his old valet, who still predominates in domestic matters, would have wished to place before his brother considerations more advantageous to the Duchess; which, however, he did not venture to do for fear of troubling his brother, contenting himself with hinting this desire to some persons who could make the most of it when the opportunity offered. And this reflection made H.R.H. all the more regret the unfortunate contingency that made the Duchess unable through illness to see her father.'

After further comforting the invalids the Cardinal, having 'dined in the Duchess's apartment in great pomp', returned to Frascati where regular bulletins were sent to him, and the very next day he was glad to hear from Dr. Mora that the Duchess was free from pain.

The official Diary of the Cardinal Duke which gives a detailed account of the early stages of Prince Charles's last illness is unable to help us in tracing the last weeks of his life, for the pages which must have described his death and his brother's succession to the empty title of King have been torn out, and no trace of these valuable missing pages has ever been found. The Prince must have rallied to a certain extent after January 11th, but before long

King Henry the Ninth

his condition was critical, and by the end of the month the last Stuart ever to set foot on British soil was dead. The time and date of his death was given as half-past nine on the morning of January 31st, 1788, though a tradition claims that he actually died on January 30th, the anniversary of the martyrdom of King Charles I, but the date was considered to be of so ominous an association that it was pretended he had lingered for another day. The Prince was sixty-seven years of age when he died. The Duchess of Albany, still in poor health, was not present at the moment of death, and the Prince is said to have died in the arms of the Master of Nairne

Henry Stuart was plunged into the deepest grief when he heard of his brother's death. Although the two princes, until reconciled by Charlotte, had been estranged for many years, the Cardinal in his distress remembered only that he had lost a dear brother, the companion and hero of his youth and once the great hope of his family, and that now he alone remained to represent the cause for which so many gallant lives had been sacrificed in vain. Though for forty years the Prince who now lay dead had been a fugitive, a man who had never known the fulfilment of his dearest ambition, so nearly won in 1745; an exile; a drunkard; a husband deserted by his wife; a king rejected by his subjects; the memory of these black years would surely fade away. A weary, half-forgotten exile had died, but the legend of Bonnie Prince Charlie would live for ever.

The Cardinal asked the Pope to grant his brother the same rites that had been accorded to his father in 1766, but in his heart he must have known that his request would not be allowed. The Holy See had never recognized Charles III and could not now grant him the honours that had been given to James III. Reluctantly Pius VI refused the request though the Cardinal had only asked that recognition as a sovereign should be given for this one solemn occasion, but it was more than the Pope could do to risk a breach with the government of King George III, and so it was decided that the funeral should take place at Frascati, for in his own Cathedral the Cardinal might do as he pleased.

While Prince Charles lay in state dressed in royal robes with crown and sceptre, the stars of the Garter and Thistle on his breast,

The Cardinal King

six altars were erected in the antechamber at which more than two hundred masses were offered for the repose of his soul by the Irish Franciscans and Dominicans who attended him in the hour of death. The body was then placed in a coffin of cypress wood and taken to Frascati where the funeral took place on the 3rd of February. The little cathedral was thronged with people, among whom were to be seen many English residents and visitors from Rome, all in the deepest mourning. A guard of honour was formed from the Frascati militia and the chief magistrates of the town were all present, though these worthies no doubt attended more out of respect for their Cardinal-bishop than for the departed, whom few of them can have known except as a name. The whole interior of the building was hung with black and adorned with texts chosen by the Cardinal himself, the most appropriate of which was taken from Ecclesiasticus: '*Ad insulas longe divulgatum est nomen tuum, et dilectus es in pace tua,*'—'Thy name went abroad to the islands far off, and thou wast beloved in thy peace.' The coffin was placed on a catafalque raised three steps from the floor of the nave and covered by a magnificent pall emblazoned with the arms of Great Britain; round about it burned many wax tapers while three gentlemen of the household clad in mourning cloaks stood on each side.

As ten o'clock struck the royal Cardinal entered the church, being carried to the door in a sedan chair heavily festooned with black crêpe. He then advanced to his throne and began to chant the office for the dead while at other altars four masses were said by the chief dignitaries of the cathedral. As the Cardinal repeated the solemn words tears were seen to run down his cheeks and more than once his voice faltered as though he were unable to proceed.

At the conclusion of the ceremonies the body was placed in a temporary vault where it remained until the Cardinal's own death when both brothers were interred with their father in the crypt of St. Peter's. Above this temporary resting place a marble tablet was erected by the Cardinal recording, in a long Latin inscription, the names and titles of the prince who lay there, the whole being surmounted by the royal arms of Great Britain in bronze. This

King Henry the Ninth

memorial tablet may still be seen in the Cathedral of Frascati by the great door at the west end of the church, though the bronze coat of arms has suffered damage in the bombardment of the town in the Second World War.

3

Prince Charles Edward Stuart, as Mr. Peter de Polnay has pointed out, had virtually reached the end of his career in so far as his political significance was concerned when he was expelled from France under the terms of the treaty of Aix-la-Chapelle in 1748. He was then only twenty-eight years old. For the next forty odd years he had to reconcile himself to the fact that the British nation had finally rejected the claims of his dynasty and that the call to return to his inheritance would never come. This fact, which was so plain to the hard-headed politicians of Versailles as it was also clear to the pious but practical Duke of York, was never accepted by the Prince. He who had come so near to achieving his ends in 1745 could never believe that the chance had gone for ever, and for this very reason he could never be content to settle down in Rome as a *de jure* sovereign as his father, James III, had done. The notion that he would one day return to his kingdom, to 'speak to his subjects in Westminster Hall', became almost a fantasy with him, and to the end of his days he kept sufficient ready money near him to defray the expenses of an immediate journey to England.

Prince Charles has been harshly judged for his conduct during those years when he wandered obscurely about Europe surrounded by opportunists and riff-raff, shunned by the graver Jacobites like Lord Marischal and General Bulkeley, often giving way to drink or engaging in unedifying quarrels with his mistresses. It should, however, be remembered that if his conduct was at times indefensible few people have had to face frustration upon so epic a scale. Betrayed, as he believed, by his friends, when he accepted their plan of retreat rather than his own instinct to advance at the fatal council of war at Derby, he could never forget that success might have crowned his efforts had he disregarded their advice.

The Cardinal King

Thus it was that this prince, so generous and magnanimous to his enemies, turned against the people who wished only to be his friends but whose hands were tied by political necessity. Louis XV, the Pope, his own father, all became enemies in his eyes. His brother, for becoming a priest, might not be mentioned in his presence. The Church itself must be abandoned if it stood in the way of his restoration to his just rights. The change of religion in 1750 must be looked upon as an entirely political move, and an utterly fruitless one at that. All it did was to break his father's heart; 'what will it avail to you all the Kingdoms in the world', he had written in anguish to his son, 'if you lose your Soul?' The Prince was not interested in the answer to that question. Until ill-health and infirmity overcame him he firmly believed that the British nation was longing for his return, and if that were so, nothing must be tolerated that might prevent his fulfilling his destiny as true and legitimate King of England, Scotland and Ireland. James III and Henry IX never became *de facto* kings because they were Catholics; Charles III would not remain a Catholic were it to prevent him from becoming a *de facto* king. Who now can doubt that the greater nobility lay in the attitude of his father and his brother?

But for all that the wonder and promise of his youth outshone all the sad years that followed. He was a brilliant commander in war; he earned the love and respect of his men who gladly fell in battle or went to the scaffold for his sake. He was brave and magnanimous. When the Hanoverians would have done anything to achieve his capture and would not have hesitated to put him to death, the Prince always refused to have anything to do with any plot that entailed personal violence against members of the family that ruled in England. While the contemptible Duke of Cumberland butchered his prisoners with unbelievable cruelty the Prince treated his captives with a clemency that was a credit to his humanity and a tribute to his bearing as a prince. Few people had known so much glory and devotion as he; few have had to suffer so long and so bitter a decline. As Lord Balmerino stood on the scaffold about to suffer execution for his part in the Forty-Five he spoke these words about the man whose cause had brought him to his present situation: 'I am at a loss when I come to speak of the Prince; I am not a fit hand to draw his character. I shall leave that to others. But I must beg leave to tell you the incomparable sweetness of his nature, his affability, his compassion, his justice, his temperance, his patience, and his courage are virtues, seldom to be found in one person. In short, he wants no qualifications requisite to make a great man.' This was a description of the prince whom England would not have as its king. Can we wonder that the experience of that rejection embittered him for the rest of his life?

4

From the moment of his brother's death Henry Stuart, Cardinal of York, never considered himself as less than a King, even though he might reign 'by the Grace of God but not by the will of men'. That he was a king he never for one moment doubted; the crown, which James II had never abdicated, was his by right of legitimate succession and the Cardinal Duke of York was henceforth Henry IX, King of Great Britain, France and Ireland, Defender of the Faith. He at once ordered certain significant changes in his style and manner of address which considerably mystified his fellow ecclesiastics. In the official documents of the church in which, as Vice-Chancellor, his name had often to appear, he had always been described as 'Cardinal Duke of York' but from now on the form was changed to 'Cardinal *called* Duke of York' (*Dux Eboracensis nuncupatus*, or in Italian *Duca di Yorck denominato*). The point of this change, Henry explained to those curious enough to enquire, was that the title Duke of York was now simply a title of incognito which he assumed for obvious reasons of state, but to continue to be known as Duke of York without the qualifying word would be to deny his legitimate right. In addition to this alteration in his style the Cardinal King also made slight changes in his armorial bearings, where the crescent, the mark of difference or cadency for a younger son, was removed, and the prince's coronet was replaced under the Cardinal's Hat by the closed crown of a sovereign.

These changes were slight and simple enough and in character

The Cardinal King

with the peaceful nature of the Cardinal; but he felt that he must take one more step to show to the world that he in no way abandoned the rights to which he was now heir even though he had no intention of demanding any public recognition as his brother had done with results so humiliating to their cause. This step was to issue a Memorial of his claims which was presented to foreign courts, and was worded in similar terms to the one he had prepared and forwarded to the Vatican at the time of his brother's serious illness in 1784. The Memorial makes plain that the Cardinal in no way renounced any of the rights of his family and that he recognized no successor to himself as *de jure* monarch other than the prince upon whom his rights would devolve by lawful descent, which in this case was Charles Emmanuel IV, King of Sardinia, the great-great-grandson of Henrietta Stuart, daughter of Charles I.

'We, Henry Benedict Maria Clement, Cardinal Duke of York, second son of James the Third, King of England . . . hereby declare and protest in the most solemn form and in the clearest manner possible and with every means that may prove useful and profitable to the duties that We owe to Our Royal Person and Our Country, that We claim in Ourselves the right of Succession . . . over those kingdoms of England, etc. And against these rights, either before God or before men, We cannot oppose the sacred office of a Bishop, which We at present hold. But inasmuch as the critical position of Our Royal House requires prudent measures and We do not wish to embarrass Ourselves further, We intend of Our own free will to retain the title of Duke of York (which will in reality be no longer Our true title) with all its adjuncts, as We have hitherto done. Thus under this incognito We now declare with every necessary protest and in the most solemn way that in the retention of this title (which We have spontaneously assumed) We have no intention of ever renouncing these rights of succession and fealty which We hold and ever intend to hold over these Kingdoms and over all else appertaining to Us, as true, last, and legitimate Heir of Our Royal House. . . . Finally, We declare that, when Our Lord God shall be pleased to dispose of Our Person, these rights of Succession to the Crown of England,

THE CARDINAL OF YORK AS KING

King Henry the Ninth

etc., will pass in their full and unimpaired force to that Prince, to whom they will lawfully revert by proximity of blood.'

Having thus asserted his rights the Cardinal was content to let matters rest. The Memorial, as may be imagined, brought no response whatsoever from the Courts to which it was addressed. Only the Holy See, perhaps out of feelings of personal respect for the Cardinal Vice-Chancellor, sent a reply but even this, possibly for reasons of state, acknowledged the document as having been sent in 1784, rather than in its present form. Completely evading all the points in the Memorial the reply of the Secretary of State, written on behalf of the Pope, was a masterly example of the non-committal.

'*From the Vatican, February* 1, 1788.

'Most obliging is the attention rendered to us by the Lord Cardinal Duke of York, in communicating to us before anyone else the protest made by him on the 27th of January 1784, for which you will return him lively thanks in our name. Having read the protest, we have found it moderate and prudent, and we have therefore nothing to say against it. At the same time you will add our condolences on the loss of his elder brother, for whom we shall not cease to intercede. And, meanwhile, we very heartily give you our paternal benediction.'

Thus, as 'true, last, and legitimate Heir' of the royal House of Stuart Henry IX began his reign in the sixty-third year of his age, having been for over forty years a Cardinal and a bishop for nearly thirty. His reign was to last for nineteen years, five months and fourteen days.

5

The Duchess of Albany was not destined to survive her father for long. After his death, still herself in a weak state of health, she moved to the Palace of the Cancelleria where her uncle provided her with rooms. From this address she wrote to her mother on the 2nd of February, 1788.

'I am so crushed by sorrow, my dear mother, that I have hardly strength to hold my pen. On Thursday at nine o'clock I lost the

The Cardinal King

best and tenderest of fathers. Alas, my dear mother, my heart is torn with indescribable pain at this moment. . . . My health is not improved by the agitations which are going on round me, but I spare myself, and Heaven will give me the necessary strength. Be at rest, my dear mother, about your future, depend on my heart which only longs to make you as happy as you deserve.'

The grief she expresses in this letter was very probably sincere, written as it was only a few days after her father's death and the day before his funeral. But the grief for this father whom she had never deeply loved did not last long and the letters to her mother that followed are more concerned with details about proper mourning and the coat of arms she intends to use than with further expressions of sorrow. On the question of arms she intends to use the same as her father and to carry his books emblazoned with the crown. This, she adds rather pertly, is the only way out unless she declares herself heir to the throne, which 'cannot happen without an Act of Parliament'.

Her father's will was found to be largely in her favour. Among his effects were certain crown jewels which included a sceptre, a collar, badge and Star of the Order of the Garter, and the cross of the Order of the Thistle set in diamonds that had once been worn by James II: these were left to the Cardinal.

Charlotte never returned to France but spent the remaining months of her life in Rome or travelling in the Papal States. In October 1788 the young Duke of Berwick arrived in Rome and was presented to Charlotte by the Spanish ambassador. The Duchess took him out to Frascati where he met the Cardinal King who, Charlotte tells her mother, 'has always favoured that branch more than that of Fitzjames, because of King James's preference for the Berwicks.' The Cardinal was delighted with his young cousin: 'le petit Berwick was very well received by my Uncle. He looks charming and is perfectly brought up. My Uncle regrets that he should be so young because it might be a suitable marriage for me. As a Grandee of Spain he will have a rent roll of three hundred thousand.'

Alas, any thought of marriage was out of the question. A year after the young Duke of Berwick's visit she was already on the

King Henry the Ninth

very threshold of death. From Nocera, where she had hoped the baths might relieve her illness, she went on to Bologna where she stayed at the house of the Marchesa Lambertini-Bovio, a member of the distinguished family that had given Benedict XIV to the Papacy, who was a friend both of her and of the Cardinal. Here, in November, the fatal tumour was finally diagnosed and some sort of operation attempted. News of her desperate condition following this operation reached the Cardinal in a letter from the Marchesa dated November 13th, 1789.

ALTEZZA REALE EMINENTISSIMA,

It is with the deepest grief I have to inform your Highness and Eminence of the very bad condition of the poor Signora Duchess. To-day she has had a serious relapse with terrible chills and high fever. The doctors in treating the wound have drawn off a great quantity of matter of very bad colour and odour, whilst her pulse is far above normal. I cannot sufficiently express my anxiety. It is the height of my affliction (and I much lament it) to have to write such melancholy news to your Highness, though I hope tomorrow to be able to send a better account. Have no fear for the excellent Christian sentiments of your respected niece. Yesterday with the greatest edification she made her devotions at her own desire, whereby your Highness can realize how fully resigned she is to the Divine Will ...

Your very humble and most obliged servant,

GIULIA LAMBERTINI-BOVIO.

P.S. The courier from Turin has delayed in passing through Bologna, so I can give your Highness the latest news of the Signora Duchess. To-day, then, at fourteen o'clock, I must tell you that the fever increases every moment, so that we fear to lose her very shortly. My Lord the Cardinal-Archbishop remains constantly with her, nor does he mean to leave her bedside so long as she is alive.

On November the 17th she died. Less than two years after the funeral of his brother the Cardinal was presiding at a requiem for his 'royal niece' in the Cathedral at Frascati. She was buried at

The Cardinal King

Bologna in a church that was later destroyed by the French during the revolutionary wars, and no trace of her final resting-place has survived.

6

Louise of Stolberg, we are told by Alfieri, was overwhelmed with grief when the news of her husband's death reached her in Paris where she was living with her lover in the Rue du Bourgogne. We may assume that he was using a little poetic licence in this phrase for it is difficult to suppose that the fickle heart of Louise, who had previously longed for the death of this man 'who seemed to be formed of iron' and who had told Alfieri's mother, with unsurpassed smugness, that if she did not hate him it was only on account of her 'Christian charity and because we are desired to pardon', was really moved to tears at this death to which she had once so eagerly looked forward. If she was indeed so stricken with sorrow she chose a curious way to assuage her grief, for it was at this time that she began to assume those absurd airs of royalty that so amazed the uninitiated visitors to her salon. Not only was this apartment adorned with a throne but people were expected to bow themselves out backwards from her royal presence. These royal pretensions, which must surely have caused a good deal of amusement in the Paris of the late 'eighties and early 'nineties, were rigidly insisted upon, and even Madame de Staël addressed her as *chère souveraine*. It is not surprising, after all, that Louise was not particularly eager to exchange the rôle of Queen Dowager for that of mere Countess Alfieri, while the poet himself, whose republican sentiments were on the wane, found it more agreeable to his self-esteem to be the lover of a Queen than the husband of an obscure German princess. Horace Mann's prophesy that she would 'marry the Count a week after she becomes a widow' was not to be fulfilled.

7

The year that began with the death of Prince Charles was to end with the death of King Charles III of Spain. Since the days when,

King Henry the Ninth

as a youth, he had taken the young Prince Charles to the siege of Gaeta this monarch had always retained a kind interest in his unfortunate Stuart cousins, and after his removal from the throne of Naples to that of Spain he had contrived to give them what help he could. He bestowed the revenues of rich benefices in both Spain and Mexico on the Cardinal and at the time when all the Catholic powers were turning their backs on Prince Charles after his father's death in 1766 the King of Spain had openly rebuked the Nuncio at Madrid for his master's cowardice in refusing to recognize the heir of the dead king. It should be added, none the less, that he was not prepared to recognize him himself.

King Charles III was the last representative of the benevolent despots who had dominated Europe during the eighteenth century from the courts of Vienna, Versailles, St. Petersburg, Potsdam and Madrid. Though Catherine the Great was to live for another eight years the end of her reign was to be overshadowed by the storms that were gathering in Europe and by ideas which, translated into political action, were to leave this former correspondent and professed admirer of Voltaire bewildered and hostile. The great age of monarchy was over. As the year 1788 died and the fatal year 1789 dawned the knell began to toll for crowns and sceptres all over the continent, and kings, be they Catholic, Most Christian, Faithful or Apostolic, felt the first tremblings of the eruption which was to send so many of their thrones toppling into the dust. New and dreaded formulas like the rights of man and the sovereignty of the people were being discussed in the very antechambers of royal palaces and revolutionary ideas were gradually spreading among the masses of the people. The whole of Europe was soon to be turned into a battlefield in the name of Liberty, Equality and Fraternity. If the same crimes, the same tyrannies, the same stupidities and the same oppressions were to be exercised under republican forms as had previously been suffered under the yoke of absolute monarchy, at least the new enfranchised citizens had the consolation of knowing that now they had only themselves to blame.

The Sovereign Pontiff, as temporal ruler of the States of the Church, was soon to feel the full violence of the storm. Pius VI,

The Cardinal King

whose reign had opened with such splendour, was destined to die a prisoner of the revolution at Valence in 1799. In the meantime he was to hurl his anathemas in vain at the new ideas that spread from France down the Italian peninsula towards Rome itself. One immediate effect of the events in France following the storming of the Bastille was to draw the monarchs of Europe into a closer association. For the first time an unofficial envoy from the British Court appeared in Rome in the person of Sir John Coxe Hippisley, a man who was later to play an important rôle in the affairs of the Cardinal of York, while the Pope sent the future Cardinal Erskine, who as a young man had been placed at the Pontifical Scots College as a protégé of the Cardinal Duke, to London. These exchanges, though unofficial, resulted in a changed relationship between the House of Hanover and the Holy See. Some old points of dispute between them had already died a natural death. The practice of James III of nominating bishops to vacant sees in Ireland had never been exercised by his elder son, though Prince Charles had demanded it as his right, and the Cardinal had never asked to exercise a privilege which had been denied to his brother. Furthermore, the delicate situation resulting from the move for Catholic emancipation in England made the Vatican most unwilling to stir up any unnecessary trouble in its relations with the British Government, which had not been in so satisfactory a state since the Reformation. Questions about appointments to colonial sees and to the English, Scots, and Irish colleges in Rome (all traditional hotbeds of Jacobitism) were settled in an amicable way, and it was a natural outcome of this *rapprochement* that the Pope should acknowledge George III as King of Great Britain in the official Gazette of the Holy See (where his name had previously only featured as 'Duca di Hannover') and in documents of state which must, inevitably, come under the eye of that other sovereign of Great Britain, King Henry IX, Cardinal Vice-Chancellor of the Holy Roman Church.

This act of Pius VI which took place in 1792, though it was the logical outcome of the policy of the Papacy since 1766, drew a cry of protest from the Cardinal King. The recognition of George III came as a bitter blow to Henry Stuart who had hoped that the

King Henry the Ninth

Holy See might at least wait until his death before it finally and irrevocably turned its back on the claims of his House. 'Amidst the continual sorrows and bitter trials that my Royal House has been decreed to suffer for over a century,' he wrote to the Pope, 'two circumstances gave it, by way of compensation, a special degree of comfort and support. The first was the reflection that our every sacrifice was made for God, for the Faith, and for that unshaken Loyalty we have ever displayed towards the Primacy of Peter and the Holy See. The second was our own sense of the Holy See's devotion to our Royal House. . . .' He went on to recall how Clement XI had absolutely refused to recognize any sovereigns of England save those of their own 'legitimate Catholic succession' and that this policy of Clement came to be regarded as a 'maxim of the Holy See that could never be abrogated'. It was true, he admitted, that Clement XIII had '*negatively* deprived of royal recognition' his brother, but that it had none the less been made clear that he would be unable to recognize any other King of England whatever outside their own House of Stuart 'without breaking a maxim of the Holy See that was at once fully recognized, intact, established and irrevocable'. Having thus stated his case the Cardinal ended on a pathetic note of outraged dignity and hurt pride which must have caused a slight twinge of conscience in the urbane and well-meaning Pius VI as he read it:

'But, O God, what a blow! what anguish of soul for me to note in a Pontifical Brief, which must of necessity fall before my own eyes, that, by a stroke of the pen, as it were, I myself have been betrayed and deprived of the benefit of that maxim, which had been upheld by the Holy See with unswerving fidelity for upwards of a century! Under these circumstances it would be useless for me to deny that the wound rankles in me, since it has been dealt me by the hand of a Father whom I love and venerate—and shall love and venerate whilst my life continues. I confess that I used to flatter myself that during these very few last remaining years of my life my Royal House would be allowed to expire in me without this fresh act of humiliation, but (inasmuch as we ought always to ascribe every event to the operation of the Divine Will) it seems

The Cardinal King

that I did wrong in resting so certain that the Holy Father would never dream of snatching from me the possession of that which in one sense can be termed a natural right, a right of compensation that protected me from many indignities. Now, as in consequence of this abjuration of a maxim of the Holy See I should be obliged to suffer insult on any occasion that I might venture to enter Rome, henceforth I intend to pass my last few years of life in deep retirement amongst my flock at Frascati.'

Alas, future events of which he had as yet little inkling were to make any hope of passing his last years in deep retirement at Frascati quite out of the question. When one remembers that these lines were penned at the height of the French Revolution one realizes how completely out of touch the Cardinal had become with the political situation outside his own small world. Since his 'accession' the Cardinal King had continued unchanged that life of 'splendid tranquillity' which he had enjoyed for so many years. He was now addressed as 'Your Majesty' by his servants though in official circles he still continued to be His Royal Highness and Eminence. His assumption of royal rank had brought few if any changes to his mode of life beyond those minor adjustments in arms and title to which we have already referred. He would sometimes, as successor to King Edward the Confessor, touch for the King's Evil, using a silver-gilt touch-piece engraved with a ship in full sail on one side and an angel on the other. This mystical aspect of royalty to which the phlegmatic Hanoverians had never laid claim was probably, with the single exception of Charles X of France, practised for the last time in human history by Henry IX. He was certainly the last person claiming the English crown to perform this rite which can be traced back to Saxon times. If the Pope's recognition of George III had come as such a blow to the placid and innocent life of this mildest of pretenders he was in for a deeper and more bitter blow in a very short time. His protest, the last to be made by the unfortunate House of Stuart, was signed at Frascati on the 4th of November, 1792. Less than three months later, on the 20th of January, 1793, King Louis XVI was guillotined by his subjects in the Place de la Révolution. The House of

King Henry the Ninth

Bourbon had suffered the fate of the House of Stuart. The news of the death of the King of France, which sent a chill through every court in Europe, was received in Rome with horror and dismay, and not least by the great-grandson of King Charles I.

10

Revolution and Ruin

I

The Protest of the Cardinal King against the recognition of George III appears all the more unreal when it is set against the background of the international tension that marked the years immediately preceeding it. The distraught Pius VI, faced with the loss of Avignon and the persecution of the Church in France, must have felt little sympathy with these laments raising almost forgotten controversies that sprang from the close of the seventeenth century. What hope had this voice from the past in the face of that new voice which rang out from beyond the Alps crying for vengeance and bloodshed; the new and terrible Voice of the People? The Pope, faced with apostacy in France, indifference among his allies and the threat of revolt in his own states, had little time to bother himself with disputes which had by now no more than an academic interest. A Pontiff faced with the devastating impact of the French Revolution could hardly be expected to waste his time over problems arising from the English Revolution of 1688—especially when that country, with which he was eager to be on the friendliest of terms, persisted in thinking of their own Revolution as 'Glorious'.

Since 1790 the Papal Government had been watching with increasing alarm the sequence of events in France which, with growing momentum, had brought the threat of disaster ever nearer to the dominions of the Church. The Cardinal of York must have noted with approval one of the first steps it took to stem the tide of revolutionary ideas: on June 18th, 1790, a decree was issued banning as subversive the tragedies of Count Vittorio Alfieri. There is a certain irony in this decree, for the poet, living

Revolution and Ruin

at the very centre of the Revolution, was finding that he had himself little sympathy with his former liberal opinions, and when he witnessed the effect of these noble sentiments upon the Paris mob he found that there was nothing he wanted to do more than to leave the stronghold of Liberty with all possible speed. After some difficulty and not a few dangers he escaped with the Countess to England, becoming more of a reactionary with every mile he placed between himself and Paris. From England the pair eventually returned to Florence where the former champion of republicanism made a point of turning his back on any representative he met of the One and Indivisible Republic.

In the spring of 1791 two distinguished refugees had arrived in Rome in the persons of Mesdames Adelaide and Victoire, the elderly daughters of Louis XV, who had escaped from Paris in February and reached the States of the Church by way of Savoy. It is thanks to them that we get an intimate picture of the Cardinal of York as he appeared in 1792 when he was sixty-seven years old. In that year Madame Adelaide was visited by her former Lady in Waiting, the Marquise d'Osmond, who brought with her a small daughter, the future Comtesse de Boigne. This little girl, then only eleven, has left a vivid picture in her *Récits d'une Tante*, written many years later, of the visits she paid with her parents to the last of the Stuarts. Her mother was received by the Cardinal with extreme kindness for she was the grand-daughter of Dicconson, who had been in the service of James III at Saint-Germain. 'He requested her to visit him at Frascati during the summer,' the Comtesse wrote, 'and in the winter he insisted that she and my father should dine with him frequently.'

'He was to be found [the Comtesse continues] in a large, sparsely furnished palace without a fire anywhere, a hood over his head and his body covered with two great-coats, his feet on a foot-warmer and his hands in a muff. His guests would have been glad to adopt the same costume for it was icily cold at his house. Out of kindness to my mother he caused a few pieces of wood to be lighted in a fourth salon and claimed that even at that distance his breathing was stifled. It should be pointed out that he had a charcoal heater under his feet. But it was necessary to observe an atmosphere of royalty, if only in the way of eccentricity! His household addressed him as Your Majesty. His guests avoided the use of any title which the use of the third person in Italian made all the easier.

'He spoke nothing but this language and a little English, but that so badly that one found him difficult to understand, a fact which annoyed him extremely.

'All his affection was centred on Consalvi, whom he treated as a son; he was not able to do for a moment without Ercole, as he constantly called him, and the poor Ercole found this rather tedious.

'The Cardinal was at this time furious with his sister-in-law, the Countess of Albany, who had accepted a pension from the Court of London; he spoke about her with an air of wounded royal dignity.'

This picture of the royal Cardinal is not a very prepossessing one. The handsome appearance and dignity of manner which other visitors noticed obviously did not impress itself on this eleven-year-old witness who remembered only a querulous old invalid with his hands in a muff. Emotional excitement always affected the Cardinal's health, and the anxieties of the times coupled with his fury at the Countess of Albany's conduct seem to have brought on an attack of asthma, a complaint often of a nervous origin and one from which his mother had also suffered. It is perhaps not surprising that the Cardinal's command of the English language had deteriorated in the course of the years for he now had few occasions on which to speak it. Even with his brother he tended, towards the end, to correspond in French or Italian, and the Duchess of Albany spoke no English and only a little Italian, though towards the end of her life she made some attempts to master the language of her forefathers. It was, however, probably more his pronunciation than anything else that made his speech so unintelligible, for to the end he was able to write in English with considerable clarity and effect, as his letters to Sir John Coxe Hippisley show.

Revolution and Ruin

2

The calamities that engulfed the Holy See as the tide of revolution spread soon made a dead letter of Henry's threat to retire in high dudgeon to his episcopal seat at Frascati. Himself a descendant of Henry IV of France the fate which befell the House of Bourbon had for him an added poignance both from its parallel to the misfortunes of his own Stuart ancestors as well as from the feelings of personal grief he felt at the plight of his cousin Louis XVI. A Requiem Mass of great solemnity for the repose of the soul of the Most Christian King was sung in the Cathedral of Frascati at which the Cardinal assisted in all his splendour as a Prince of the Church. It was a requiem not only for a king but for an age, and it was fitting that a king in exile should preside at it. As the Cardinal King pontificated from his throne on this sad occasion he must at last have been conscious of the collapse of the very foundation of life as he had known it and lived it for the past sixty years. *La douceur de vivre*, of which Talleyrand was later to speak, and which the Cardinal in his pleasantly cultured and quietly luxurious mode of life had experienced to the full, was to vanish for ever from the face of the earth. The eighteenth century had come to an end: that elegant and serene century, the age of the powdered wig and the brocaded coat; of the minuet, the sarabande and the gavotte; the age of grace and reason, in which a Cardinal-prince could move with dignity, accepting as his due the respect which was without question accorded to him; this ordered and familiar world was now disintegrating rapidly as war and chaos spread before the victorious forces of republicanism.

In this old world the Cardinal of York was supremely at home. It was the only world he had known and it had dealt exceptionally kindly with him. For all the misfortunes of his House he himself had never lacked the luxuries and attentions which were considered the prerogatives of so exalted a position, living in stately splendour 'as a great Prince should', notwithstanding that he brought to his sacred office a sense of duty and vocation rare in that urbane epoch. So far he had been little more than a privileged

The Cardinal King

spectator of affairs but now the days were numbered before he too would be caught up in the flood of events. Already the horizon was dark with gathering clouds. As the words of the *Dies Irae* rang out in the Cathedral of Frascati they foretold a day of wrath not only for the Cardinal but for the Apostolic See and for the very person of the Pope himself.

3

In the month in which Louis XVI went to his death the delicate relations between the Holy See and the new government in France were seriously strained by an ugly and unfortunate incident which took place in Rome. There was living there at that time a sort of unofficial representative of the French Republic called Hugon de Bassville, a man who had caused considerable embarrassment to the Papal authorities by his open encouragement of revolutionary elements in the population. This envoy's rather hysterical advocacy of the new ideas reached a climax on Sunday, January 13th, 1793, when he rode down the Corso in an open carriage in which he and his friends sat with large tricolour cockades in their hats while one of them defiantly waved a silken tricolour flag. The Roman population took exception to this gratuitous exhibition of republican sentiment and soon the carriage was surrounded by an angry mob. Insults were exchanged between the occupants of the carriage and the crowd and a few stones were thrown. By the time the Piazza Colonna was reached the mob had become more menacing and a pistol shot was fired, though no one was actually hit. The Frenchmen, who were more accustomed to having the rabble on their side, now panicked when there seemed some chance of their becoming victims of the mob themselves. Followed by a yelling crowd they took hasty refuge in the Palazzo Palombara which was the residence of a French banker called Morette. On entering the Palazzo a scuffle took place in the course of which Bassville was wounded from a knife-thrust in the stomach. Two days later he died from the effects of this wound.

As Bassville lay dying the Roman mob went about smashing the windows of houses where Frenchmen were known to be living and an attempt was made to burn down the French Academy of Art where only a short time before the students had destroyed a statue of Louis XIV and erected one of Brutus in its place. Now these same students found their academy surrounded by an angry mob yelling such unfamiliar slogans as '*Viva il Papa!*' and 'Long live the Catholic religion!' which must have struck a discordant note on ears attuned to the cry of mobs yelling for the death of kings. While these disorderly scenes took place Bassville, at the final ebb of life, was abjuring his oath to the Civil Constitution of the Clergy and receiving the Last Sacraments from the curé of San Lorenzo in Lucina. The Papal troops soon restored order but it was a bitter day for French aspirations in the States of the Church, for as the Venetian Ambassador informed his government on January 14th: 'The revolution that was to be started in Rome has misfired; there were no supporters of it anywhere.'

France was soon to seize this incident as a weapon against the Church, and on February 2nd, 1793, the National Convention passed a resolution demanding vengeance for Bassville who was now regarded as a martyr to the cause of republicanism. France, surrounded by enemies on all sides, was not then in a position to put her threat into execution so for the moment the affair had to be shelved. It was not, however, forgotten. The French Government had to wait until 1796 before it was able to launch its armies into Italy. By then France not only had a new and more stable government in the Directory but she had in her service a general of such ability that he was destined not only to avenge Bassville but to replace the Directory by an even newer government headed by himself. Into the Italy in which the grandson of King James II still occupied his high offices in the Roman Church there now entered men whose names were as remote from the ancient claims still advanced by the Cardinal King as one age can be from another; the names of Augereau, of Berthier, and of Napoleon Bonaparte.

Bonaparte invaded the Italian peninsula in May with an army of ten thousand men. In a few days Milan had fallen, and from this city the victorious general issued his proclamation. 'We are the friends of every nation,' he announced, using a phrase that was to become the slogan of almost every act of aggression for the next

The Cardinal King

hundred and fifty years, 'especially the descendants of Brutus and the Scipios. Our intention is to restore the Capitol, to set up there in their honour the statues of the men who won renown, and to free the Roman people from their long slavery.' If the opening sentence of this proclamation savoured of insincerity there was nothing insincere in the last sentence, and nothing of comfort in it for the Cardinals whom the Pope now called to advise him in the hour of peril. There can have been little room for thought of those old 'maxims of the Holy See' in the mind of the Cardinal of York as he made his way to the Quirinal to add his counsels to those of his brethren in these dangerous days. In no time the French were in occupation of Ravenna, Ferrara and Bologna, and the representatives of the Holy See were compelled to sue for peace. At Bologna the conqueror issued his terms, making it clear that they would have been even more severe but for the intervention of the King of Spain, who was at that time the rather reluctant ally of the Directory.

By the terms of the Armistice of Bologna the Holy See was obliged to close the ports of Ancona and Civita Vecchia to the ships of the anti-French coalition, certain Papal territories were to be under military occupation, and a 'tribute' amounting to twenty-one million *scudi* was to be paid within three months, while one hundred works of art and five hundred manuscripts were to be surrendered to the invader. Furthermore the Pope was to apologize for the murder of Bassville and undertake to free all political prisoners. Notwithstanding these apologies, when the new agent of the French Government arrived in Rome to execute the terms of the armistice he took care to make as few public appearances as possible.

If the Pope thought that he had bought peace at this exorbitant price he was soon to learn his mistake. An uprising in the neighbourhood of Ferrara, encouraged by false reports of an Austrian victory, was rigorously suppressed by General Augereau, and gave Bonaparte his excuse to resume hostilities against the Church. In January 1797 the news of the fall of Mantua brought dismay and confusion to Rome where many leading citizens and highly placed ecclesiastics made preparations for flight. Certain of the

Revolution and Ruin

Cardinals begged the Pope himself to seek asylum in the Kingdom of Naples, but Pius VI steadfastly refused to leave Rome. Cardinal York, too, considering himself safe at Frascati where he was surrounded by the affection of his flock, made no attempt as yet to escape from the advancing foe. Meanwhile the Sacred College dispatched a delegation headed by Cardinal Mattei and the Duca Braschi-Onesti, the Pope's nephew, to negotiate with Bonaparte at Tolentino.

The terms of the Treaty of Tolentino, which General Bonaparte dictated to these envoys were even more humiliating than those of Bologna, which seemed mild and magnanimous in comparison. After asserting that all the demands of the previous armistice still held good, the Pope was now made to renounce Avignon together with the legations of Bologna, Ferrara and the Romagna, while the 'tribute' already due was augmented to the tune of forty-six million *scudi*. The young conqueror treated the envoys of the Pope with supreme contempt and refused to mitigate the huge financial burden or any other of the harsh terms of the treaty for all that, as the Duca Braschi reported to the Pope, 'more than once poor Cardinal Mattei threw himself at Bonaparte's feet, fighting for a long time against such terrible conditions for Rome.'

There was some doubt as to whether the Papal government would be able to fulfil its obligations when the terms of the Treaty of Tolentino were made known in Rome. The treasury was exhausted, and though fresh taxes had been levied it was necessary to call in many sacred vessels from the churches to be melted down, and the treasure of Pope Sixtus V was withdrawn from the Castel Sant' Angelo to help pay off the indemnity. The Pope sold many of his own personal treasures and ordered that some of the Papal vestments should be stripped of the pearls and other precious stones that decorated them. This example was followed by Roman nobles and by many of the Cardinals, and in this the Cardinal of York set an example that rivalled all the others. Always generous to the poor and to those who applied to him for alms, the Cardinal was now able to come to the aid of the institution which he held in respect and veneration even above his own claims to an earthly crown; he was able to place almost his entire private fortune at the disposal of the Apostolic See. This spontaneous act of generosity was made despite the fact that the revolution had already deprived him of the revenues he enjoyed from his French benefices, while his income from Spain was soon to vanish in the same way. The resentment he had felt when Pius VI had recognized the *de facto* King of England, if indeed it still lingered, was swept aside in this magnificent and kingly act when the Cardinal ordered the disposal of all his family treasures to buy off the despoilers of the Church and the murderers of his Bourbon cousins. Among the historical and irreplaceable objects that were sacrificed at his orders were the solid gold embossed shield which the Holy Roman Emperor had presented to his great grandfather King John Sobieski after he had saved Vienna from the Turk, and the Great Ruby of Poland, another Sobieski heirloom, said to be the size of a pigeon's egg and valued at above fifty thousand pounds. Thus the money was raised to pay the invader, leaving the city impoverished of its treasures, its coffers empty, and many of its leading families ruined. But the respite, bought at so dear a price and upon so humiliating terms, was again to be short-lived.

4

In August 1797 Joseph Bonaparte, later to be raised by his brother to the thrones first of Naples and then of Spain, was sent as Ambassador of the French Republic to the Holy See. He took up residence in the Palazzo Corsini, which soon became a centre of anti-Papal intrigue and republican propaganda. This future monarch had been specially instructed by the Directory to encourage revolutionary and republican activities within the States of the Church, but events, similar to those connected with the death of Bassville, were destined to make his stay in Rome last only a few months. In December of the same year serious riots broke out and there were skirmishes all over the city between the rioters and the Papal troops. The mob, accustomed now to look to the French embassy for protection, made a dash towards it when a patrol fired on the crowd killing two men. At this critical moment one of the ambassador's guests, a French officer called

Revolution and Ruin

General Duphot, rushed from the Palazzo Corsini with his sword drawn and flung himself in defence of the crowd. It was a foolish histrionic gesture and cost the General his life. The French government, as in the Bassville affair, lost no time in making use of this unfortunate incident for a final assault on Rome. Joseph Bonaparte demanded his passport and left abruptly despite the attempts of Cardinal Doria, the Secretary of State, to apologize and make him remain at his post. It was the opportunity the French had wanted to break with the Holy See and on January 11th, 1798, General Berthier was ordered to march on Rome. The French army occupied the city on February 15th, the anniversary of the election of Pius VI, and the Roman Republic was proclaimed. The Republican General, later to be created by his fellow general Prince of Neufchâtel and of Wagram, bade the Roman citizens to 'accept the homage of free Frenchmen on the Capitol where you so often defended the rights of the people and celebrated the Roman Republic.' After this solemn inauguration and the inevitable planting of a Tree of Liberty a period of terror ensued during which the Cardinal of York's dear friend and pupil Ercole Consalvi was confined in the Castel Sant' Angelo and six Cardinals were placed under house arrest. The Pope, aged over eighty and in poor health, was placed under 'protective custody' prior to his banishment. The Cardinal of York fled from Rome the day before General Berthier arrived.

5

While the old Pope was escorted north to end his days a political prisoner at Valence the Cardinal of York sped south to seek sanctuary in the dominions of the King of Naples. Once more a Stuart prince was forced to go on his travels but this time, unlike Charles II after the Battle of Worcester or Charles Edward after Culloden, he was not a prince with youth and robust health to support him but an old man past his seventieth year.

No sooner had the Cardinal left Frascati than revolution broke out there, as in Rome, though in the little town in the Alban Hills the revolt had the rare distinction of being instigated by a Canon of the Cathedral, a man who owed his advancement to the royal

The Cardinal King

bishop who was now fleeing for his life. This man, who occupied the chair of Theology in the Cardinal's seminary, now exhorted his fellow citizens to throw off their chains and to greet the restoration of the rights of man which had previously been 'filched by despots'. If he included the Cardinal King among the despots, as no doubt he did, he might have reflected that one of this tyrant's particular acts of despotism had been to establish the seminary in which he held a position as professor, and to make it one of the best and most respected in Italy. The art of reflection is not, however, an attribute of revolutionary thinkers. For the moment this priest was intoxicated with the new spirit and considered it much more important to plant yet another Tree of Liberty on 'the broad and pleasant hillside of our own Tusculum' than to devote himself to his possibly more useful task of instructing the young in the science of theology.

It is a sure testimony to the affection in which the fleeing 'despot' was held by some at least of his spiritual subjects to record that those of his treasures which he was unable to take away with him were hidden in the houses of poor dependants who gladly ran the risk of guarding their beloved bishop's possessions until the return of better times. But the bulk of his belongings had to remain in the palace and these, his collection of pictures and works of art with many valuable books and manuscripts, were all plundered when the French army entered the town. What remained of his treasures after his own generous donation to pay off the indemnity demanded by Bonaparte and the subsequent pillage by the French were later put up to public auction by the government of the Roman Republic. Thus, from being the richest prelate of the Roman curia, the Cardinal of York now found himself with nothing beyond what he could take with him in his flight.

The Cardinal eventually reached Naples accompanied only by Monsignor Cesarini, his loyal and devoted secretary, and Eugenio Ridolfi, his valet. In Naples, where the Bourbon sovereigns were his distant relatives, he found various other members of the Sacred College who had also taken refuge in this city which was still protected by the army of the Austrian General Karl von Mack, a commander in whom King Ferdinand IV and Queen Maria

Revolution and Ruin

Carolina had a profound but quite unjustified confidence. Before the disasters that befell General Mack's army caused the Cardinal to continue his travels he was able to hear the first tidings of good news since the beginning of this long series of disastrous events. While he was still in Naples the news of the victory of Lord Nelson at the Battle of the Nile reached that city and the tidings of it were actually conveyed personally to Henry IX before they reached the ears of King George III. This picturesque and touching incident has been described by Cornelia Knight who was in Naples at the time and left an account of it in her autobiography.

'Cardinal York was then at Naples [she writes] having fled from Rome to avoid falling into the hands of the French. Sir William Hamilton, on his return from the palace, met him in his carriage, called on the cardinal's coachman to stop, and, getting out of his own carriage, he went up to the cardinal's and said: "I beg pardon of your eminence for stopping your carriage, but I am sure you will be glad to hear the good news which I have to communicate."

'The Cardinal, rather surprised, asked, "Pray, sir, to whom have I the honour of speaking?"

' "To Sir William Hamilton."

' "Oh! to the British Minister," rejoined the Cardinal. "I am much obliged to you, sir, and what is the news?"

'Sir William then gave an account of the victory as succinctly as he could. The Cardinal, agitated and rejoiced, said, "But may we depend on the truth of this great affair? There are so many false reports." Sir William then introduced Captain Capel, saying, "This gentleman, a brother of Lord Essex, was in the action, and is going home immediately with the despatches."

' "In that case sir," said the Cardinal to Captain Capel, "when you arrive in England, do me the favour to say that no man rejoices more sincerely than I do in the success and glory of the British navy." '

This little incident is surely one of the happiest in the long career of the Cardinal King. There is something very moving in the scene as the grandson of James II, whose achievements as Lord High Admiral were so much more glorious than the short and disastrous episode of his reign, hears the news of Lord Nel-

The Cardinal King

son's great victory. We can imagine his delicate Stuart features looking from the window of his carriage 'agitated and rejoiced' as Sir William unfolded the story of the rout of the French fleet. There were times when the report of a French defeat would have been sad news for an exiled Stuart, but those times were dead. As the Cardinal drove on he must have been highly satisfied that this news should first have reached the ears of the last descendant of England and Scotland's ancient line of kings; and Nelson too, who had pointedly refused to attend the celebrations for the centenary of the 'Glorious' Revolution, may well have been pleased to learn that the House of Stuart was able to hear of his great exploit before the House of Hanover. It also does credit to the imagination and goodness of heart of Sir William Hamilton that he should have thought of stopping the Cardinal's carriage to impart this welcome information. He never entertained any bitterness or hatred for the banished dynasty like his former colleague in Florence. It is impossible to imagine Sir Horace Mann in such a situation.

6

But this was just a passing moment of sunshine in a bitter and stormy exile. After ten months in the Neapolitan capital the Cardinal had again to look round him for a means of escape from the advancing Revolution. The inability of General Mack to hold the French in check made escape again essential, and this time the flight was led by the Royal Family, who were taken across the straits to Palermo in the British man-of-war *Vanguard*, the flagship of Lord Nelson. In Naples, forsaken by its ruling house, yet another Republic was proclaimed in the wake of the fleeing royalty, with all the terrors that had come to be associated with such changes, while Trees of Liberty sprang up all over Italy in a positive frenzy of egalitarian afforestation.

The Cardinal did not, as has sometimes been stated, cross over to Sicily in one of the escorting vessels of the British fleet but hired a small coasting ship, and in this tiny craft sailed for Messina in one of the worst storms that had been known in those parts for as long as men could remember. There is no evidence that Cardinal

Revolution and Ruin

York and Lord Nelson ever met, though they must have been in Naples at the same time, and there is a tradition that the Cardinal was able to present to the victor of the Nile a silver-mounted dirk which had once belonged to Prince Charles. Whether this story is true or not it is a fact that Henry Stuart left Naples the day before the flight of the Neapolitan royal family and made not for Palermo but for Messina.

The weather, which rarely smiled on a Stuart in moments such as this, was so tempestuous that it took the ship twenty-three days in the passage from Naples to Messina, at the conclusion of which the old fugitive was utterly exhausted and at the end of his strength. His physical misfortunes were not over, however, for while he was in Messina he managed to bruise his right shin when entering a coach and this abrasion, probably due to his general state of weakness and exhaustion, refused to heal and eventually developed into an open sore which finally made his right leg permanently crippled.

At Messina the Cardinal of York found three other members of the Sacred College. These were Cardinal Doria, formerly Secretary of State, Cardinal Pignatelli, and Cardinal Braschi, a nephew of Pius VI. To save expense the four of them lived in the same house for the months they remained in Sicily. A great problem almost at once faced these Princes of the Church; the problem of a conclave to elect a new Pope in the event of the death of Pius VI, an event which, considering the great age and fragile health of the prisoner of Valence, might happen at any moment. Before the Sacred College had been dispersed from Rome there had already been some discussion on this question, and it was finally decided that should the Cardinals be unable to return to Rome the place of meeting should be Venice, which was now under Austrian rule. Rather than wait for news of the Pope's death, in which case they might not be able to reach Venice in time, Cardinal York and his companions agreed that no moment should be lost in reaching the city on the Adriatic, for it was essential that a sufficient number of Cardinals should assemble there, and with the members of the Sacred College scattered all over Europe (some of the French Cardinals had taken refuge in England while others who were subject to the Austrian crown had retired to Vienna) the mere collection of a sufficient number of qualified electors was a major problem, especially as republican France would do everything in its power to prevent the election of another Pope. Thus in February 1799 the Cardinal crossed over to Reggio on the coast of Calabria and from there was able to hire a Greek merchant-vessel whose master was persuaded to carry the Cardinal of York, together with Pignatelli and Braschi, to their destination.

The voyage to Venice, like that from Naples to Messina, was not without its perils and again the ship containing the three Cardinals was caught in a great storm off the coast of Apulia and was compelled to put in to the island of Corfu for protection. Here better luck attended them for this beautiful island, then part of the Sultan's empire, had recently been cleared of the French invaders and was now occupied by Russian and Turkish armies. The idea of these two hereditary enemies holding the island as allies was hardly more surprising than the sudden appearance of three Princes of the Church, one the claimant to a kingdom, in a storm-tossed merchant vessel. Had it not been for the melancholy nature of their plight the sight of these three prelates being received by Abdul Cadir Bey, the Ottoman viceroy, on this Greek island full of Russian soldiers might have suggested a scene from a comic opera by Rossini.

After some time resting on the island of Corfu the three travellers continued their journey to Venice where the elderly Henry Stuart arrived 'infirm as well as destitute' and took lodgings in a private house near the Rialto. His poverty had now reached such a state, however, that he was soon compelled to move from this refuge and was grateful to accept the hospitality that was offered him by a neighbouring monastery. He was now reduced to selling his few remaining pieces of plate in order to provide for the necessities of existence.

7

While the Cardinal of York was suffering these privations he would have been surprised to know that the cause of the Stuarts had emerged once more, though this time only as a weapon of irony, in the game of international politics.

In Paris Monsieur de Talleyrand now sat in the Ministry of Foreign Affairs having returned from his self-imposed term of exile in the United States of America. In 1799, this year of such anguish for Henry Stuart, a note was sent to England hinting at the desire of Napoleon Bonaparte, now First Consul and dictator of France, for peace between the two countries. To this note the British Government replied that they could consider no offer of peace with France as being sincere until that country, as a guarantee of the purity of her intentions, should immediately recall her legitimate monarch to the throne. On receiving this snub the French Foreign Minister lost no time in pointing out the absurdity of the case of the British cabinet in invoking the principles of legitimacy (which Talleyrand was later himself to champion) while the legitimate grandson of James II was still living in exile in Italy. The ability of the British to ignore unwelcome facts seemed to the French something much more like hypocrisy, and Talleyrand, in the words of Duff Cooper, 'was not slow to remind the English Cabinet of the true nature of their master's claim to the throne.'

To this we might add that it was not so surprising as might at first appear that Monsieur de Talleyrand, alone among European politicians, should remember the existence of the Cardinal of York; he was, after all, a bishop himself.

8

Pope Pius VI died at dawn on the 29th of August, 1799. His reign of twenty-four years was the longest there had been since that of St. Peter. The last words he spoke were of forgiveness for those who had caused his exile and imprisonment as with a dying gesture he imparted for the last time the Apostolic blessing of the city and the world—the city from which he had been driven into exile and the world that was content to leave him to his fate.

This Pope, who had once hoped to reign with all the glory of a Leo X and who had performed with such relish the splendid ceremonies of his exalted office; who had once sat so serenely upon

The Cardinal King

the throne of the Apostle and gathered round him the artists and men of genius who flocked to Rome in the early years of his reign, now breathed his last in a small squalid building closely guarded by sentries who were instructed to refer to him as 'the former so-called Pope'. In the face of the terrible disasters that befell him Pius VI showed a spirit of heroic fortitude. The man who now lay dead in the little room at Valence was a changed man from the handsome Pontiff who had displayed a shapely foot at his coronation in 1775. His spiritual stature had increased as his sufferings had multiplied and at the end he had become, in the words of Freiherr von Pastor, 'an heroic follower of Christ with whom he kept faith unflinchingly and in whose footsteps he trod as few others had done.' The Revolution had tried to crush the Papacy out of existence; it had forgotten that it was founded upon a rock.

Meanwhile the Cardinals were converging upon Venice from all parts of Europe to elect a successor to the vacant throne. Far and away senior to any of them in age and seniority of appointment were the two old friends who now met again in such unhappy circumstances, Giovanni Francesco Albani, Dean of the Sacred College, and Henry Benedict Stuart, Cardinal of York, who had been close friends since the reign of Benedict XIV. As the prelates assembled Cardinal York had the joy of being united with a younger friend, for in the suite of the Benedictine Cardinal Chiaramonti came Ercole Consalvi, now freed from his captivity in the Castel Sant' Angelo from which he had been sent into banishment at Civita Vecchia. He was almost at once made Secretary of the Conclave, and though not a Cardinal exercised a considerable influence in the deliberations that preceded the election of a Pope.

The island monastery of San Giorgio was chosen as the site of the Conclave and here, on November 31st, 1799, the doors were closed on the electors. They did not open until March 14th, 1800, when the fifty-eight-year-old Cardinal Luigi Barnabo Chiaramonti was elected Pope and took the name of Pius VII as a mark of respect and attachment to his predecessor. One of his first acts as Pontiff was to bestow the red hat on Consalvi and to appoint this brilliant protégé of Cardinal York to the office of Secretary of

Revolution and Ruin

State. For the remainder of Cardinal York's life his former pupil and dear friend would be the leading personality in the Roman Church.

It was while this lengthy conclave was in progress that King George III discovered the sad plight to which the last of the Stuarts was reduced. Very soon the Cardinal was to learn how his distant cousin at St. James's had acted on hearing of his distress.

11

The Pension

I

Before entering into an account of the schemes that resulted in a pension being paid to the Cardinal of York a word should be said about the financial obligations still undischarged by successive British governments, and owed to the exiled Royal House, which had been the cause of much fruitless negotiation since the death of James II in 1701.

At the time of the accession to the throne of James II he had granted under Letters Patent a jointure of £50,000 to be paid to his Queen Consort, Mary of Modena, in the event of his death. As King William III, after his usurpation of the throne, never disputed the legal acts of his predecessor as King there can be no doubt that the payment of this dowry was binding on the conscience of both William and his parliaments, though no money was ever received by Mary of Modena after 1688, despite the fact that William III promised that the money should be paid while negotiating the Treaty of Ryswick, a promise which he confirmed personally in the presence of the Swedish Ambassador. He even went so far as to assure Marshall Boufflers, who questioned him on behalf of Louis XIV, that the matter of paying the jointure had never been in dispute. The promise of William III proved to be of little value and not one penny of the money ever reached the Queen. A similar promise made by Queen Anne on December 13, 1713, was equally devoid of fulfilment and in May 1718, Mary of Modena died leaving nothing but her debts and had to be buried at the expense of the French Government. By then the accumulated arrears owed to her by the British Government amounted to £1,500,000.

The Pension

It could hardly be expected that the Government of George I would hand over so large a sum to Mary's son knowing that the money would immediately be used to finance schemes against both them and their *de facto* monarch, and the Act of Attainder passed against James in 1701 gave them a good excuse for doing nothing whatsoever about it. The Este family of Modena, the Dowager Queen's next heirs, seem not to have known of the money or to have been unwilling, from political or family reasons, to put in any claim for it.

No serious attempt was made by the heirs of Mary of Modena to claim their inheritance until the year 1785, over sixty years after her death, when Prince Charles, urged by his daughter Charlotte, sent the Jacobite peer Lord Caryll to Paris where he hoped to obtain the good offices of Louis XVI in obtaining a recognition by the British Government of the Prince's claim to the money. Meanwhile Charles wrote to his brother the Cardinal at Frascati asking for his assistance as co-heir in obtaining this sum of well over a million pounds.

June 7th, 1785.

My Lord Caryll, on whose zeal and devotion we can count absolutely, has for some time past been charged by me with a commission to re-claim the debt which is due to us in England concerning the dowry of the late Queen, widow of James II. He has just written to me that it is necessary for him to show Monsieur le Comte de Vergennes a similar commission on your part, since the moment is favourable for negotiating this matter, and the Minister is disposed to serve us to the best of his power, without touching the honour of our family, my own position and my own rights. . . . As the matter is pressing, and we are awaiting your consent, you will, my very dear Brother, forgive my importunity,

CHARLES R.

The Cardinal Duke gave his consent without much enthusiasm having been warned by his own agent that 'the warmth of Lord Caryll's zeal is apt to raise his hopes beyond what there is reason to expect'. The result of Caryll's representations did, however,

The Cardinal King

get the matter raised by the Count de Vergennes and the question of the long delayed payment was presented to Pitt by the Earl of Pembroke, though the Minister flatly refused to bring the subject to the notice of George III.

Having failed to get any further by ministerial intervention it was decided to get legal advice and the opinion of Francis Plowden (the ex-Jesuit who had entered the Middle Temple after the suppression of his Order) was sought, and this distinguished lawyer declared without equivocation that 'the length of time that has elapsed since the death of her late Majesty is no bar to the recovery of the arrears of her jointure which was due to her at the time of her death'. As the Queen's co-heirs were unable to sue in person he recommended that they should bring an action through their Este cousins, but this suggestion seems to have been distasteful both to Charles and to the Cardinal Duke, for no approach seems to have been made to the Court of Modena. In any event the death of Prince Charles occurred only a few months after Plowden's opinion had reached him and the Cardinal at that time was still in the full enjoyment of his vast ecclesiastical revenues, and so no action of any sort was taken.

Prince Charles did, however, bequeath his rights to his share in this fortune to his daughter the Duchess of Albany who in her turn left it to her Uncle. Thus at the time of his own great poverty when he reached Venice the Cardinal was the sole undisputed heir to well over a million pounds legally owed to his family by the British Government, and that Government, in which Pitt was still a Minister, was fully aware of the fact.

2

It will be remembered that at the time of the Cardinal King's protest at the recognition of King George by the Holy See a certain Sir John Coxe Hippisley had been appointed as an unofficial envoy of Great Britain in the States of the Church. Despite their differences on matters of loyalty a friendly relationship had sprung up between the Cardinal and the representative of King George and it was this diplomat, now returned to London, who initiated

The Pension

the attempt to bring some financial aid to the impoverished Stuart prince. Feeling that it would be inappropriate for himself to approach either the Cardinal or his own Government upon so delicate a subject on his own authority, he looked round for some disinterested party who could raise the question in such a way that he could tactfully pass on the information to the British Government; and with this purpose in view he wrote, on the 16th of August, 1799, to Cardinal Stefano Borgia, the Secretary of the Propaganda, an old friend of Cardinal York's and one who shared his passion for collecting ancient manuscripts and art treasures, asking for his co-operation. It was Sir John's plan that Cardinal Borgia should be the person to explain his colleague's distress to those most able to help him, and in his letter he suggested how this might best be done.

'I take the liberty of addressing myself to your Eminence and asking of you the favour that if you have any knowledge of the Duke's circumstances you will write me a letter on the subject, saying that this would be a fitting opportunity for our Government to take into consideration the losses and sufferings of an unfortunate descendant of the throne of England. Such a letter placed before such persons of influence would, I feel sure, produce a good effect. Should your Eminence deem the Cardinal Duke to be in need of such help, it would be well for any proposal to come, not as suggested by me, but as an idea originally conceived by your Eminence, and as arising in the course of our correspondence.'

Cardinal Borgia, only too pleased to help his old friend, rose magnificently to the occasion and despatched a long letter on September 4th, 1799, to Sir John from Padua where some of the Cardinals were living prior to the opening of the Conclave in Venice, while the Archbishop of Siena also wrote in support of Borgia's letter. After telling how the Cardinal of York had been barbarously stripped of all his property by the French, Cardinal Borgia also referred to the old prince's bad state of health, pointing out how he had barely survived his flight both by land and sea 'the miseries of which . . . greatly injured his health at the advanced age of seventy-five, and produced a very grievous sore in one of his legs.'

The Cardinal King

'Those who are well informed of the most worthy Cardinal's affairs [the letter continues] have assured me, that since his flight, having left behind him his rich and magnificent valuables, which were all sacked and plundered both at Rome and Frascati, he has been supported by the silver plate which he had taken with him, and of which he began to dispose at Messina; and I understand, that in order to supply his wants during a few months at Venice, he has sold all that remains.

'Of the jewels that he possessed very few remain, as the most valuable had been sacrificed in the well-known contribution to the French, our destructive plunderers; and with respect to his income, having suffered the loss of 48,000 Roman crowns annually by the French Revolution, the remainder was lost also by the fall of Rome; namely, the yearly sum of 10,000 crowns assigned him by the Apostolic Chamber, and also his particular funds in the Roman bank.

'The only income he has left is that of his benefices in Spain, which amount to 14,000 crowns; but this, as it is only payable in paper at present, is greatly reduced by the disadvantage of exchange, and even that has remained unpaid for more than a year, owing, perhaps, to the interrupted communications with that kingdom. But here it is necessary that I should add that the Cardinal is heavily burdened with the annual sum of 4,000 crowns for the dowry of the Countess of Albany, his sister-in-law; 3,000 crowns for the mother of his deceased niece, and 1,500 for divers annuities of his father and brother. Nor had he credit to supply the means of acquitting these obligations.

'This picture, nevertheless, which I present to your friendship, may well excite the compassion of every one who will reflect upon the high birth, the elevated dignity, and the advanced age of the Personage whose situation I now sketch in the plain language of truth, without resorting to the aid of eloquence. I will only intreat you to communicate it to those distinguished persons who have influence with your Government; persuaded as I am that English Magnanimity will not suffer an illustrious Personage of the same nation to perish in misery.

'But here I pause, not wishing to offend your natural delicacy

The Pension

which delights to act from its own generous disposition, rather than from the impulse and urgency of others . . .
'Your true friend and servant,
'STEFFANO, CARDINAL BORGIA.'

When this letter reached England Sir John Coxe Hippisley, assisted by Andrew Stuart of Castlemilk (who was the author of a book called *The Genealogical History of the Royal Stuarts* which he later presented to the Cardinal) at once got in touch with Dundas, afterwards Lord Melville, a Secretary of State, who placed it before Pitt, who as Chancellor of the Exchequer was the responsible Minister. On this occasion Pitt showed a little more generosity of character than he had displayed over the question of the jointure of Mary of Modena and brought the whole matter to the notice of the King. Meanwhile other Ministers, when they heard of the case, hastened to give it their warmest support. 'Sir John Coxe Hippisley', a Memorandum in the Braye MSS records 'had the pleasure to receive letters from the Duke of Portland, Lord Chatham, Lord Spencer, and Mr. Secretary Windham (all Ministers of State) strongly expressing their satisfaction in acquiescing in any measure that could offer relief to the illustrious and venerable Cardinal of York. It was sufficient that the knowledge of his sufferings should reach the Throne, to assure both sympathy and relief.'

Bearing in mind the considerable sum of one million five hundred thousand pounds which the Cardinal could legitimately claim from the British Government the reader may well find the spectacle of Cabinet Ministers congratulating themselves on their generosity with public money as a little wanting in sincerity, but in their defence it may be said that their action at least lacked something of the calculated cynicism of modern vote-catching politicians, for these Ministers had nothing to gain from their recommendations in favour of the last of the Stuarts for the simple reason that to the mass of the population his very existence had long been forgotten. Indeed, only a year or two later a bet was recorded in the wager book of Corpus Christi College, Oxford, as to whether the Cardinal of York were still alive. What Dons

The Cardinal King

doubted the general public could hardly be expected to know and the members of the British Cabinet could flatter themselves on a unique display of 'English Magnanimity' such as Cardinal Borgia's letter had urged upon them.

The information received by Sir John from these distinguished persons made him feel sufficiently optimistic of a favourable outcome to write to Cardinal Borgia on the progress of their plan and to arrange for a letter of credit to be sent to help the Cardinal of York in his immediate needs. The letter, with its post-script, was for some mysterious reason unsigned, and reached Venice just as the Cardinals were about to enclose themselves in the Conclave in which Cardinal York, as Sub-Dean of the Sacred College, would occupy a place of honour which his present reduced circumstances made it all the harder for him to sustain.

Londres, 22 Nov. 1799.

MONSEIGNEUR,

I have been hoping to be able to give your Eminence a final account of the success of our mission, but matters are too confused at this moment to allow of an immediate settlement. I am, however, persuaded that in a few days' time this interesting matter will be laid before the eyes of *the High Personage* from whom flows every grace; and I do not doubt but that the impartial sentiments of his high soul will prove propitious to our desires. I hope meanwhile that your Eminence will give all the consolation that is possible to your Illustrious Friend, and will try to prevent his being obliged to despoil himself of *the remainder* of the precious objects which have been for so many years in his family, and which have gained thereby a sentimental value that is higher than their intrinsic worth. I think I can promise in eight or ten days to give your Eminence news that we shall be able to ward off another similar catastrophe, and it will perhaps be as well during this interval for us to despatch under *your Eminence's name* a letter of credit for £500 sterling which will be sent by to-day's courier to Mr. Conrad Martens in Venice, and which your Eminence can acknowledge. I hope that by this arrangement, though a poor one, your Eminence will be able to stop for the time being the

The Pension

progress of these misfortunes which have afflicted your high mind for so long a space of time. Your Eminence will, of course, understand that this small sum—so inadequate to its real object—is only sent *per interim*, and in a private manner; but it often happens that a small sum promptly sent is worth more than a larger one sent later. *Bis qui cito dat.* I flatter myself in any case, Monseigneur, that I can soon give you news from London of a *settlement* which will not be unworthy of its interesting object, and I have no doubt as to the discreet and graceful manner whereby such an arrangement will be notified to the Personage in whose favour it will be made. Nobody better than your Eminence can render justice to the true motives which rule in this case, and nobody better than yourself can make it acceptable and pleasant to the sensitive soul of your Illustrious and respectable Colleague.

Nov. 26.

I have the satisfaction to inform your Eminence that a life-annuity, which will, I trust, be found adequate for the Personage for whose benefit it is intended, is shortly to be arranged. Of this your Eminence will be informed either through myself, or through another and worthier channel. I hope in a few days' time that £1,000 sterling will be remitted for the same object, either to your Eminence, or to your Illustrious Friend by another hand.

It must have caused great pleasure to Cardinal Borgia, armed with the assurances of success which this letter promised, to be able to tell his 'Illustrious and respectable Colleague' that help was coming to him from so unexpected a quarter; while the Cardinal of York himself, perplexed to know where his next penny was to come from, must have been deeply touched to learn of the kind efforts that his friends had been making on his behalf without his knowledge.

3

King George III, meanwhile, had been approached by Pitt and, after consulting with his son the Duke of Sussex (who had visited the Cardinal in Rome where, in April 1793, he had married Lady Augusta Murray in defiance of his father and the Royal Marriage

The Cardinal King

Act) gave his immediate consent for an annual pension of £4,000 to be awarded to his third cousin twice removed whose poverty deeply touched his generous heart. It was, indeed, not the first time that King George had shown an interest in the distant cousin who claimed to be the rightful holder of his kingly office. Mr. Coutts, the banker, who combined the office of court banker to the House of Hanover with a more than sentimental devotion to the exiled Stuarts, had enjoyed the unique privilege of being received very cordially by his two sovereigns, George III and Henry IX, and after describing his reception at Frascati to his king at Windsor had later sent an account of King George's audience to the other monarch in Italy. The Cardinal had presented Mr. Coutts with one of his 'Henry IX' medals, and this the banker later produced for the inspection of King George. 'He questioned me on the likeness,' the banker wrote in his report of this interview to the Cardinal, 'and said he was much pleased to have seen it, and imply'd that few he supposed would have mentioned the subject to him, but that they were much mistaken who imagined he did not very sincerely regard the family of Stuart, who were worthy of all good men's attention, were it only for their misfortune.' After expressing these sentiments which in his grandfather's reign would have ranked as downright Jacobitism, King George accepted from Mr. Coutts the medal which the latter had received at the hands of the Cardinal King.

The action of King George in granting a pension to the Cardinal of York was one of pure generosity entirely free from any motive other than the desire to relieve the sufferings of a distinguished and unfortunate prince. Of the negotiations about the jointure of Mary of Modena, which Pitt had refused to lay before him, it may be said that he probably knew little or nothing, and was unaware that the House of Stuart had any financial claims against the Government of Great Britain. He suffered from no twinge of conscience, as Queen Anne had done, in respect to the claims made by the kings over the water, regarding the Protestant Succession as his firm and undisputed title to the throne. Indeed it was the fear of an attack upon this principle, which his never very lucid mind saw in the movement for Catholic emancipation, that

The Pension

was soon to be one of the main causes for the overthrow, not of his throne, but of his reason. One cannot imagine either of his predecessors coming so speedily or so practically to the assistance of his rival claimant; of George III it may fairly be said that one cannot imagine him doing anything else.

4

The good news of the King of England's consent to a pension was at once communicated to Cardinal Borgia in a letter from Sir John Coxe Hippisley dated exactly four months after his original request for Borgia to write an account of his colleague's misfortunes designed for the eyes of the British Cabinet. Unlike the unofficial, unsigned note which the Cardinal had already received, this letter gave authoritative confirmation of the success of their benevolent plot.

'Although I was informed some time ago that Lord Minto, H.M. Envoy and Minister at Vienna, had received instructions from Lord Granville, Secretary of State for Foreign Affairs, concerning the matters about the object which is of such great interest to us, I have thought it best not to inform your Eminence thereof, until Mr. Pitt, as Chancellor of the Exchequer, had given me leave to communicate it to your Eminence. It is thus with very great satisfaction that I take up my pen . . . to tell you, Monseigneur, that Mr. Pitt has himself authorized us to inform your Eminence that Lord Minto has received definite orders to fulfil the object which we have so very much at heart. . . . It is my duty to tell your Eminence, that I may do the justice which is due to our Ministers, that neither Mr. (Andrew) Stuart nor I have doubted for a single moment as to the impression which your Eminence's letter would make on their feelings, and the goodness of heart of our august Sovereign is too well known for me to need to praise it.

'I have already made known to your Eminence the favourable views expressed by those of our Ministers who were in London when your letter reached me. They put on one side every consideration, however thorny and delicate, so as to regard only the misfortunes which appealed so strongly to their hearts.

The Cardinal King

'Your Eminence will be so good as to be the friendly channel for explaining to your illustrious colleague these steps in the most delicate way, and that most fitting to the sensitiveness of his disposition. He may always count with assurance on the tender interest which the British nation will take in his misfortunes, and that nation will never allow such a person to sink beneath the weight of distress which a faithless race has prepared for him in the height of its atrocity.'

When this letter reached Venice the Conclave was already in progress, but with the special consent of the Cardinal Dean the messenger was allowed to enter and acquaint their Eminences with the news he brought from London. It proved a pleasant diversion for the electors in this long and so far inconclusive conclave and the old Cardinal of York was deeply moved by the enthusiasm with which this welcome news was received. All the Cardinals were delighted to think that the troubles of their royal colleague were now over and thronged round pressing upon him their compliments and congratulations. To the Cardinal himself it was a moment of heart-felt emotion. 'It would be impossible for me to express to you all the satisfaction felt by this exalted person at the assurance which you give me as to the security of the annual pension which has been allotted to him . . .' Borgia replied to Sir John: 'My colleagues have learned of the British generosity towards the illustrious Cardinal of York, and have all applauded the nobility of this action, and have justly praised the national liberality and all those who have co-operated in the success of so interesting a matter.' It must have seemed quite dull for the members of the Sacred College, walled up in their island monastery, to return to the endless canvassing of *papabili* after this exciting interruption. The older Cardinals, no doubt, would recall that there had been no such diversion in their labours since the historic occasion when the Emperor Joseph II had invaded the Conclave that had elected Clement XIV when a mock election had been provided for his entertainment.

The Pension

5

Shortly after this a letter arrived by the hand of Charles Oakeley, Secretary to the British Embassy at Vienna, from the Earl of Minto, who was Ambassador there, to inform the Cardinal of York personally of his pension. It was the first direct intimation he had had about the subject on which so much secret negotiation had already taken place without his knowledge.

Vienna, 9 Feb. 1800.

MY LORD,

I have received the orders of His Majesty the King of Great Britain to remit to Your Eminence the sum of £2000 sterling, and to assure Your Eminence that you will cause him great pleasure by accepting this mark of interest and esteem. I have at the same time been commanded to communicate to Your Eminence His Majesty's intention to transmit from him a like sum of £2000 sterling in the month of July, should circumstances continue such as to make Your Eminence desire it.

I have therefore the honour to inform you that the sum of £2000 sterling has been placed at the house of Messrs. Coutts and Company, bankers, London, at the disposal of Your Eminence. In carrying out the commands of the King my Master, I trust that Your Eminence will believe me to be infinitely alive to the honour of being the agent for the noble and touching sentiments that have dictated to His Majesty the mission on which he has deigned to employ me: sentiments that have been inspired in him as much by his own virtues and by the high qualities of the August Personage who is the object of his bounty, as by his wish to repair in every way possible the disasters by which the Universal Scourge of our times seems desirous of destroying by preference all that is most worthy of veneration and respect.

I beg Your Eminence to accept the assurance both of my respected homage and of the profound Veneration with which I have the honour to be Your Eminence's very humble and very obedient Servant,

MINTO,
Env. Ex. & Min. Plen, de S.M.B.
à la Cour de Vienne.

The Cardinal King

Having at last been addressed directly in this matter which concerned him so closely the Cardinal was now able to write himself to express his gratitude for all that had been done. Gone indeed were the days when any reference to the King of Great Britain, such as that in the opening phrase of Lord Minto's letter, could have come under his gaze without a spirited protest; even the omission of Royal Highness is now accepted with a good grace by the sincerely grateful old Cardinal. The letter which he addressed to Lord Minto shows by its quaint phraseology that though able to express himself clearly enough in his native language (for he answered in English to the letter which the Ambassador inscribed to him in French) his command of idiom was strange and sometimes archaic.

Venice, February 26th, 1800.

With the arrival of Mr. Oakeley, who has been this morning with me, I have received by his discourse, and much more by your letter, so many Tokens of your regard, singular Consideration, and attention for my Person, that oblige me to abandon all sort of ceremony, and to begin abruptly to assure you, My Dear Lord, that your letter has been most acceptable to me in all shapes and regards. I did not in the least doubt of the noble way of thinking of your generous and beneficent Sovereign; but I did not expect to see in writing so many and so obliging expressions that, well calculated by the Persons who receive them and understand their force, impressed in their minds a lively sense of tenderness and gratitude which, I own to you, obliges me more than the generosity spontaneously imparted.

I am in reality at a loss to express in writing all the sentiments of my heart, and for that reason leave it entirely to the interest that you take in all that regards my Person to make it known in an energetical and convenient manner all I fain would say to express my thankfulness which may easily be by you comprehended after having perused the contents of this letter.

I am obliged to you to have indicated to me the way I may write unto Coutts the Court Banker, and shall follow your friendly insinuations. In the meantime I am very desirous that you should

The Pension

be convinced on my sentiments of sincere esteem and friendship with which, My dear lord, with all my heart I embrace you,

HENRY, *Cardinal.*

His reference to Lord Minto's 'generous and beneficent Sovereign' shows that the Cardinal had no hesitation in recognizing the kind intentions of King George III in the affair. For this he was not always given credit, for Joseph Forsyth, whom the Cardinal later received hospitably after his return to Frascati, when commenting on the pension in his *Remarks on Antiquities, Arts, and Letters during an Excursion in Italy,* writes inaccurately of this correspondence that 'York, while he acknowledges in bad English the obligation conferred on him, studiously avoids any mention of his Majesty.' The Cardinal, in fact, had no scruple in expressing his thanks for the kind action of the King. It was, indeed, a new experience for him to be receiving charity instead of dispensing it, for no one was more generous than he was when he had money at his disposal. As an article in the *Annual Register* for the year of his death records: 'His purse was always open to suffering humanity; and British travellers particularly, when ruined by misfortune or by imprudence, found in him, on all occasions, a compassionate benefactor.' A person accustomed to act the benefactor does not always find it easy to return thanks gracefully when he finds himself in the position of the needy. Cardinal York, for all the 'sensitiveness of soul' he displayed, found no difficulty or reluctance in returning thanks for the very welcome help extended to him by the man whom he could never consider as being more than the Elector of Hanover.

Having written to Lord Minto the Cardinal then sent a long and cordial letter to Sir John Coxe Hippisley showing the deep sense of obligation he felt towards him as the originator of the whole plan that had now reached so happy a conclusion. He begins by thanking Sir John for 'the cordial interest you take in all that regards my Person', adding that he was happy to acknowledge 'that I principally owe to your friendly efforts, and to those of your friends, the succour generously granted to relieve the extreme necessities into which I have been driven by the present dismal circumstances.' He then goes on to describe the arrival of Mr. Oakeley with Lord Minto's letter which was 'written in so extremely obliging and genteel a manner, and with expressions of singular regard and consideration for me, that, I assure you, excited in me most particular and lively sentiments, not only of satisfaction for the delicacy with which the affair had been managed, but also of gratitude for the generosity with which it has been provided for my necessity.'

'I own to you [the Cardinal continues] that the succour granted to me could not be more timely, for, without it, it would have been impossible for me to subsist on account of the absolutely irreparable loss of all my income, the very funds being also destroyed; so that I would otherwise have been reduced during the short remainder of my life to languish in misery and indigence. I would not lose a moment's time to apprize you of all this, and am very certain that your experimented good heart will find proper means to make known in an energetical and proper manner these sentiments of grateful acknowledgement.

'The signal obligations I am under to Mr. Andrew Stuart for all that he has, with so much cordiality on this occasion, done to assist me, render it for me indispensable to devise, that you may return him my sincerest thanks, assuring him that his health and welfare interest me extremely: and that I have with great pleasure received from Gen. Acton the genealogical history of our family, which he was so kind as to send me; I hope that he will, from that gentleman, have already received my thanks for so valuable a proof of his attention for me.

'In the last place, if you think proper, and an occasion should offer itself, I beg you make known to the other gentlemen also who have co-operated my most grateful acknowledgements; with which, my dear Sir John, with all my heart I embrace you.

'Your best of Friends,

'HENRY, *Cardinal.*'

To this touching letter Sir John replied assuring the Cardinal that 'severe as have been your Eminence's sufferings, they will nevertheless find some alleviation in the general sympathy of the

The Pension

British nation: with all distinction of parties, with all differences of communion, among all conditions of men, but one voice is heard: all breathe one applauding sentiment: all bless the gracious act of the Sovereign in favour of his illustrious but unfortunate relation.' These moving lines could not go unanswered, and again the Cardinal wrote to express his gratitude for the 'benevolent conduct of your Ministers, your gracious Sovereign's noble and spontaneous generosity.' His mind, he said, was full of the most lively sensations of tenderness and heartfelt gratitude. 'What return', he asked, 'can I make for so many and so signal proofs of disinterested benevolence? Dear Sir John! I confess I am at a loss how to express my feelings.'

6

In the middle of all these rejoicings a slight hitch occurred which occasioned a letter from Lord Minto to Hippisley and Andrew Stuart. In his original instructions from Lord Granville the British Ambassador at Vienna had only been authorized to make two payments, and he now wrote to say that he could make no further advances until more specific authority was received from England.

'If his Eminence has already received the sum I now allude to [Lord Minto wrote] I am concerned to acquaint you that my powers are entirely exhausted. These powers were not only so precise, but were given to me so formally (by the King's sign manual), that there is no room for any latitude in their interpretation, and a fresh authority will be indispensable for carrying on the payments. It appears, indeed, so clear that his Majesty's intention was to extend this bounty during the continuance of those necessities which gave occasion to it, that I cannot think anything will be risked by an application for the subsequent payments or even by the request suggested by his Eminence that they may be put on some regular and permanent arrangement which may save this old and venerable personage from the inconvenience, as well as the anxiety of uncertainty, and purge this noble and beneficent act of every hesitation or modification that could diminish its lustre.'

The Cardinal King

All, however, ended happily, and on the 30th March 1801 Sir John heard from Lord Hawkesbury to the effect that 'care will be taken that future payments of the allowance to the Cardinal of York shall be regularly made.'

Thus, on this highly satisfactory note, ended the only successful negotiation that had ever taken place between the exiled House of Stuart and the British Government since the deposition of James II in December 1688. It is not surprising that so unusual an episode should have resulted in congratulations on all sides. The cordial reception by the College of Cardinals of this singular piece of good fortune to one of their most distinguished and venerable members has already been described. In England the news was received with equal pleasure. The *Times* newspaper having depicted the life of the aged Cardinal as 'placid, humane and temperate', went on to tell how 'the malign influence of the star which had so strongly marked the fate of so many of his illustrious ancestors was not exhausted' and told the story of the disasters which had brought poverty and distress to this last member of the Royal House. The newspaper then expressed its warmest approval of the pension which would now help to soften the many misfortunes which the Cardinal had to bear. It only remained for the Muse of minor poetry to set the seal on this happy occasion, and as usual the Muse was not slow to oblige.

> *Illustrious Isle, fair Freedom's last retreat!*
> *The Throne of Honour! pure religion's seat!*
> *Object of Europe's envy and her hate!*
> *Still shalt thou stand among the nations great;*
> *Still shall the persecuted Stranger find*
> *Thy happy shores the refuge of Mankind!*
> *And the* last Prince of Darnley's House *shall own*
> *His debt of gratitude to* Brunswick's Throne!

12

The End of a Dynasty

I

The improved state of international affairs and the French First Consul's desire for better relations with the Holy See made it possible for the Cardinal of York to start on his journey back to Rome shortly after Pius VII had been elected. But even before he began this long journey he sent instructions to the Chancellor of his diocese ordering various measures to be taken for the welfare of the flock from which he had been separated for so long. His renewed financial security, thanks to the pension from George III, enabled him also to give directions for the palace to be prepared for his return. After being plundered by the French and standing empty for so long a time the old fortress of La Rocca was badly in need of refurbishing and repair, and this was undertaken with little regard for the reduced circumstances of the Cardinal, for despite the pension he was still very much poorer than he had been before the Revolution. The palace was almost entirely refurnished, six new beds were installed, and five new carriages, twelve horses and two mules were purchased. At Rome the Cardinal's suite on the second floor of the Palazzo della Cancelleria was also splendidly refurnished in readiness for his return.

In the course of his journey, which the aged Cardinal took by easy stages, he stayed for a few days at Siena where he was the guest of the Archpriest. News of his expected arrival there had somehow reached the ears of Louise of Albany, who was then living at Florence, still in the company of Vittorio Alfieri. The thought of this elderly invalid did not give rise to any charitable ideas in the shallow mind of his sister-in-law, nor did his poverty which was to some extent due to the dowry he paid her out of his greatly reduced income, suggest to her anything but a subject for ridicule. Only rich relations were of any use to Louise. In a letter of unusual malice, which in her circle passed for wit, she wrote a vicious account of the poor Cardinal to her friend Teresa Mocenni which has survived to give us a true picture of the petty nature of the Countess rather than to belittle, as it was intended to, the character of her brother-in-law.

'I write to warn the good Archpriest that the Cardinal of York is going to settle at Siena. It will be very pleasant for the poor Archpriest who will be ruined if he has to keep this incubus for any length of time in his palace. . . . He is very whimsical and very dull, and he bores everyone he meets. When he was on the open sea he wanted to have the ship stopped at his pleasure, as if such a thing were possible! He belongs to a race of amphibious creatures who are intended to be seen from a distance, but whom an evil chance has brought close to our eyes. All that class would appear similar if one had to live with any one of them, as in the case of that stage-figure, my brother-in-law.'

Louise of Albany, queening it over her admiring circle at Florence, could afford to jeer at her distinguished relation and make fun of his recent sufferings, for as well as the money which she still expected to receive from his pocket she too had managed to secure a pension from England. But this did not prevent her, at a later date, when news of the Cardinal's illness in 1804 reached her, from rushing to Rome with all speed not, as might be thought, to enquire after the health of her brother-in-law, but to arrange with Cesarini for the continued payment of her dowry in the event of his death.

After resting for some time at Siena the Cardinal continued his journey, ignorant of the vituperation with which Louise had hailed his arrival there, and eagerly looking forward to the prospect of returning once again to his beloved Frascati. He reached Rome on the 25th of June, 1800, and made his way in triumph to the Palace of the Cancelleria.

The End of a Dynasty

2

The return of the Cardinal King to his palace was made the occasion for a public demonstration. The provisional government which had been set up pending the election of a Pope and which continued in office until Pius VII arrived in July had not particularly endeared itself to the people owing to its unwise policy of revenging itself on the former rulers of the city; and so any event which heralded the return of the Pope was greeted with acclaim, if only because it meant that the days of the provisional government were numbered. Thus large crowds turned out to cheer the Cardinal of York's coach as it passed along the Corso, while his arrival at the Cancelleria was greeted by the gay music of a military band. As he stepped down from the coach members of his household rushed forward to kiss his hand and tears were shed on all sides as the Vice-Chancellor of the Holy Roman Church took possession of his Palace after his years of exile.

But dearer to his heart than these noisy and emotional greetings was the welcome of the masses of the people who, remembering his charity and benevolence, hailed him as the Protector of the Poor. Such a tribute as this was one which the Cardinal valued above all others as he had shown on that occasion when he had been rebuked for not quitting the ecclesiastical state and providing heirs for his royal House. The angry Cardinal had indicated the poor of Frascati and those whom he had saved from a life of sin and replied that they were his true heirs and that he desired no others. This incident, which has already been referred to, is important because it shows the true character of the priest behind the often worldly-seeming appearance of the prince and answers those critics who had once accused him of entering the Church merely for the revenues and position which his rank would assure for him as a member of the Roman curia.

But warm as was his reception in Rome it was to Frascati that the Cardinal longed to return, and after dinner and a short rest, he set out on the familiar road towards the Alban hills two hours before sunset.

The Cardinal King

Here again the people gave their returning Bishop a splendid welcome. 'His entry into Frascati', records the *Diario*, 'was a true triumph for His Royal Highness, since the joy and show of affection that every class of person manifested proved to him how distasteful to his people had been the long absence of their loving Father, whom this day they saw with delight returning to their midst.' Once again the brass bands brazened out their marches as the Cardinal drove through the shouting crowds that thronged the narrow streets. Everywhere he was greeted by illuminations, cheers, and the ringing of bells as the people pressed on him from all sides to receive his blessing. When the palace was at last reached he found the clergy and leading citizens standing ready to receive him; all, that is, except for Canon Arini, for this worthy professor of theology and equality who had been so eloquent in denouncing the Cardinal-bishop and urging the people to plant a Tree of Liberty on their broad and pleasant hillside had very prudently run away into hiding after being deprived of all his offices and threatened with much worse should he ever be caught.

3

Almost at once the Cardinal had to return to Rome to take part in the preparations for the arrival of Pius VII in his capital, but after the Pope's triumphal entry into Rome, and the ceremonies that welcomed him had been completed, the Cardinal withdrew again to Frascati where he hoped to pass his remaining years in peace and semi-retirement.

His income, for all the help he received from England, was still very much less than it had been before the revolution, but this did not prevent the Cardinal from continuing to live in considerable state. He began again to entertain as lavishly as before and was as generous as ever in the gifts he showered on his friends and the alms he gave to the poor. When the Pope bestowed the Red Hat on Consalvi and made him Secretary of State the Cardinal of York marked the occasion by presenting his protégé with a carriage.

The new Pope, now that he was installed in his capital, was

The End of a Dynasty

especially eager to show some particular mark of respect to the royal Cardinal, not only as the last representative of his House but also as one of the oldest and most distinguished members of the Sacred College. In fulfilment of this desire he decided on the unprecedented course of paying an informal visit upon the Cardinal at his palace at Frascati. The Cardinal's cousin and heir, Charles Emmanuel IV, King of Sardinia, was also in Rome at the time and as he also wished to congratulate the Cardinal King on his safe return from exile, both Pope and King travelled out to Frascati together.

Henry Benedict Stuart and Charles Emmanuel of Savoy had more than a family relationship in common for both were deeply religious men who counted their faith above their royal blood. The reason for the presence of the King of Sardinia in Rome was not merely because he wished to pay his respects to his Stuart cousin at Frascati but because, like Henry, he wanted to follow a religious vocation. Shortly after his visit to Frascati he abdicated in favour of his brother, Victor Emmanuel I, and later was ordained to the priesthood. It would probably have surprised that canny Scotsman, King James VI & I, had he known that of these two descendants of his one would become a priest because he saw no chance of becoming a king while the other would renounce a kingdom for the sake of becoming a priest. It certainly would never have occurred to the author of the dictum 'No bishop, no king,' that the last representative of his House would be both king and bishop, and that if England did not recognize him as king it was equally certain that the Cardinal of York would not have recognized his ancestor's prelates as bishops.

Though the visit of Pius VII and Charles Emmanuel IV was supposed to be impromptu the Cardinal heard of it in time to be ready to meet the Papal procession some miles outside the town where he waited with three gala coaches. As the papal equipage came into sight the Cardinal got down from his carriage and went to meet the Pope on foot. It was now that Pius, with a charming gesture, was able to demonstrate his respect for the aged host who, with difficulty resulting from his lame leg, now knelt at his feet. Alighting from his own coach he embraced the Cardinal cordially

The Cardinal King

and leading him back to the papal carriage insisted that Henry Stuart should sit next to him, an honour that was only accorded to crowned heads. The significance of this gracious act was not lost on the Cardinal King.

The procession then continued up the steep hill and at the entrance to the town the keys were formally presented to the Pope. Charles Emmanuel, meanwhile, had gone on ahead and received the Pope at the Cathedral where, as a mark of homage, he fell on his knees to kiss the papal slipper. Edified by this spectacle of what they now no doubt considered to be the proper relationship between the spiritual and the temporal power, the people of Frascati, all thoughts of Trees of Liberty safely banished from their minds, saw their venerable bishop lead the Sovereign Pontiff and the King of Sardinia to the Seminary, the great pride of his heart and the chief monument of his episcopacy, where he showed them round his famous library, producing from the shelves rare manuscripts and ancient codices for the Pope and King to admire. It was the crowning moment of Henry Stuart's reign as Bishop of Frascati and set the seal on his triumphant return to his flock after fleeing from the perils of revolution.

On leaving the Seminary the distinguished party went to the house of Monsignor Cesarini, the Cardinal's devoted secretary whom the Pope was soon to consecrate, at Henry Stuart's special request, as titular Bishop of Milevi, and here they were offered refreshments. Finally a great banquet was held at the palace of La Rocca where Henry was able to lavish all his skill as a host on the unique privilege of entertaining the supreme Head of the Church as well as the Sovereign of Italy's chief independent Kingdom. The Pope sat at the head of the table with the Cardinal King on one side of him and Charles Emmanuel on the other. When the banquet was over and the time came for the Pope to begin his journey back to Rome, Henry accompanied him to the outskirts of the town. So the visit came to an end; it was a great moment in the history of the palace and of the town, and the people of Frascati shared in the delight of their bishop at the honour that was done him.

The next day the Cardinal of York sent his chamberlain to

The End of a Dynasty

enquire after the Pope's safe return and the following Sunday, despite his great age (for this visit took place in 1802 when he was seventy-seven years old), the Cardinal himself drove into Rome to offer his thanks in person at the Apostolic Palace. On his return to Frascati he ordered a marble tablet to be placed in La Rocca recording in a Latin inscription the great occasion of the Pope's visit.

4

News from the outside world occasionally brought back memories of earlier days to the old Cardinal as he passed his last years quietly at Frascati surrounded by his little court and the works of art, books and manuscripts which he had started to collect again now that he was restored to his old home and to some of his former riches.

In 1802 he heard of the death of the Countess of Alberstrof, better known as Clementina Walkinshaw. She died at Fribourg in Switzerland where she had gone to seek refuge from the revolution. To the end she had received a small annuity from the Cardinal which he had managed to provide even during the years of his own poverty, but despite this help she must have been reduced to very straightened circumstances for her whole estate at the time of her death amounted to no more than twelve pounds, six silver spoons, a work on geography, three books of devotion, and a small gold box. The Cardinal, who had always deplored his brother's relationship with her and whose only contact with her had been during her unwelcome visit to Rome at the time of Prince Charles's marriage, can hardly have felt any personal regrets at the news of the death of this lonely old woman.

Another death of more interest to the Cardinal took place on the 8th of October, 1803, when Count Vittorio Alfieri ended his eventful life in Florence at the age of fifty-four. His last years had been spent in learning the Greek language, a task which had not been made any easier for him by his rapidly declining health. To reward himself for this labour he had instituted an Order of Homer the insignia of which was to be a gold collar of his own design, and of this interesting Order he became the one and only member.

The Cardinal King

His death caused Louise to cry out: 'I am now alone in the world. I have lost all, consolation, support, society, all—all!' This was something of an overstatement. Some time before the great poet died the Countess of Albany had met a young French painter called François Xavier Fabre, then unknown to fame. He became a frequent visitor at Alfieri's palace on the Lungarno where he painted the lovers' portraits both separately and together. Already there had been a certain amount of gossip about the keen interest shown by the princess in the work of the painter, and it was hinted that her interest in him was not entirely confined to matters of art. No one, therefore, was particularly surprised when Louise, who had so recently lost all in the death of Alfieri, installed François Xavier Fabre in his place only a few months after the former had died. Louise was then fifty-one; the painter thirty-seven. He was to remain with her until she died in 1824 when he inherited all her possessions including many Stuart relics. Fabre's portrait of Alfieri, which now hangs in the Uffizi Galleries in Florence, is possibly unique in being the picture of a lover painted by the man who was destined to succeed him in the arms of his mistress.

The Cardinal must have known very little about his sister-in-law's mode of life during the years of her second residence in Florence. They had long ceased to communicate. He had, however, no wish to bear malice for the shabby treatment he had received from her at the time of her separation from Prince Charles, and when he died he bequeathed her a watch and a picture in his will.

5

The last of the Stuarts had now become something of a legend and British travellers of all ranks came to see him when they visited Rome or happened to pass through Frascati. The revolutionary wars had made foreign visitors—other than unwelcome invaders—rare in Italy, but after the Peace of Amiens the Cardinal again found himself acting as host to travellers from the distant kingdom whose crown he claimed to wear. Fortunately some of the people who enjoyed his hospitality at the Palace of La

The End of a Dynasty

Rocca left accounts of the Cardinal King as they saw him in the last years of his life.

Not the least interesting of these visitors was Valentine Lawless, second Lord Cloncurry, who was travelling in Italy after a period spent as a guest of King George III, not, as one might imagine, at Windsor Castle or St. James's, but in the Tower of London, where he had been serving a sentence of imprisonment for taking too active a part in the inflammatory politics of his native Ireland. This Irish patriot was all the more welcome at Frascati where he went out of his way to flatter the old Cardinal whose hospitality he found a good deal more entertaining than King George's.

Lord Cloncurry soon became a favourite with the Cardinal 'probably', as he blandly remarks in his *Personal Recollections*, 'by virtue of addressing him as "Majesty", and thus going a step farther than the Duke of Sussex, who was on familiar terms with him, and always applied to him the style of Royal Highness.'

According to Cloncurry, whose visit took place in 1803, the Cardinal was now in fairly affluent circumstances again, his income being in the neighbourhood of eight or nine thousand pounds a year, the remainder over and above his pension coming from his ecclesiastical benefices. 'The revenue was then, in Italy, equivalent at least to £20,000,' he continues, 'and it enabled his Eminence to assume somewhat of royal state.' He then goes on to describe the manner of life lived in the bishop's palace at Frascati where he was often a guest.

'He was waited upon with all suitable ceremony, and his equipages were numerous and splendid, and freely placed at the disposal of his guests. He was in the habit of receiving visitors very hospitably at his villa at Frascati where I was often a guest, and was frequently amused by a reproduction of the scenes between Sancho Panza and his physician, during the reign of the squire in the island of Barataria. His Eminence was an invalid, and under a strict regimen; but as he still retained his taste for savoury meats, a contest usually took place between him and his servants for the possession of each rich dish which they formally set before him, and then endeavoured to snatch away, while he, with greater eagerness, strove to seize it in its transit. Among the Cardinal's most favourite attendants, was a miserable cur dog, which, having probably been cast off by its master, being neither useful nor ornamental, one day attached itself to his Eminence at the gate of St. Peter's, an occurrence to which he constantly referred, as a proof of his true royal blood—the cur being, as he supposed, a King Charles spaniel, and, therefore, endowed with an instinctive, hereditary acquaintance with the house of Stuart. Upon the occasion of my visit to Frascati, I presented the Cardinal with a telescope, which he seemed to fancy, and received from him, in return, the large medal struck in honour of his accession to his unsubstantial throne.'

At about the same time as Lord Cloncurry's visit the Cardinal received Joseph Forsyth, the antiquarian, who was then making the tour of Italy which was later to provide the material for his *Remarks on Antiquities, Arts, and Letters* to which reference has already been made. 'I was introduced to Cardinal York by an Irish gentleman residing at Rome,' he tells us. 'When my name and country were announced, he said he had heard of second sight in Scotland, but never of Foresight, and this poor joke drew a laugh from all that understood English, which his Holiness [*sic*] talks pretty well for a foreigner.' If this rather pompous Scotsman's dignity was offended by the Cardinal's harmless joke amends were soon made, for the Irish gentleman who had brought about the introduction explained that Forsyth's grandfather had fallen in the Stuart cause, upon receiving which information the Cardinal could not hide his feelings: 'the recollection of that cause drew a tear into his eye, an emotion to which he is very subject.' The Cardinal, according to Forsyth, 'says little, and in that little there is nothing', but one cannot help thinking that the Cardinal very probably found conversation rather an arid undertaking in the presence of this erudite but mirthless Caledonian when compared to the garrulous and flattering Irish peer.

Forsyth noted that the Cardinal stooped a good deal and walked with difficulty on account of his bad leg, but the other limb had 'still the first shape of his great uncle Charles II's.' Though then seventy-seven or eight years old his face was still handsome and

The End of a Dynasty

showed little sign of his age, having few wrinkles except on the forehead. The dog which Lord Cloncurry had seen was still in evidence, for it was brought in after dinner and allowed to play on the table where it performed a few tricks while the host remarked 'very significantly' to his guest: 'This is a King Charles's dog.' Henry certainly seems to have been lavish in his entertainment of the visitor, for he ordered his Master of the Horse—'a polite young man'—to show Forsyth round the different villas of Frascati, placing a carriage and four at his disposal for the purpose.

'On our return to the Rocca [Forsyth writes] we found a numerous company convened for dinner, a Neapolitan duke, several Roman noblemen, a bishop and a few prelates. I owed to my poor grandfather a distinction not due to me. I sat next to His Royal Highness at table, and of the little that was said, the greater part was addressed to me. I could perceive at dinner a residue of royal state. There was a space between him and us sufficient for another cover. After a pause in the conversation, none began till he spoke. He had a salt-cellar to himself; but it was stoneware, and the rest silver; he had his own soup; but it was served in a porringer, and ours in a tureen. There was a distinction even in his coffee-cup and saucer; but they were of a much inferior china to ours.'

He goes on to tell of the visits of the Duke of Sussex, to which Cloncurry also referred, adding that the two princes 'Royal Highnessed' each other incessantly. There is something rather delightful in the thought of George III's son and the old Stuart prince exchanging these courtesies and compliments.

Cloncurry and Forsyth, the Irish nobleman and the Scots scholar, who have left us these intimate glimpses of the life of the aged Henry IX, had one other experience which they shared in common; both passed part of their lives as political prisoners. Cloncurry, as we have seen, had not long been released from the Tower of London when he arrived in Italy. Forsyth was to be arrested shortly after his visit to Frascati. When hostilities again broke out between England and France General Bonaparte ordered the arrest of all Englishmen at large in his dominions. Forsyth was apprehended at Turin on May 25th, 1803. Cloncurry

The Cardinal King

had only served two years in the Tower but the unfortunate antiquarian was not released until April 1814. It was during his years as a prisoner of war that he wrote his book on Italy which contains the account of his visit to the Cardinal of York.

6

In September 1803 another death not only removed one of the Cardinal of York's oldest friends but was responsible for his advancement to the first place in the hierarchy of the Catholic Church after that of the Vicar of Christ himself. This promotion resulted from the death of Cardinal Giovanni Francesco Albani who had been a friend of Henry Stuart since he had first joined the Sacred College. With the death of Albani the Cardinal of York, who had been a Cardinal for fifty-six years, became the senior member of the Cardinalate and thus succeeded to the office of Dean of the Sacred College.

While the old man must have been pleased to take first place after the Pope his succession as Dean brought about one change which caused him a pang of real sorrow, for by tradition the Cardinal Dean was always Bishop of Ostia and Velletri, and so, after forty-two years as Bishop of Frascati, he was compelled to resign from the position which had probably brought him greater pleasure than any other of the high appointments which he had held. But while it was necessary for him to resign his See the Cardinal, who was not far off his eightieth year, felt that he could not leave the town which had been his home for almost half a century and take up residence in some strange place. And so, with the approval of Pius VII and the glad consent of Cardinal Doria, who succeeded him as Bishop of Frascati, he was allowed to remain in possession of the Palace of La Rocca until the time of his death.

But if he was to continue living at Frascati the people of Velletri were not to be done out of a pageant to welcome their new royal bishop when he came to take possession of the See on the 20th of November, 1803. In their enthusiasm at having a king as their bishop they had actually added the name of an additional kingdom to the list of those to which the Cardinal King laid claim, hailing

The End of a Dynasty

him as the 'sole surviving son and heir of the unconquered and immortal James III, King of Great Britain, of Scotland and of Jerusalem, and valiant Defender of the Catholic Faith.' The omission of Ireland from this galaxy of western and oriental kingdoms was to be remedied later in the day.

The Cardinal entered his new diocese under a triumphal arch, and after the religious ceremonies were over and the inevitable banquet consumed, a mock tournament was held in his honour in the piazza of the town. As darkness fell lanterns were lighted all over the town and these were seen to have the royal arms of Great Britain painted on their glass windows. Finally a great set-piece of fireworks rising ninety feet into the air was set off in honour of the Bishop. As this burst into a thousand flashing stars and glittering sparks the delighted spectators saw appear at the very top of it the figure of a cherub playing upon a harp over which hovered and shimmered a royal crown outlined in dazzling lights. It was the harp of Ireland as it appeared (without the attentive cherub) in his Royal Highness's coat-of-arms. The Cardinal sat on a balcony surrounded by his friends to watch the display, and warmly applauded the appearance of this heraldic emblem of the country where his grandfather had fought his last battle.

Exhausted by the festivities in his honour the Cardinal was too tired to receive the many deputations or to reply in person to the addresses of welcome, and these duties were undertaken by Monsignor Cesarini, who now rarely left his master's side. After ten days spent at Velletri the Cardinal returned once more to Frascati.

7

About the time that he became Dean of the Sacred College the Cardinal of York received a visit from a German nun who was to recall her meeting with 'Henry of England' many years later when, in extreme old age, she passed her last years in a French convent.

This woman's mother had come to France in the entourage of Marie Antoinette, and she herself, as a young girl, had been the intimate of the tragic Dauphin (Louis XVII) and Madame Royale, later Duchesse d'Angoulême. When the revolution broke out this

The Cardinal King

girl had been separated from the Royal Family, and after many adventures had found refuge in a convent in northern France where her aunt was the Superior. Later on, having made her profession as a member of the community, she came over to England with them when conditions in France grew worse. In England the nuns settled near Portsmouth and while living there Sister Louise, as the nun was called, was brought to the notice of George III as having been a friend of the unfortunate Royal Family of France.

When King George visited Portsmouth for a naval review he expressed a wish to meet the nun and 'with fear and trembling' she was led into his presence.

'I could not speak English fluently, and wondered if his Majesty could speak French. I was conveyed to the hotel where the King and Queen were staying, and was at once taken to the royal presence. In my early days I had been so accustomed to the pomp and luxury of the French Court, the beautiful Queen, the smart pages, the gorgeous dresses of the household, and the splendour of the royal apartments, that on first going into the room I could not believe it was a royal apartment and that the homely couple sitting side by side on a horsehair sofa were the Sovereigns of a mighty and powerful kingdom. Afterwards it was explained to me that this apartment was only a private sitting-room in the hotel, and that they had only come down for the night to review the fleet.'

The King greeted Sister Louise with his customary affability and presented her to the Queen. 'The royal French was very bad,' the nun noted, 'both had a strong German accent, and the King spoke with a sort of hesitation or stammer which, I was told, always became worse when he attempted to speak French.' So, turning to the Queen, Sister Louise admitted that she could speak German, which greatly surprised both the King and his Consort, who asked if she was of German nationality. To this question she replied, rather pertly, that nuns had no nationality. However, in spite of the 'fear and trembling' with which she had been ushered into the royal presence the kindness of the King and Queen soon put her at her ease, and by the end of the interview she was full of

The End of a Dynasty

enthusiasm and admiration, having answered their many questions about the Royal Family and the situation in France.

'The King was an ugly man [she wrote] with a red face, and a loud voice which seemed to get louder as he became interested in his subject. All his hesitation went after a time.

'Both he and the Queen were *bourgeois*; she was essentially German looking, whilst the King was a regular Englishman in appearance. They seemed a devoted couple, always appealing to each other, and the King was full of little attentions to his consort —even stooping to pick up the pocket-handkerchief which she had dropped.'

When this audience ended Sister Louise returned to her convent thinking that her contacts with the English Royal Family were over. But she was destined, in a few years' time, to find herself in the presence of another King of England under very different circumstances from those that had brought her into the presence of King George.

When conditions again made continental travel possible Sister Louise and the Abbess were sent by their convent to Rome, where they had to take certain relics, and while there Sister Louise was presented to the Cardinal of York. No doubt the Cardinal, hearing that the nuns had come from England, had arranged the meeting, for Sister Louise had no idea who he was. After hearing an account of her reception by King George, 'to my surprise', she says, 'the Cardinal then asked me if I knew that he himself was the rightful King of England, Henry IX.' The nun, who did not know this, replied at once: 'Monseigneur, you look like a King!' showing that she had learnt a little more tact since she had snubbed George III on the question of her nationality. She then knelt down to kiss his outstretched hand. 'He gave me an audience of quite an hour,' she adds, 'talking incessantly, like his cousin King George; but while King George had made me sit down in the royal presence, the Cardinal never once thought of offering me a seat.' However, she seems to have felt something of the Stuart charm which the Cardinal was still able to show to his visitors.

'My whole heart seemed to have gone out to the royal Cardinal; he was so handsome and saintly-looking. He was more excited

The Cardinal King

by hearing about my interview with King George than by hearing of the royal family of France, and I had to repeat to him over and over again all King George had said to me. I told him that King George gave me the idea of being a thoroughly good and honest King; in fact, if I had seen more of him, he would almost have inspired me with affection, but that his personal appearance, abrupt manners, and hesitation of speech would never inspire me with feelings of enthusiasm.'

Nevertheless her account of George III may have sounded a little too enthusiastic for the ears of Henry IX, for when she had referred to him the Cardinal had turned to his chaplain 'with a cold smile' and remarked: 'She means the Elector of Hanover.' Memories of Pope Pius VI's recognition of the *de facto* King still hurt his pride in spite of all that had happened in the meantime.

At the end of the audience Sister Louise knelt once more to receive the Cardinal's blessing. 'You have been received by Henry of England,' he told her. Before she left Rome she was to see him once more.

'I only saw him once again, and that was at a grand procession held at St. Peter's at Rome when the Pope entered, surrounded by his Cardinals. First and foremost among them, with a far-away look in his eyes, was Henry of York. He was much loved and respected in Rome. People said that he had no ambition to be King of England, preferring to be a Cardinal in Rome. He knew that it was hopeless to try to bring back England to his own faith, and he had the greatest horror of blood being shed for him. He often came to see the Lady Abbess, and very often talked with her about England; she told him how few and far between the Roman Catholics were, how England was Protestant to the backbone, and that the only way for him to regain his throne was to deny the faith of his fathers—a course which was simply impossible. Of all the Stuarts he was the most devoted adherent to the Church.'

He had not, Sister Louise considered, the physique of his brother Prince Charles, 'but with the exception of the martyr King, Charles I, he seems to have been the most refined-looking of all that line of Princes.'

The End of a Dynasty

8

It was very possibly the occasion of the feast of St. Peter and St. Paul in 1804 when Sister Louise saw the Cardinal of York entering St. Peter's in procession 'with a far-away look in his eyes'. He received the Pope at the head of the College of Cardinals when the Pontiff arrived at the Vatican Basilica from the Quirinal palace, and headed the procession up the vast church to the foot of the pontifical throne. Henry Stuart always enjoyed these splendid ecclesiastical ceremonies and despite the fact that he had entered his eightieth year he still insisted on attending the more important church festivals in St. Peter's despite the efforts of the members of his household to persuade him not to over-tax his failing strength. Certainly on this day in 1804 he would have been wise to have listened to their advice for the long rite of the pontifical High Mass proved to be too much for him and before it was over he was compelled to retire to the sacristy in a fainting condition.

When the Mass was over the Pope himself came to enquire after his health and suggested, out of kindness, that the Dean of the Cardinals should return to Frascati and never leave it again. The old man seems to have take this well-intentioned remark amiss, for the suggestion, says the *Diario*, was one 'that His Royal Highness appeared not to relish'—which perhaps also accounts for the fact that he insisted, with undiminished Stuart obstinacy, on attending the same festival in the following year, though it was to prove to be his last visit to St. Peter's and to Rome. The Pope's advice in 1804 was given only on account of the Cardinal's obvious exhaustion, for even after resting in the sacristy he was too weak to walk to his carriage and had to be carried on a litter by members of the Swiss Guard.

The chief excitement in Rome at this time was caused by the arrival of the summons from Paris for the Pope to go there and crown Napoleon Bonaparte as Emperor of the French. The Cardinal of York, in his capacity as Dean of the Sacred College, was also to receive the imperial summons to attend, but his age prevented him from obeying the command whatever his own feelings on the question may have been. It is unlikely that this last champion of the theory of the divine right of kings would have felt much sympathy for the Corsican Usurper who had justified his assumption of royalty by the remark: 'I found the crown of France in the mud; I picked it up and put it on my head.' The Cardinal, who had lived to see more than one crown fall in the mud, was probably unimpressed in this case either by the crown or the head on which it was to be placed, though having had reason to tremble before the might of the greatest military genius of the age he was wise enough to keep his opinions on the subject of the new Emperor to himself.

In fact his only reaction to the invitation to attend the coronation at Nôtre Dame was characteristic of his obsession with the claims of his own family to the exclusion of everything else so far as political changes or worldly events were concerned. He objected to being addressed as 'Cousin' in the imperial letter instead of 'Brother' as was the customary practice in communications between princes. This omission of his right to be treated as a royal personage caused him to make an angry complaint to Cardinal Fesch, Napoleon's uncle and ambassador in Rome, who promised to take the matter up with his imperial nephew.

These excitements had their usual bad effect on his health and he was seized with an attack of lethargy which made his friends despair for his life. It was now that the Countess of Albany hurried from Florence to confer with Cesarini about the payment of her jointure in the event of her brother-in-law's death. Other friends were less heartless or self-seeking when they heard of the old man's collapse. The Duke of Sussex wrote to enquire after the invalid and was soon to hear that the Cardinal was rallying though he had lost his sense of taste and could 'no longer relish his chocolate of a morning'. Though indeed he made something of a recovery his health never fully returned, and by 1806 his memory also began to fail him. It was now just a matter of time before the long life of the last of the Stuarts should come to its end.

The End of a Dynasty

9

In the middle of the year 1807 the Cardinal, who had been growing more frail and senile as the months progressed, caught a feverish chill while staying at his villa at Frascati, and it soon became evident to his friends that the end was near. For a fortnight he lay ill, each day growing weaker, and on the morning of July 13th he died. It was the forty-sixth anniversary of his enthronement as Bishop of Frascati.

As this aged prince breathed his last in the eighty-third year of his age the Stuart dynasty came to an end. He had lived longer than any of his predecessors and his peaceful death was in marked contrast to the tragic and stormy history of his royal line. Of the descendants of Robert II, from his death in 1390 to the accession of James VI to the throne of England in 1603, hardly one had died a natural death and only one had lived beyond his fiftieth year. Robert III had died of grief after one son had been starved to death and another captured by the English; James I was brutally murdered; James II was killed by the explosion of a cannon at the siege of Roxburgh; James III was thrown from his horse and done to death by his own rebellious subjects; James IV was killed on Flodden field; James V had died of a broken heart after hearing of the rout of Solway Moss; his daughter Mary died on the scaffold. The tragedy which had haunted this family down the ages did not leave it when the crowns of England and Ireland were united to the unhappy crown of Scotland, for as Kings of England only two died in their beds. Now at last, in the peaceful death of this old priest, the long and terrible history of the House of Stuart was ended.

James III, acknowledged as King by half of Europe, had been buried with all the pomp appropriate to a reigning sovereign; Charles III also, though only in private, had been buried as a king. It was, however, simply as a churchman that Henry IX was laid to rest, for there was now no surviving 'Pretender' to see that royal honours were paid to the last descendant of James II. Three days after his death the body of Henry Stuart was taken into Rome to lie in state at the Palace of the Cancelleria. The crown

The Cardinal King

and sceptre, which the Cardinal's father and brother had worn in death, were not seen at the obsequies of the Cardinal King, who lay in bishop's robes with a mitre on his head, a crozier by his side, and the Red Hat at his feet. The only sign of royal rank was the large escutcheon displaying the arms of Great Britain which was placed at the foot of the catafalque: the leopards of England, the lion of Scotland, the harp of Ireland and the lilies of France glowing in their bright heraldic colours against the sable of the pall. Many thousands passed through the hall of the palace to pay their last respects to the dead Cardinal, but as it was the height of summer there were not many foreigners in Rome, so that few, if any, travellers from the distant northern kingdom came to look for the last time on the face of their *de jure* king.

The funeral took place in the church of St. Andrea della Valle, a church close to the Cancelleria and dedicated, appropriately enough, to the patron saint of Scotland. Here, under the dome, the second highest in Rome after that of St. Peter's, twenty-seven Cardinals gathered with the Pope to assist at the last rites. The body of the Cardinal King was later taken to St. Peter's where the entombment took place. Henry Stuart was buried beside his father in the crypt of the Basilica and soon afterwards the body of Prince Charles was brought from its temporary resting place at Frascati to join them. On these simple tombs marble tablets were placed on which the three Stuart princes were referred to for the last time by the royal titles to which they had laid claim: James III, Charles III, and Henry IX. Here they remained until recent years, when the bodies were reinterred in a marble tomb upon which rests a replica of St. Edward's crown. A single inscription, similar to that on Canova's monument to the last Stuarts in the nave above, records the final resting place of James Francis Edward and his sons.

IACOBO III
IACOBI II MAGNAE BRIT REGIS FILIO
CAROLO EDVARDO
HENRICO DECANO PATRVM CARDINALIVM
IACOBI III FILIIS
REGIAE STIRPIS STVARDIAE POSTREMIS

The End of a Dynasty

10

After the funeral ceremonies had taken place in Rome the panegyric was preached in Frascati Cathedral by Dom Marco Mastrofino, professor of theology at the Seminary. This eulogy was delivered with all the florid decorations and grandiose flourishes which were then considered suitable for such a theme. 'Art thou fallen, last and sublimest glory of the House of Stuart?' the preacher asked. 'And we are left in darkness as in the terrible silence and shadow of nature under the quaking and eclipse and the horrors of desolate night. As the royal prophet wept in Ziglag over Saul and Jonathan, fallen on Gilboa, and then burst into the most pathetic of elegies, so let my tearful words over the cold ashes of our beloved dead be a tribute of reverent and mournful praise. I have flowers to strew upon his grave, balsams incorruptible that will at least preserve his memory. The field from which I gather them is wide, and abundant is the harvest, but sincerity is moderate and brief; scant and broken the voice of supreme grief. May just praise echo up to you, O sublime soul, and assure you of the gratitude of a people and a clergy who adored you.'

As the preacher droned out his sonorous platitudes we may reasonably allow ourselves to think that the minds of his congregation began to wander. What were the real thoughts of the people who listened to Dom Marco Mastrofino as he thundered on about the virtues of the departed prince? We may be sure that few of them thought about him as a pretended king, for the royal claims of Henry IX were never taken seriously outside the confines of his own household. Of this fact the Cardinal himself was fully aware and while he refused to abandon a just claim one may say that it was only out of loyalty to the memory of his father and brother and as witness to the justice of a cause known to be lost rather than from any personal ambition or desire for recognition that Henry Stuart persisted unpretentiously in asserting his claim to the British crown. He was content that his mild protest should be made known, but beyond this he had no wish to go, and he was always careful to avoid those embarrassing situations which had

The Cardinal King

once resulted from his brother's stubborn refusal to abandon any of those demands on an unwilling Europe for a recognition which every court had long since ceased to consider either possible or desirable.

The Cardinal had smarted at the ludicrous and humiliating situations which the obstinacy of his brother's policy in later life had brought upon their family and was determined that no further opportunities to snub his royal claims should be offered; nevertheless he never doubted those claims or abandoned them in any way. It has been said that Henry IX 'bequeathed' his rights in the British crown to King George III as a mark of gratitude for the pension he had received from the House of Hanover. This, of course, is quite untrue. Not only would such an act have made all his previous career as *de jure* claimant to the throne quite pointless but it would also have been an act of disloyalty to the memory of his father and brother which the Cardinal would have been quite incapable of committing; nor would a man of his integrity have accepted a pension at the cost of abandoning the principles of a lifetime any more than George III would have demanded such a sacrifice from him. Furthermore, Henry Stuart knew well enough that if his claim to the crown was legally valid it followed that there was no precedent by which a crown could be bequeathed to anyone but the prince upon whom it devolved by proximity of blood. The only heir acknowledged by Henry IX was his cousin the King of Sardinia. His gratitude to the reigning dynasty in England was expressed by the gift of certain crown jewels to the Prince Regent; an act devoid of any political significance. Henry Stuart died in the full conviction that no one but himself had the right to be called King of England, and that no one could succeed him in that office but his nearest relation by legitimate succession.

But to the congregation in the Cathedral at Frascati it was as a bishop and as a Prince of the Church that Henry Stuart would be remembered; as a devout son of the Catholic Church. If they thought at all in terms of royal claims or of historical parallels they might indeed have looked upon the pure and blameless life of Henry IX as a reparation for the apostacy of Henry VIII whose concupiscence had disrupted the unity of Christendom. Henry

The End of a Dynasty

Stuart, who once told Louis XV that he took pride in bearing the name of those eight monarchs who had sat upon the English throne, could hardly have claimed a single thought in common with the bluff Tudor by the marriage of whose sister with the King of Scots the English crown had eventually passed to the House of Stuart, yet the fact remained that Henry VIII represented a type which is dear to the English heart, a fact which could not be said of the pious and cultivated Henry IX whom Richelieu had once described as an 'Italian bigot' and other people had condemned as haughty and proud. Yet he had also been known as the protector of the poor and his generosity of heart made him the all too easy prey of the importunate. This side of his character was known best to his intimate circle who saw him as a kindly and paternal bishop, a generous and splendid host, a connoisseur and patron of the arts, a proud and dignified prince. He was, as the *Annual Register* later expressed it, 'a studious and well-informed prince, and a sincerely pious prelate'. If few would have followed him to war many found in him a true man of peace.

When Dom Marco had finished his panegyric and the people left the cool of the *Duomo* for the bright sunshine of the piazza their last thought, perhaps, for their departed bishop was that he had been a great figure of the eighteenth century. The battle of Jena in the previous year and the victory of Friedland only a month before the Cardinal's death were facts to remind the mourners that the age to which Henry Stuart had belonged was gone for ever. So too, it must have seemed, were the ideals for which he had stood; legitimacy, divine right, the altar and the throne. Yet even at the very heart of the new order the voice of the old Cardinal of York was still to be heard. Consalvi, brought up in the legitimist atmosphere of the *entourage* of the last Stuart, was to stand up to the blusterings of Napoleon and finally triumph over him when the Papal States were restored in 1815. ('You realize that I could destroy the church whenever I wish,' the Emperor had said to him. 'Even we priests, sire, have not been able to do that after eighteen centuries,' Consalvi had replied.) Yet in the triumph of the spirit of legitimacy in 1815 there was no Stuart left to take part; and had any descendant survived he would have

The Cardinal King

found no place in the restored, order for by the irony of fate the Hanoverian usurper had himself become the champion of the legitimist cause.

As for the doctrine of divine right, that too had gone for ever, and much else that might have been thought divine had gone with it. Only in France was it to emerge for a brief epilogue in the short reign of King Charles X, a monarch who was to complete the parallel between Stuart and Bourbon by suffering the fate of James II as his brother had shared in the tragedy of Charles I. As Charles X fled from his capital in 1830 the last scene was acted in the tragic drama which had started in December 1688. It was the end of the cause for which the Stuarts had spent over a hundred years in exile and for which the Bourbons, to whom the Stuarts had once looked for help, were now to join them in the shadowy company of the dispossessed. Europe was never to hear of it again.

Bibliography

ALFIERI, VITTORIO. *Memoirs of the Life and Writings of.* London, 1810.
Annual Register for the Year 1807.
BOIGNE, COMTESSE DE, *Récits d'une Tante: Mémoires de la Comtesse de Boigne.* Vol. 1. Paris, 1907.
BUCHAN, S. *Funeral March of a Marionette.* London, 1935.
CLONCURRY, LORD. *Personal Recollections of the Life and Times of Valentine Lord Cloncurry.* Dublin, 1850.
DORAN, DR. *'Mann' and Manners at the Court of Florence.* London, 1876.
Decline of the Last Stuarts, The. (Despatches of the British Envoys to the Secretary of State.) London, 1843.
DUMONT-WILDEN, L. *Le Prince Errant: Charles-Edouard le dernier des Stuarts.* Paris, 1934.
EWALD, A. C. *The Life and Times of Prince Charles Stuart, Count of Albany.* London, 1876.
FALLS, A. M. *On the Banks of the Seine.* London, 1900.
FORSYTH, JOSEPH. *Remarks on Antiquities, Arts and Letters during an Excursion in Italy.* London, 1825.
FRANCIS, GRANT R. *Scotland's Royal Line.* London, 1928.
ISAACSON, CHARLES S. *The Story of the English Cardinals.* London, 1907.
KELLY, BERNARD W. *Life of Henry Benedict Stuart, Cardinal Duke of York, With a Notice of Rome in his Time.* London, 1899.
KNIGHT, CORNELIA. *Autobiography.* Vol. 1. London, 1861.
LANG, A. & SHIELD, A. *The King over the Water.* London, 1907.
LEE, VERNON. *The Countess of Albany.* London, 1884.
LANG, ANDREW. *Prince Charles Edward Stuart, the Young Chevalier.* London, 1903.
MACKENZIE, SIR COMPTON. *Prince Charlie and His Ladies.* London, 1934.
Prince Charlie. London, 1932.

Bibliography

Nobili-Vitelleschi, Marchesa. *A Court in Exile*. London, 1903.

Pastor, L von. *History of the Popes*. Vols. XXXVIII–XL. London, 1951.

Petrie, Sir Charles. *The Jacobite Movement, The Last Phase, 1716–1807*. London, 1950.

Pirie, Valerie. *The Triple Crown*. London, 1935.

Porcelli, Baron. *The White Cockade*. London, 1949.

Polnay, Peter de. *Death of a Legend*. London, 1952.

Roberts, Cecil. *And so to Rome*. London, 1950.

Roome, H. D. *James Edward the Old Pretender*. Oxford, 1904.

Ruvigny and Raineval, Marquis of. *The Jacobite Peerage, Baronetage, Knightage and Grants of Honour*. Edinburgh, 1904.

Seton, W. W. *Relations of Henry, Cardinal York, with the British Government*. Aberdeen, 1920.
Some Unpublished Letters of Henry, Cardinal York. Glasgow, 1919.

Shield, A. *Henry Stuart, Cardinal of York, and His Times*. London, 1908.

Skeet, F. A. J. *H.R.H. Charlotte Stuart, Duchess of Albany*. London, 1932.
Catalogue of Jacobite Medals and Touch-pieces. Leeds, 1938.

Tayler, A. & H. *The Old Chevalier*. London, 1934.
The Stuart Papers at Windsor. London, 1939.
1745 and After. London, 1938.

Tayler, H. *Prince Charlie's Daughter*. London, 1950.
Jacobite Epilogue. London, 1941.

Vaughan, H. M. *The Last Stuart Queen*. London, 1910.
The Last of the Royal Stuarts. London, 1906.

Walpole, Horace. *Letters to the Countess of Ossory*. London, 1903.

Wiseman, Cardinal. *Recollections of the Last Four Popes and of Rome in their Times*. London, 1858.

Index

Acquaviva, Cardinal, 17, 38, 65
Adelaide, Madame, 114, 209
Albani, Cardinal Alessandro, 43, 64, 70, 94, 99
Albani, Cardinal G. F., 67, 91, 131, 224, 254
Albany, Charlotte Stuart, Duchess of, 75, 126–7, 156, 168, 169–71, 172, 174, 176–87, 188, 191, 192, 193, 199–202
Alberoni, Cardinal, 17, 50
Alfieri, Count Vittorio, 66, 135, 139–42, 143, 145, 146, 148, 149, 152, 153–6, 157, 158, 159, 161, 167, 179, 180, 208, 243, 249–50
Alford, Lord, (John Graeme), 77, 78
Argenson, Marquis d', 46, 50, 55, 56
Aubeterre, Marquis d', 93, 95
Augereau, General, 213, 214

Bassville, H. de, 212–13, 214, 216
Benedict XIII, Pope (Orsini-Gravina), 20
Benedict XIV, Pope (Lambertini), 36, 43, 57, 63, 73, 78, 79, 98, 105
Bernis, Cardinal de, 88, 107, 110, 128, 131–2, 138, 155
Berthier, General, 213, 217
Berwick, Duke of, 20
Boigne, Comtesse de, 114, 209–10
Bonaparte, Joseph, 216, 217
Borgia, Cardinal Stefano, 229–31, 232, 233, 235
Bouillon, Duc de, 53
Bouillon, Duchesse de, 14, 28
Brosses, Président de, 20, 25

Caryll, Lord, 120, 122
Charles III, King of Spain, 25, 202–3
Charles X, King of France, 206, 266
Charles Edward, Prince ('Charles III'). Birth, 14, 17; first letter, 23; tour of Italian cities, 28; called to Paris, 37; early disagreements with Henry, 37–8; departure for France, 38–41; leaves for Scotland, 42; his return, meeting with Henry, 53–4; further disagreements, 54–7; learns of Henry's appointment as Cardinal, 57; expelled from France, 70; with Clementina Walkinshaw, 74–7; birth of natural daughter, 75; returns to Rome, 96; reunion with Henry, 97; audience with Clement XIII, 101–2; description of, 103–4; appears drunk at opera, 104; visits Paris, 119; marriage, 122; anger at attitude of Papacy, 124–5; thinks Henry will be elected Pope, 133; settles at Florence, 133–5; assumes style of Count of Albany, 134; ill health, 135; ill-treatment of wife, 145; deserted by Louise, 145–6; reconciliation with Henry, 157; apoplectic seizure, 161; signs deed of separation, 166–7; recognises his daughter, 168; demands Henry's recognition of Duchess of Albany, 173; gives daughter Order of Thistle, 176; agrees to meeting between brother and daughter, 182; persuaded to return to Rome, 184–5; returns to Muti Palace, 186; life at Rome, 188–90; last illness and death, 191–3; funeral, 194; his character, 195–7
Charles Emmanuel IV, King of Sardinia, 198, 247–9
Chesterfield, Earl of, 34, 68
Cesarini, Angelo, Bishop of Milevi, 108, 184, 218, 248, 255, 260
Clement XI, Pope (Albani), 13, 205
Clement XII, Pope (Corsini), 24, 84
Clement XIII, Pope (Rezzonico), 80, 81, 83, 90, 93, 95, 98, 101, 105, 109, 124, 134, 153, 205
Clement XIV, Pope (Ganganelli), 107, 113, 124, 128–30
Clementina, Princess Sobieska, 14, 17, 18, 19, 21, 23–4, 25, 69
Clermont, Count, 52
Cloncurry, Lord, 251, 252, 253
Consalvi, Cardinal Ercole, 114, 116, 191, 210, 217, 224, 246, 265
Corsini, Prince, 134, 151
Coutts, Thomas, 234, 238
Crisp, Samuel, 27
Cumberland, Duke of, 40, 54, 196

Doria, Cardinal, 72, 217, 221, 254
Dunbar, Earl of (James Murray), 29, 31, 32, 71

Fabre, François Xavier, 250
Fesch, Cardinal, 260

Index

Fitzjames, Duc de, 118, 119
Forsyth, Joseph, 239, 252-4
Frederick II, King of Prussia, 34-5, 140

Gaetani, Duke of, 38
George I, King of Great Britain, 16, 22, 78, 82
George II, King of Great Britain, 22, 35, 40, 42, 81
George III, King of Great Britain, 68, 82, 83, 95, 149, 186, 204, 206, 208, 225, 233-5, 239, 256, 257, 264
Gesvres, Duc de, 46, 48
Gloucester, Duke of, 120-1, 129, 137
Gori, Francesco, 161, 165
Gustavus III, King of Sweden, 138, 161-2, 165, 166

Hamilton, Sir William, 109, 219
Henry Benedict, Cardinal Duke of York ('Henry IX'). Birth, 13, 20; baptism, 20; appearance and character as child, 25-8; keeps journal, 27; character at seventeen, 29-31; excluded from plans for brother's departure, 38-40; leaves for France, 43; at Avignon and Paris, 45; audience with Louis XV, 46-8; commands army at Dunkirk, 49-51; distrusted by Richelieu, 49-50; at siege of Antwerp, 52; tries to get Charles back from Scotland, 53; their reunion after the '45, 53-4; quarrels with Charles in Paris, 54-7; leaves for Rome, 57; created Cardinal, 57; receives Tonsure, 63; and Red Hat, 64; devotion to Music, 67; disagreements with father, 67, 71-4; ordained priest, 69; Archpriest of St. Peter's, 77; Camerlengo, 78; first Conclave, 79-80; consecrated Archbishop of Corinth, 80-1; made Bishop of Frascati, 83; enthronement, 85; character as bishop, 86-7; created Vice-Chancellor of the Roman Church, 87; tries to make Charles return to Rome, 90; death of father, 91; fails to get Charles recognized as king, 93-6; meeting with Charles, 97; angers Pope, 98; deplores Charles's drinking, 100; presents Charles to Clement XIII, 101-2; his second Conclave, 105-7; attempt on his life, 111-12; injured in collapse of floor, 112-13; collection of books, 113; dress and appearance, 115; hears of brother's marriage, 117; meets sister-in-law, 123; visits Clement XIV in last illness, 128; his third Conclave, 131-3; hears of Louise's flight, 138; places her in convent at Rome, 146-8; meets Alfieri, 152-3; reconciliation with Charles, 157; forbids Louise to receive Alfieri, 157-9; objects to separation between Charles and Louise, 162-5; issues Protest against Charlotte, 174-7; first letter to Charlotte, 178; they meet, 183; entertains Charles at Frascati, 189; hears of Charles's fatal illness, 191; fails to secure Charles's burial as a sovereign, 193; at brother's funeral, 194; regards himself as king, 197-9; protests at recognition of George III, 204-6; described by Comtesse de Boigne, 209-10; sells his treasures, 216; flies from Rome, 217; reaches Naples, 218; hears of battle of Nile, 219; flight from Naples to Venice, 220-2; reduced to poverty, 222; attends last Conclave, 224-5; receives pension, 228-42; returns to Rome, 245; visited by Pope and King of Sardinia; 247-9; by Lord Cloncurry, 251-2; by Forsyth, 252-4; Dean of Sacred College, 254; visited by Sister Louise, 255-8; last illness, 261; death, 261; funeral, 262
Hippisley, Sir John Coxe, 204, 228-42

Ildefonso, Father, 29, 31, 71
Inverness, Earl of (John Hay), 21

James Francis Edward, Prince ('James III'). Proclaimed king, 14; attitude to religion, 15; marriage, 16; character and appearance, 18-20; receives Imperial ambassador, 36; alarmed at behaviour of sons, 37-8; sees Charles for last time, 38; described by Benedict XIV, 42-3; writes to Henry in France, 50-1; tries to reconcile sons, 56; informs Charles of Henry's acceptance of Hat, 58-9; life with Henry in Rome, 66-9; their quarrels, 71-4; ill health, 77; quarrels with Pope, 78; final illness, 89-90; death, 90; funeral, 92-3, 116, 196, 261, 262
John III, Sobieski, King of Poland, 16, 216
Joseph II, Emperor, 106, 137, 160, 236

Keith, Marshal James, 27

Leopold, Grand Duke of Tuscany, 106, 146, 182
Lercari, Monsignor, 71, 72, 74
Ligonier, Viscount, 141, 142
Louis XIV, King of France, 14, 15, 45, 181, 226, 231
Louis XV, King of France, 40, 42, 43, 45, 46-9, 52, 55, 70, 107, 108, 130, 140, 173, 265

Index

Louis XVI, King of France, 206, 211, 212, 227
Louise, Sister, 255–8, 259
Louise of Stolberg, Countess of Albany, 117; ancestry and education, 119–20; appearance, 121; first meeting with Charles and marriage, 122; 'Queen of the Apostles', 123; meets Henry, 123; life in Florence, 134–45; meets Alfieri, 135, 143; leaves husband, 145–6; appeals to Henry, 146; arrives in Rome, 148; moves to Cancelleria, 151; with Alfieri in Rome, 151–6; Henry discovers her relations with Alfieri, 156–60; legal separation, 161–6; mentioned in Charlotte's letters, 178, 179, 180, 181; hears of husband's death, 202; her opinion of Henry, 244; relations with Fabre, 250
Lumisden, Andrew, 104

Mann, Sir Horace, 43, 44, 50, 57, 60–1, 65, 69, 76, 89, 94, 96, 102, 107, 109, 118, 121, 129, 133, 135, 146, 157, 160, 161, 170, 186, 220
Marefoschi, Cardinal, 122, 124
Maria Theresa, Empress, 35, 119, 120
Marischal, Earl, 27, 75, 195
Marlborough, Duke of, 14
Mary of Modena, Queen, 14, 15, 188, 226–8
Mastrofino, Dom Marco, 116, 263, 265
McDonnell, Father Myles, 61
Merolli, Giacomo, 111–12, 115
Miller, Lady Anne, 103, 104
Minto, Earl of, 235, 237, 238, 239, 241

Napoleon I, Emperor of the French, 213, 215, 223, 259, 265

Nelson, Viscount, 219, 220, 221

Orléans, Duc de, Regent of France, 14
Orléans, Duc de (Philippe-Egalité), 138

Philip V, King of Spain, 26
Pitt, William, 228, 231, 233, 235
Pius VI, Pope (Braschi), 132, 136, 137, 146, 151, 153, 158, 160, 173, 183, 193, 203–4, 208, 215, 223–4
Pius VII, Pope (Chiaramonti), 108, 224, 243, 246–9

Richelieu, Duc de, 33, 49–51, 265

Santa-Croce, Princess, 131, 155
Saxe, Marshal de, 40, 41, 46, 47
Sheridan, Sir Thomas, 40–1
Sobieski, Prince James, 16, 28
Stanley of Alderley, Lord, 189
Strickland, Francis, 37
Sussex, Duke of, 68, 233, 251, 260

Talleyrand, Prince de, 211, 223
Talmond, Princesse de, 74, 90
Tencin, Cardinal, 36, 37
Towneley, John, 37

Vernon, Admiral, 51
Victoire, Madame, 114, 209

Walkinshaw, Clementina, Countess Alberstrof, 74, 75, 76, 102–3, 126–7, 249
Walpole, Horace, 43, 60, 78, 94, 106, 118, 121, 126, 161, 169, 173
Walpole, Sir Robert, 36
William III, King, 14, 226
Wogan, Charles, 16